What Life Was Like

ON THE BANKS OF THE NILE

Egypt
3050 ~ 30 BC

What Life Was Like

ON THE BANKS OF THE NILE

Egypt
3050 ~ 30 BC

BY THE EDITORS OF TIME-LIFE BOOKS, ALEXANDRIA, VIRGINIA

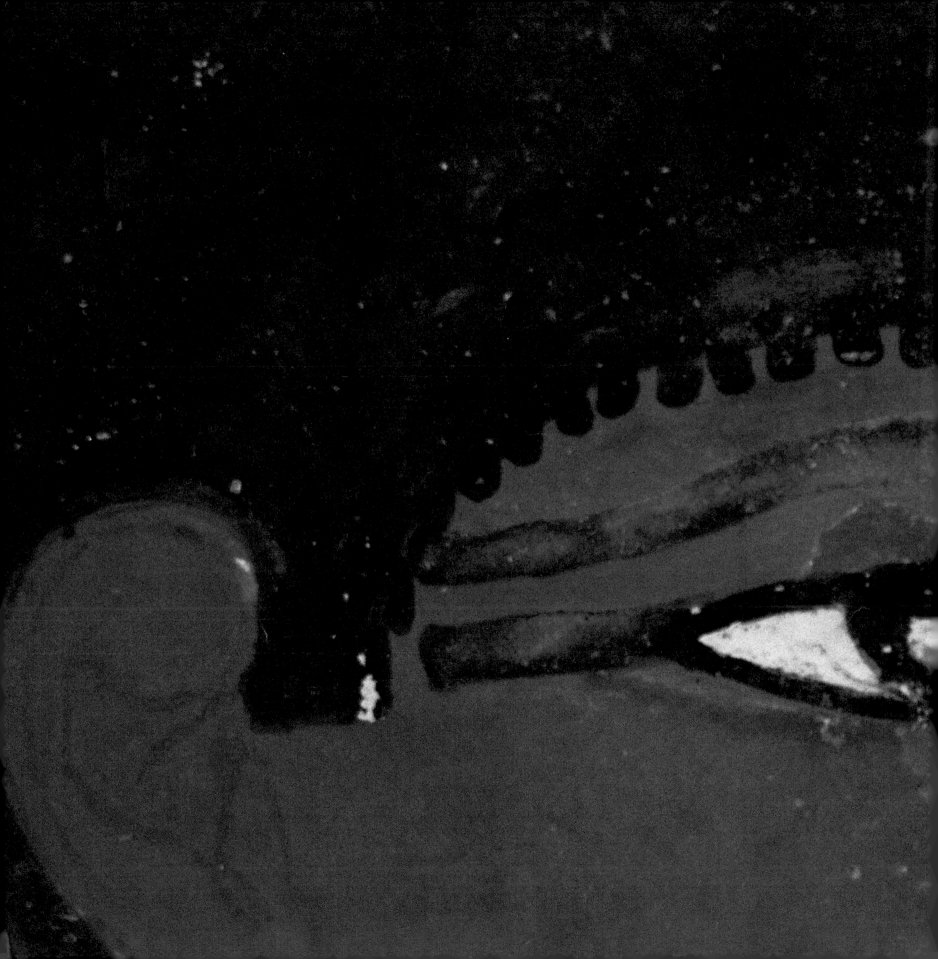

CONTENTS

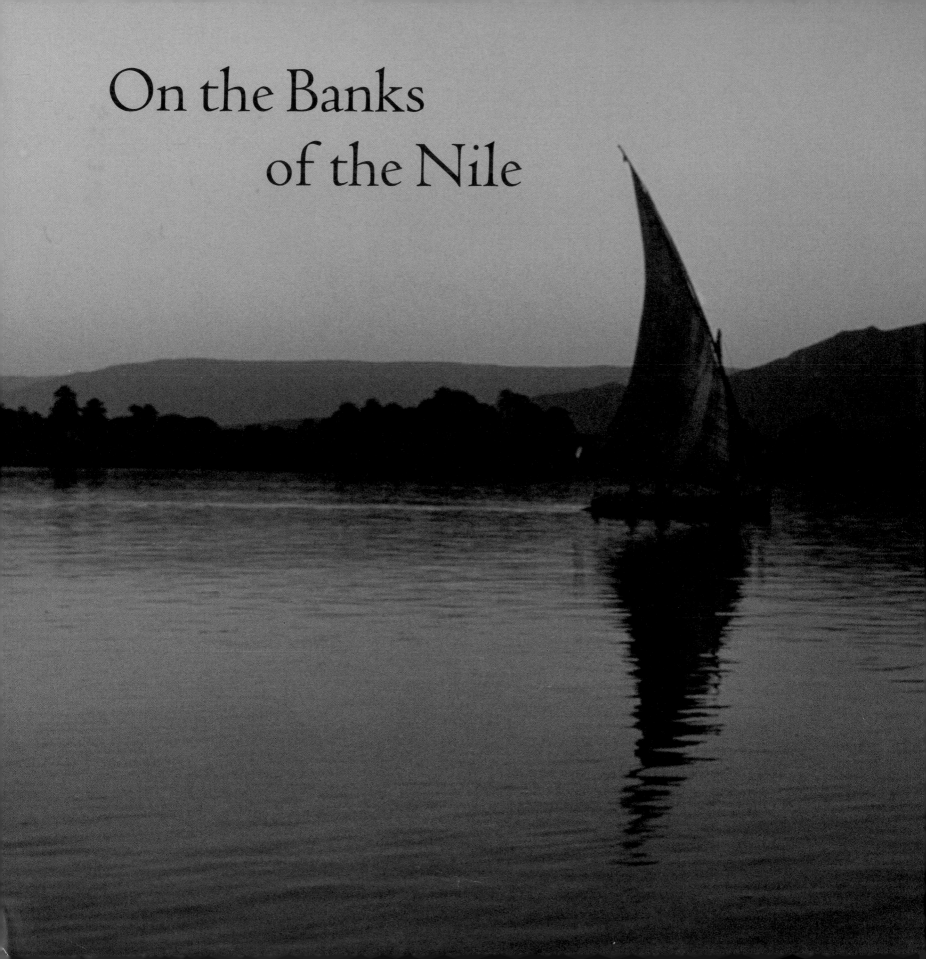

On the Banks
of the Nile

3,000 Years of Splendor

NARMER

KHUFU

Each summer, when the Nile overflowed its banks and replenished the parched earth, the people of ancient Egypt witnessed anew the miracle of creation. In the beginning, Egyptian legends attested, floodwaters engulfed the world. Nothing stirred amid that dark and dismal expanse. Then, miraculously, a lotus blossom surfaced and opened its petals to give birth to the sun. Rising from the blossom like a golden bird, the sun subdued the waters and coaxed life from the emerging land. Ever after, when the Nile receded and the growing season began, people gave thanks to the sun god Re and to his earthly counterpart, the pharaoh, who claimed divine powers and kept the country fruitful.

Like the earth itself, the mighty kingdom of Egypt emerged from cloudy depths of confusion and discord. The rulers who brought order out of the chaos 5,000 years ago may have had the gods on their side, but they had many obstacles to overcome. The land along the Nile was really two countries—Upper Egypt to the south, a long river valley hemmed in by steep cliffs and

desert; and Lower Egypt to the north, encompassing the broad, marshy Nile Delta *(map, page 13)*. In the delta, settlements were dispersed along the river's many branches. In Upper Egypt, by contrast, the Nile formed a single artery of communication for villagers, easing the task of political consolidation.

By 3100 BC, Upper Egypt was under the control of rulers based at the town of Hierakonpolis, devoted to Horus, a falcon-headed god who would become closely identified with Re. Kings of Upper Egypt proceeded to conquer the delta and unify the country. The last of those conquerors, King Narmer, recorded his achievement on a splendid palette that bears his name. His successor, Aha (also named Menes), founded a new capital at Memphis, strategically located where the Nile Valley meets the delta.

Aha and his heirs made up the first of many dynasties to govern Egypt over the next 3,000 years. Each dynasty consisted of a succession of related kings and ended when a king died without heirs or when outsiders seized power. According to legend, Aha

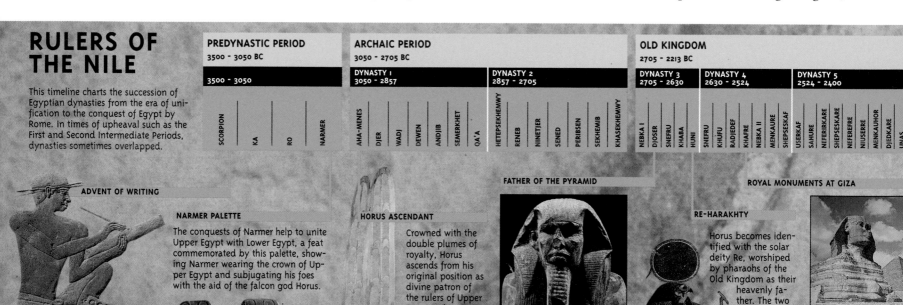

RULERS OF THE NILE

This timeline charts the succession of Egyptian dynasties from the era of unification to the conquest of Egypt by Rome. In times of upheaval such as the First and Second Intermediate Periods, dynasties sometimes overlapped.

PREDYNASTIC PERIOD 3500 – 3050 BC	ARCHAIC PERIOD 3050 – 2705 BC		OLD KINGDOM 2705 – 2213 BC		
3500 – 3050	DYNASTY 1 3050 – 2857	DYNASTY 2 2857 – 2705	DYNASTY 3 2705 – 2630	DYNASTY 4 2630 – 2524	DYNASTY 5 2524 – 2400
SCORPION / KA / RO / NARMER	AHA-MENES / DJER / WADJ / DEWEN / ANDJIB / SEMERKHET / QA'A	HETEPSEKHEMWY / RENEB / NINETJER / SENED / PERIBSEN / SEKHEMIB / KHASEKHEMWY	NEBKA I / DJOSER / SNEFRU / KHABA / HUNI	SNEFRU / KHUFU / RADJEDEF / KHAFRE / NEBKA II / MENKAURE / SHEPSESKAF	USERKAF / SAHURE / NEFERIRKARE / SHEPSESKARE / NEFEREFRE / NIUSERRE / MENKAUHOR / DJEDKARE / UNAS

ADVENT OF WRITING

Egyptian scribes begin using hieroglyphs to record dates, events, and the names of rulers (examples of which appear in the margins above).

NARMER PALETTE

The conquests of Narmer help to unite Upper Egypt with Lower Egypt, a feat commemorated by this palette, showing Narmer wearing the crown of Upper Egypt and subjugating his foes with the aid of the falcon god Horus.

HORUS ASCENDANT

Crowned with the double plumes of royalty, Horus ascends from his original position as divine patron of the rulers of Upper Egypt to become the supreme god of a united kingdom.

FATHER OF THE PYRAMID

Djoser, shown wearing the pharaoh's ceremonial beard, inaugurates an era of monumental construction in stone by erecting the Step Pyramid to hold his remains, setting a precedent for the true pyramids to come.

RE-HARAKHTY

Horus becomes identified with the solar deity Re, worshiped by pharaohs of the Old Kingdom as their heavenly father. The two gods together are known as Re-Harakhty, or Re-Horus, portrayed with the head of a falcon beneath a solar disk.

ROYAL MONUMENTS AT GIZA

Khafre, son and successor of Khufu, builder of the Great Pyramid, constructs his own pyramid at Giza as well as the 240-foot-long Sphinx, endowed with a lion's body and Khafre's face.

8

was carried off by a hippopotamus while hunting, but his dynasty lived on through the descendants who succeeded him.

Pharaohs of the first two dynasties solidified their hold on the country, preparing the way for a long era of stability known as the Old Kingdom. By then Egyptians had refined the gifts that would make theirs one of the most durable and distinguished of civilizations—a system of writing, using characters called hieroglyphs, that transmitted wisdom and learning from one generation to the next; an administrative genius that brought together the resources of far-flung communities for building projects or military expeditions; and a profound concern for the afterlife that expressed itself in towering monuments and sublime works of art.

The soaring ambitions of the pharaohs—god-kings who expected to reign in heaven after death—reached a peak in the Fourth Dynasty, when King Khufu ordered construction of the Great Pyramid at Giza, near Memphis, to hold his mummified remains. Based on a plan evolved in the Third Dynasty, it consisted of 2,300,000 massive blocks of stone, hauled into place over two decades by thousands of laborers. In the words of one sacred text, the lofty pyramid enabled the dead pharaoh's spirit to "ascend to heaven as the eye of Re." Nearby, Khufu's successors built two smaller pyramids and the brooding figure of the Sphinx.

Eventually, pharaohs of the Old Kingdom seemed to lose the god-given ability to keep the land safe and bountiful—in part because the monsoon rains in Ethiopia that fed the Nile each year were slackening, decreasing the floods and spoiling harvests. As their hopes withered under the fierce sun, people lost confidence in the god-king, and local leaders increased their authority. A lengthy interval of civil strife ensued, known as the First Intermediate Period. "I show you the land in turmoil," related one Egyptian account written long afterward. "What should not be has come to pass." The unrest continued until rulers from Thebes in the south gained control of Upper Egypt and waged war on kings in the north, reuniting the country by force of arms.

KHAFRE

MENTUHOTEP III

SEQENENRE
TAO II

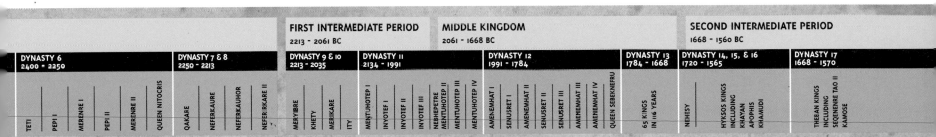

DYNASTY 6 2400 - 2250						DYNASTY 7 & 8 2250 - 2213					**FIRST INTERMEDIATE PERIOD** 2213 - 2061 BC				**MIDDLE KINGDOM** 2061 - 1668 BC																		**SECOND INTERMEDIATE PERIOD** 1668 - 1560 BC			
											DYNASTY 9 & 10 2213 - 2035			DYNASTY 11 2134 - 1991								DYNASTY 12 1991 - 1784								DYNASTY 13 1784 - 1668	DYNASTY 14, 15, & 16 1720 - 1565		DYNASTY 17 1668 - 1570
TETI	PEPI I	MERENRE I	PEPI II	MERENRE II	QUEEN NITOCRIS	QAKARE	NEFERKAURE	NEFERKAUHOR	NEFERIRKARE II		MERYIBRE	KHETY	MERIKARE	ITY	MENTUHOTEP I	INYOTEF I	INYOTEF II	INYOTEF III	NEBHEPETRE MENTUHOTEP II	MENTUHOTEP III	MENTUHOTEP IV	AMENEMHAT I	SENUSRET I	AMENEMHAT II	SENUSRET II	SENUSRET III	AMENEMHAT III	AMENEMHAT IV	QUEEN SEBEKNEFRU	65 KINGS IN 116 YEARS	NEHESY	HYKSOS KINGS INCLUDING KHAYAN APOPHIS KHAMUDI	THEBAN KINGS INCLUDING SEQENENRE TAO II KAMOSE

MENTUHOTEP III

COFFIN WITH EYES

Pyramid building subsides while other funerary efforts become more elaborate, including coffins with magical eyes that allow the dead to look west toward the setting sun, the land of Re.

STARVING TIME

Drought and famine contribute to Egypt's descent into a period of political and social chaos, known to posterity as the First Intermediate Period.

The Theban-based ruler Mentuhotep II forcefully restores Egyptian unity, inaugurating the Middle Kingdom, marked by the return of peace and prosperity and by a renewed emphasis on the pharaoh as god-king.

FORTRESS AT BUHEN

Internal stability allows 12th Dynasty pharaohs to muster their strength and launch campaigns into Nubia, where Egyptian forces build imposing forts such as this one at Buhen.

HYKSOS CROWN

Egypt lapses into the Second Intermediate Period as intruders from the east called the Hyksos assume control of the delta and crown their own kings at Avaris, where the golden diadem above was uncovered.

Thus began the Middle Kingdom, which saw pharaohs of the 11th and 12th Dynasties regain the clout of their Old Kingdom predecessors. Some rulers shrewdly economized, however, by building pyramids with cores of mud brick, encased in stone pilfered from the monuments of past pharaohs. Seeking fresh sources of wealth to the south, royal troops moved into Nubia and built fortresses there. One 12th Dynasty king boasted of his Nubian conquests: "I carried off their women, I carried off their subjects, went forth to their wells, smote their bulls."

Kings of succeeding dynasties faced a challenge of a different order to the north, where migrants from the east were streaming into the delta. Eventually, chiefs of eastern origin known as the Hyksos, or "rulers of foreign lands," came to power in the delta and exacted tribute from the lords of Upper Egypt, based at Thebes. This era of divided rule, known as the Second Intermediate Period, was regarded by later Egyptians as a time of degeneration and disgrace. But the Hyksos in fact introduced new technology to the land, including bronze weapons and chariots, both of which made Egypt more formidable in years to come.

Chafing under Hyksos domination, Theban rulers set out to regain control of Egypt. Again, forces from the south marched on the delta and hammered a divided country together. Ahmose I of Thebes claimed the final victory over the Hyksos and inaugurated the New Kingdom, which saw Egypt reach fresh heights of imperial power and splendor. The 18th Dynasty included some of the most memorable figures in Egyptian history: Hatshepsut, a woman who triumphed in the traditionally masculine role of pharaoh; Tuthmosis III, who emerged from Hatshepsut's shadow to achieve brilliance in battle; Amenhotep III, whose long, peaceful reign of diplomatic courtship and monument building represented Egypt at its prime; his son Akhenaten, who proclaimed himself high priest of a new solar cult dedicated to the sun disk Aten; and the boy king Tutankhamun, who achieved a measure of immortality through his glittering burial treasures.

NEW KINGDOM
1560 - 1070 BC

DYNASTY 18
1570 - 1293

AHMOSE I · AMENHOTEP I · TUTHMOSIS I · TUTHMOSIS II · HATSHEPSUT · TUTHMOSIS III · AMENHOTEP II · TUTHMOSIS IV · AMENHOTEP III · AKHENATEN · SMENKHARE

BATTLE-AX OF AHMOSE I

Ahmose I of Thebes—whose treasures include this ceremonial battle-ax—wages a series of campaigns to drive the Hyksos from Egypt and regain Nubian territories. His triumphs usher in the confident years of the New Kingdom.

TEMPLE OF AMUN

The god Amun, sometimes depicted at his temples in the form of a ram, emerges as Egypt's supreme deity when his cult center, Thebes, becomes the ceremonial heart of the New Kingdom.

SEAL OF TUTHMOSIS I

Tuthmosis I, one of Egypt's great warrior kings, marshals an army, including charioteers like the one that is portrayed on this royal seal, and expands the Egyptian empire.

HATSHEPSUT'S SPHINX

Hatshepsut, serving as regent for her young stepson, Tuthmosis III, assumes the role of pharaoh and has herself portrayed as a bearded king on this sphinx and on other monuments.

TUTHMOSIS III

Tuthmosis III, shown holding jars of wine as offerings, succeeds Hatshepsut and asserts his authority by leading campaigns abroad.

CULT OF THE SUN KING

TEMPLE OF LUXOR

The wealth of the New Kingdom was not confined to the palace grounds. Temples devoted to the gods grew larger and more luxurious during this period. Priests conducted rituals in sprawling complexes that included workshops and storehouses, filled with grain harvested by peasants toiling in fields set aside for the gods. Prominent among the gods so honored was Amun, who sometimes took the form of a ram but remained, at heart, elusive and indescribable. Originally the patron deity of Thebes, Amun was dear to rulers of the 18th Dynasty, who traced their origins to that town. But Theban kings tactfully honored ancient tradition by incorporating the sun god Re into the cult of Amun (much as earlier kings had incorporated Horus into the worship of Re). By one reckoning, the cult of Amun-Re controlled one-tenth of Egypt's land, including 40 workshops and 400,000 animals, all of it tended by 90,000 priests and laborers.

In principle, everything in Egypt belonged to the pharaoh, who presided as god-king over the temples, the towns, and the farthest outposts of the empire. In practice, however, most kings were shrewd enough to leave plenty of wealth and power in the hands of trusted priests, army officers, and administrators, many of whom had large estates of their own. In return, the pharaoh claimed a share of Egypt's annual harvest, the right to conscript troops and laborers for his campaigns and building projects, and tribute in the form of treasure and slaves from the foreign lands his armies subjugated. All this was more than enough to support pharaohs and their followers in grand fashion. Ramses II of the 19th Dynasty provided lavishly for dozens of his wives and scores of their children in this world and the next, as evidenced by the elaborate tomb chambers he had hewn for his dependents in the limestone cliffs west of Thebes. Indeed, Ramses and other kings of the period supported an entire community of artisans at Deir el-Medina to prepare sumptuous burial places for the elite.

Slowly in the centuries to come, however, the might of the pharaohs declined. Ramses and his successors made their capital

AMENHOTEP III

AKHENATEN

RAMSES II

DYNASTY 19
1293 - 1185

DYNASTY 20
1185 - 1070

TUTANKHAMUN · AY · HOREMHAB · RAMSES I · SETI I · RAMSES II · MERNEPTAH · AMENMESSE · SETI II · SIPTAH · QUEEN TAWOSRET · SETHNAKHT · RAMSES III · RAMSES IV · RAMSES V · RAMSES VI · RAMSES VII · RAMSES VIII · RAMSES IX · RAMSES X · RAMSES XI

MASK OF TUTANKHAMUN

The Luxor temple complex in Thebes, dedicated to Amun, grows in size and splendor under the patronage of 18th Dynasty kings, who claim descent from Amun and honor him by supporting his priests and enlarging his sanctuaries.

Akhenaten—portrayed below with his wife Nefertiti and their daughters—rejects the cult of Amun and extols the sun disk Aten, once a minor aspect of Re but now the one supreme god, identified with the king.

Spurning the legacy of Akhenaten, the boy king Tutankhamun presides over a return to the worship of Amun. He is best remembered for his magnificent funeral treasures, including this golden mask.

RAMSES THE GREAT

Ramses II, shown holding a crook as shepherd of the people, stakes a claim to greatness during his 67-year reign by propagating more monuments and children than any other pharaoh.

CAPTIVES OF RAMSES III

Egyptian forces under Ramses III overwhelm their Libyan foes and claim captives, shown shackled at right. For all his success in battle, Ramses subsequently becomes the target of a conspiracy hatched by one of his secondary wives.

ALEXANDER
THE GREAT

CLEOPATRA VII

in the delta. By the end of the 20th Dynasty, local leaders in Upper Egypt were going their own way—the high priests of Amun-Re set themselves up as rulers at Thebes—and Egypt lapsed into the discord of the Third Intermediate Period.

This time there would be no great national resurgence, for Egypt's neighbors were growing ever stronger and profiting by her distress. Libyans who had earlier infiltrated the delta took power there. Eventually, kings of Nubian origin asserted control over the entire country, initiating the Late Period, during which Egypt was held together by one foreign power after another—Nubians, Assyrians, Persians, and finally Macedonians under Alexander the Great. That conqueror inaugurated the last line of pharaohs, the Ptolemaic Dynasty, which ended in 30 BC when Cleopatra VII committed suicide and Egypt became a Roman province. To the end, the land of the pharaohs retained its distinctive culture. People continued to worship the deities of old, including the maternal Isis, goddess of renewal and resurrection.

In their abiding concern for the afterlife, the Egyptians stocked their tombs with wondrous gifts for posterity—paintings, carvings, keepsakes, and inscriptions that reflect the rich lives the people led on earth and hoped to perpetuate in the afterworld. Thanks to such compelling testimony, along with the words and pictures inscribed on monuments and letters penned on papyrus and preserved by chance through the ages, we can unravel the accounts of actual Egyptians who lived, loved, and died thousands of years ago. Using this wealth of detail, the stories told in the following chapters take on a new perspective—captivating tales of everyday life, of ambition and intrigue within the royal family, of adventure and conquest beyond Egypt's borders, and of the ultimate search for eternal fulfillment that preoccupied everyone, from the pharaoh in his palace to the farmer in the fields. We can never know if the Egyptians reached the afterworld they dreamed of. But we can follow the people of the Nile on their earthly journeys and learn what their life was like.

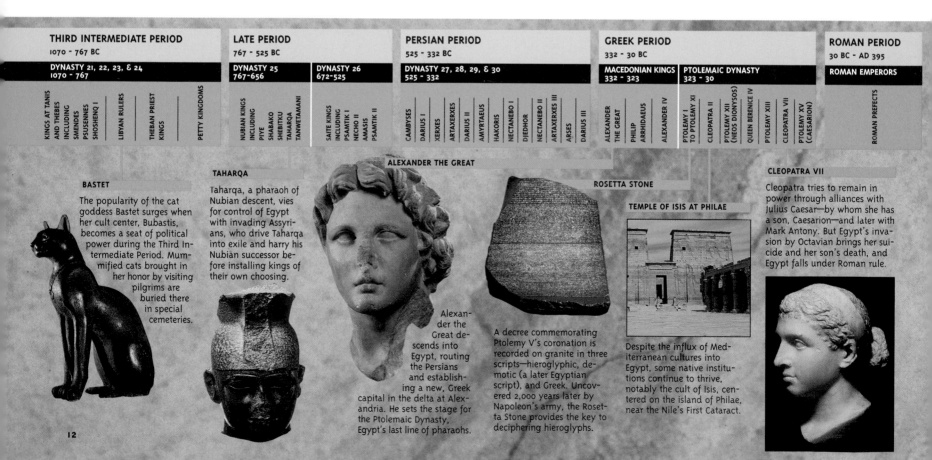

THIRD INTERMEDIATE PERIOD
1070 - 767 BC

DYNASTY 21, 22, 23, & 24
1070 - 767

KINGS AT TANIS AND THEBES INCLUDING SMENDES PSUSENNES SHOSHENQ I | LIBYAN RULERS | THEBAN PRIEST KINGS | PETTY KINGDOMS

LATE PERIOD
767 - 525 BC

DYNASTY 25
767-656

NUBIAN KINGS INCLUDING PIYE SHABAKO SHEBITKU TAHARQA TANWETAMANI

DYNASTY 26
672-525

SAITE KINGS INCLUDING PSAMTIK I NECHO II AMASIS PSAMTIK II

PERSIAN PERIOD
525 - 332 BC

DYNASTY 27, 28, 29, & 30
525 - 332

CAMBYSES | DARIUS I | XERXES | ARTAXERXES | DARIUS II | AMYRTAEUS | HAKORIS | NECTANEBO I | DJEDHOR | NECTANEBO II | ARTAXERXES III | ARSES | DARIUS III

GREEK PERIOD
332 - 30 BC

MACEDONIAN KINGS
332 - 323

ALEXANDER THE GREAT | PHILIP ARRHIDAEUS | ALEXANDER IV

PTOLEMAIC DYNASTY
323 - 30

PTOLEMY I TO PTOLEMY XI | CLEOPATRA II | PTOLEMY XII (NEOS DIONYSOS) | QUEEN BERENICE IV | PTOLEMY XIII | CLEOPATRA VII | PTOLEMY XV (CAESARION)

ROMAN PERIOD
30 BC - AD 395

ROMAN EMPERORS

ROMAN PREFECTS

BASTET

The popularity of the cat goddess Bastet surges when her cult center, Bubastis, becomes a seat of political power during the Third Intermediate Period. Mummified cats brought in her honor by visiting pilgrims are buried there in special cemeteries.

TAHARQA

Taharqa, a pharaoh of Nubian descent, vies for control of Egypt with invading Assyrians, who drive Taharqa into exile and harry his Nubian successor before installing kings of their own choosing.

ALEXANDER THE GREAT

Alexander the Great descends into Egypt, routing the Persians and establishing a new, Greek capital in the delta at Alexandria. He sets the stage for the Ptolemaic Dynasty, Egypt's last line of pharaohs.

ROSETTA STONE

A decree commemorating Ptolemy V's coronation is recorded on granite in three scripts—hieroglyphic, demotic (a later Egyptian script), and Greek. Uncovered 2,000 years later by Napoleon's army, the Rosetta Stone provides the key to deciphering hieroglyphs.

TEMPLE OF ISIS AT PHILAE

Despite the influx of Mediterranean cultures into Egypt, some native institutions continue to thrive, notably the cult of Isis, centered on the island of Philae, near the Nile's First Cataract.

CLEOPATRA VII

Cleopatra tries to remain in power through alliances with Julius Caesar—by whom she has a son, Caesarion—and later with Mark Antony. But Egypt's invasion by Octavian brings her suicide and her son's death, and Egypt falls under Roman rule.

Egypt was nurtured and defined by the Nile, which originated in the highlands of central Africa, rushed over rocky cataracts in Nubia, rolled through the fertile valley of Upper Egypt, and fanned out to form the lush delta of Lower Egypt. The ancient distinction between Upper and Lower Egypt was symbolized by the white and red crowns of the pharaoh (far right), who also wore the double crown in his capacity as Lord of the Two Lands. Rulers of the Old Kingdom made their capital at Memphis, where Upper and Lower Egypt met. During the New Kingdom, Thebes (detail, inset) became a great ceremonial center, site of royal residences, temples, and tombs. The Egyptian empire reached its height at this time, extending far south of the First Cataract—the traditional boundary with Nubia—and reaching up through western Asia as far as Syria.

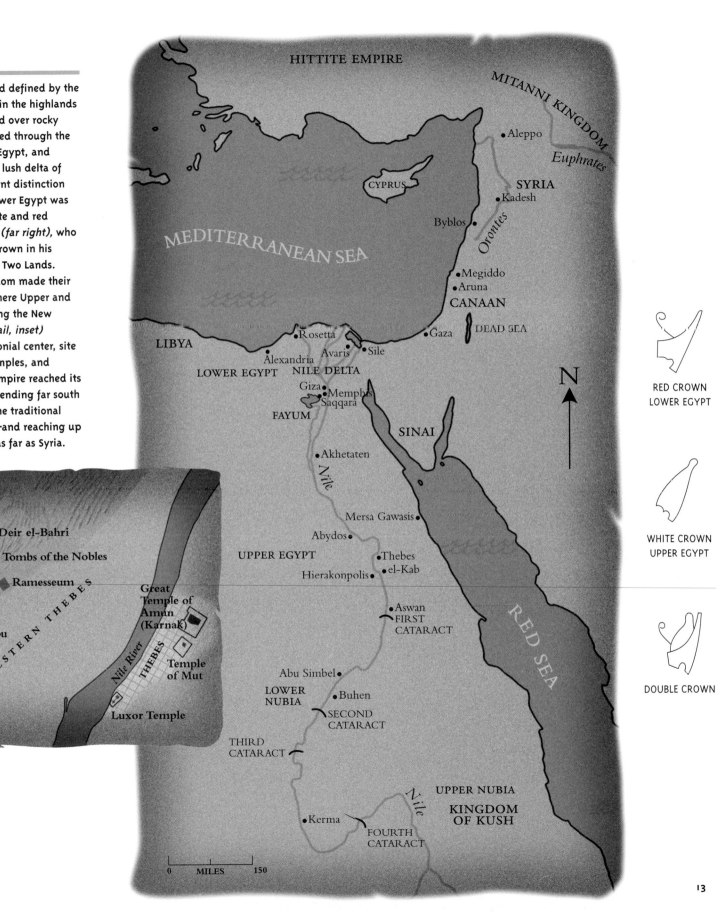

RED CROWN
LOWER EGYPT

WHITE CROWN
UPPER EGYPT

DOUBLE CROWN

CHAPTER ONE

Public Faces, Private Lives

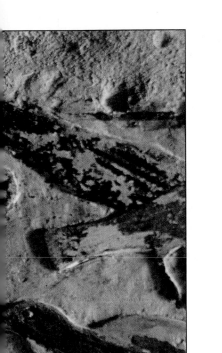

All Egyptians depended on the river for survival, but none so closely as these sun-bronzed harvesters, burdened under bound stalks of papyrus. Each year the receding Nile flood left immense thickets of papyrus, the versatile reed that was transformed into paper, rope, fabric—even food and medicine.

A light in the sky was the sign. For 70 nights of each year, the star known to the ancient Egyptians as Sopdet—Sirius, to a later world—lurked out of sight somewhere below the horizon. Finally, on a day in late June, Sopdet came forth from hiding, creeping into view just minutes before daybreak. Farther back in Egyptian history, astronomers had noticed that the star's emergence coincided with another annual event: the swelling of the Nile River, presaging a flood that would soak the land and renew it with a fresh coating of fertilizing silt. The coincidence was not exact, since the onset of the river's rise could vary by weeks, but it was close enough so that the return of Sopdet became an occasion of great ceremonial importance, launching the new year and festivals of prayerful thanks and great joy.

That joy was shared by everyone in Egypt: from the farmers, fishermen, and hunters, and the women weaving flax into soft linen garments, to the artisans and merchants in the towns; from the priests who honored Egypt's many gods in huge temple complexes along the river and the powerful families living in splendor on immense estates, to the godlike pharaoh himself, who could command the building of an entire city to sustain his retinue in this world and who, if he chose,

Nestled along a Nile tributary, the Fayum oasis evokes the ageless marriage of earth and water. Irrigation canals like those dug centuries ago stretch into the flood plain, coaxing precious green from silt-rich soil.

might erect a stone mountain to hold his remains in the next.

All were dependent on the bountiful Nile, which flowed at a stately pace of about three miles an hour, creating a ribbon of lushness that stretched across a rainless landscape of rock and sand. Hundreds of villages were strung like beads along the shores, occupying natural rises of sandy ground in the flood plain. Larger communities grew up here and there, and a few became cities. Much of the Nile's corridor of greenery, some 13,000 square miles, was densely settled, housing an estimated three million persons at its height.

These were the men and women who created the miracle of human achievement we call Egypt. Their passions and intellect were no different from our own, while their lifestyles were governed by customs, beliefs, and technologies that never fail to amaze those making the acquaintance of this captivating land for the first time. You will meet some of them in this volume—vibrant personalities who represent a cross section of the ordinary Egyptians who inhabited this world, as well as some of the most dazzling of the pharaohs and their queens and advisers.

Unfortunately, the people at the bottom of the human pyramid, the shepherds, the cattle drovers, and the peasant farmers, left no traces of how they lived. But the lives of those who were better off were chronicled in letters, lawsuits, and other records, written on papyrus and shards of pottery and engraved on stone. Only a few accounts remain, but those that do offer vivid glimpses of people expressing the full range of human emotions. Their stories do not suggest an orderly, unchanging society, as is sometimes portrayed; instead they form a colorful collage of passionate men and women, often unruly, who confronted one another in ways familiar to denizens of the modern age.

Within the selected narratives that are presented here, there is an abundant store of well-documented details that not only describe a way of life but also recount what people said and did in their dealings with one another: There was Hekanakht,

who was unable to prevent his family from mistreating his second wife; the patient foreman Neferhotep struggling to cope with his troublesome adoptive son; Paneb, a stonemason who ousted the pharaoh's chief official; Wabet, Paneb's wife; Hunro, the weaver, who maintained an affair with Paneb throughout marriages to her first and second husbands; and Naunakht, a woman who would not be taken for granted.

Among those awaiting the life-giving waters of the Nile around the year 2002 BC was a well-to-do farmer named Hekanakht, whose lands were located on the river's west bank, near the village of Nebeseyet, about 10 miles southwest of Thebes. It was early in the Middle Kingdom, during the 11th Dynasty when Sankhkare Mentuhotep III was pharaoh. The country was again united after a debilitating civil war between

Urged forward by a young herdsman clutching his coiled rope, dappled long-horned cattle are rounded up for the annual tally. Only the wealthy could afford to own cattle, which were costly to feed as well as heavily taxed. Professional herdsmen tended the animals with great care, and some of them even went so far as to give their charges names like Beautiful, Brilliant, or Good Counsel. Except at celebratory feasts, few Egyptians knew the luxury of eating beef, since most cattle were kept as draft animals, for milking, or for sacrifice to the gods.

two royal houses, and the reigning king was a strong ruler whose immediate predecessors had fostered anew trade, art, and agriculture. In the month of August, the star Sopdet had already made its heralding appearance, and the Nile was overflowing its banks, but the inundation had not peaked nor had the waters yet reached Hekanakht's property.

Hekanakht was restless and uneasy. Instead of being on his own estate during this critical period, directing his workers and overseeing a multitude of vital chores, he was far from his home, and would be away for many months fulfilling ceremonial and administrative duties for a client. Hekanakht had been appointed ka priest for Ipi, a royal official who had died, leaving estates whose produce provided the upkeep for his tomb. As ka priest, Hekanakht was paid to oversee the tomb, located near his own villa, for which he collected a fee from Ipi's estates, far to the north, which he was currently visiting.

It was his own property, however, that Hekanakht thought about as the flooding progressed. He had left a young man by the name of Merisu, most likely his eldest son, in charge of his lands and household. Yet without Hekanakht to direct him, would Merisu be trustworthy and effective?

Hekanakht was taking no chances. He had been sending a series of letters home, dispatching them with Sihathor, presumably another of his sons, who trekked to and from his estates at his command. Hekanakht may have written his letters himself, or he may have dictated them to a scribe. Assuming he summoned a scribe, the learned man arrived, clad as was Hekanakht in a kilt with an embroidered border—a rectangular piece of linen that was wrapped around his hips and tucked

A pool of life-giving water—shaded by a canopy and filled daily from a nearby canal—dominates the walled courtyard of this rural Middle Kingdom home. Built from sunbaked mud brick, the building's columned portico, narrow doorways, and high windows protected the interior from direct sunlight, while roof vents helped circulate air. Behind a pair of storage bins, steps lead to a flat roof, where the family often cooked, ate, and slept when they wanted to escape the summer heat.

under a belt—which reached to the midcalves and left his upper body uncovered.

The two men exchanged a few traditional greetings: "Welcome in peace!" and "In peace, in peace!" Then after cutting off from a roll of coarse, straw-colored papyrus a sheet about 10 inches square, the scribe brushed his reed pen across a cake of water-moistened black ink and started taking down the words dictated by Hekanakht. With each dip of his brush, he created about nine signs.

Hekanakht began by admonishing Merisu to "be very active in cultivating. Take great care that the seed of my grain be preserved and all my property be preserved since I am holding you responsible for this." In one caustic comment after another,

Hekanakht laid out instructions, warned Merisu of the ills that would befall him if his orders were not precisely followed, declared his anxieties about a quarrel that was disturbing his household, expressed his affection for another of his sons, Snefru, and chided Merisu for past failures.

Among these lapses was one that affected Hekanakht's daily sustenance: On his current business trip, Hekanakht was required to provide some of his own food, so he requested grain from his stock back home. But instead of good, fresh grain, Merisu had sent him stale, dry barley. Hekanakht was outraged at being slighted in this way and thought longingly of his table back home. In the dining room of his comfortable house, a splendid chamber with its walls painted in two colors divided by a decorative border, Hekanakht enjoyed his dinner, joined by Iutenheb, his second wife; Ipi, his elderly mother; Hetepet, a female relative who lived with them; his chief retainers and their families; and his daughters and sons with their respective spouses and children.

The diners sat on stools or mats around small tables, while household servants presented them with reed dishes piled high with portions of roast duck or goose, perhaps chosen from among the fattest of the fowl raised in his own pens, and surrounded by delicious vegetables. As the steaming hot food was brought in from his kitchen, in an open-air room at the back of the house, the aroma of its seasonings—onion, garlic, dill, parsley, thyme, coriander, marjoram, or cumin—wafted through the room.

Yet here he was, far from home, and his son could not even provide him with fresh barley! How then could Merisu be trusted to run the entire estate? Hekanakht added words of bitter complaint to his letter: "Is it not the case that you are happy eating good barley while I am neglected?"

His thoughts then turned back to the oncoming Nile flood. It was during this interval before the level of the flood was known that the Egyptians negotiated a number of land-renting deals, and Hekanakht had such a transaction in mind. He instructed Merisu to order two of his men to take some of the cloth that the women of his household had recently woven and use it to rent additional land, to be cultivated with emmer wheat and barley. "Don't settle on just anybody's land," he cautioned Merisu; "ask for some from Hau the Younger."

Hekanakht contemplated the added land with satisfaction. After the inundation had ebbed, when the ground was firm enough to walk on, his peasants would loosen the soil with simple hoes to prepare it for sowing. Typically an advancing line of workers, carrying the seed in a leather bag or basket, scattered it across the ground,

The impish household god Bes dances in time to his tambourine, keeping evil spirits at bay. His noisy merrymaking and gargoylish looks acted to frighten away all manner of misfortune, from poisonous serpents to unfavorable spells. Despite his apparent ferocity, Bes was a popular domestic guardian who was worshiped at the family altar, and craftsmen painted his likeness on furniture, pottery bowls, and cosmetic jars. Particularly associated with childbirth, Bes kept pregnant women and their babies safe during labor, and young children wore protective pendants bearing his image.

while supervisors urged them to "make haste," perhaps mindful of Hekanakht's command to "make the most of my land, strive to the utmost, dig the ground with your noses!" To prevent birds from eating the seeds, the laborers brought sheep and goats to the field to tread them deep into the soil.

In order to bury the seed further, as well as to aerate the soil, the farmers plowed the fields with an implement composed of a blade of hardwood that splayed into a pair of handles. Usually the plow was pulled by a pair of oxen; but at times, other workers would do the pulling.

The success or failure of Hekanakht's current harvest, however, rested with Merisu. "Sow that farm with barley," Hekanakht now dictated, but "if it turns out to be a big inundation, you shall sow it with emmer." Some acreage, no doubt, would be set aside to grow flax that subsequently could be woven into cloth; the ripened seeds of the mature flax yielded another important product, linseed oil, one of several plant oils used for lamps, cooking, and cosmetics.

It was not only farming matters that weighed heavily upon Hekanakht. Within his large, fractious household, domestic squabbles often erupted, and disgruntled relatives and retainers wrote him letters recounting their grievances. His youngest son, Snefru, for example, was his special favorite, but he sensed that the boy was not being properly cared for in his absence. He reminded Merisu of how much Snefru meant to him. "Greet Snefru a thousand times and a million times," he declared effusively. "Take great care of him. Give him an allowance," he commanded, adding, "There is no one more important than he in the house including yourself." After Snefru has finished the cultivation work assigned to him, said Hekanakht, "send him on to me."

He then turned his attention to a conflict that was ripping apart his family. At the center of the acrimony was

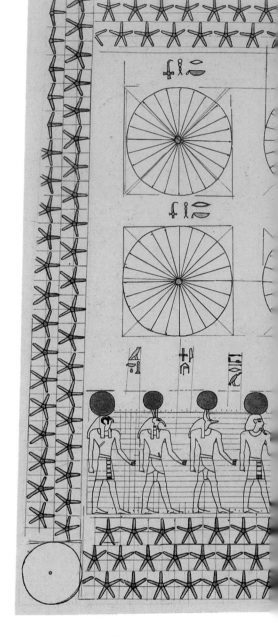

MARKING TIME

Like most early civilizations, the ancient Egyptians measured the passing of time by the phases of the moon. Their first calendar was based on the lunar cycle—the 29 or 30 days from one new moon to the next. A year consisted of three four-month seasons, and the new year was heralded by the star they called Sopdet that appeared just above the horizon at dawn around the time of the annual Nile flood.

The lunar calendar was not without problems: The first day of each new month was unpredictable, and no one knew in advance exactly how many days a particular month would have. Days or even weeks might pass between the end of the last lunar month of the year and the reappearance of Sopdet. For most people in this agricultural society, these were minor inconveniences, but the civil bureaucracy needed a more consistent system—a year with a fixed number of days, not subject to the variations of moon and stars.

Around 2900 BC, a civil calendar was adopted based on a solar year of 365 days. It had 12 months of 30 days each—with three 10-day weeks—plus five days between the old and new years set aside for religious feasts. Years were numbered consecutively within the reign of each pharaoh.

But like any calendar divided into days, it missed the sun's exact annual cycle by about six hours. The result was that, over the course of four years, the civil calendar crept one full day ahead of the true solar year. Once its inaccuracy became obvious, the civil calendar was probably just ignored by farmers and other simple folk, even though the government was tied to its errant schedule. Eventually, about 2500 BC, an official lunar calendar was installed side by side with the civil calendar. It served mainly to schedule religious events and the lunar feast day that gave each month its name.

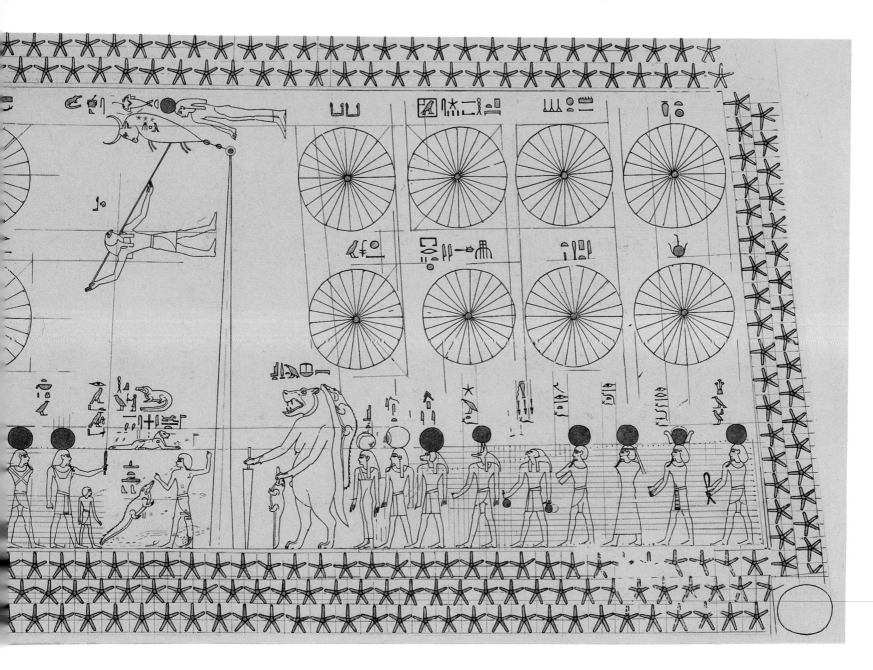

Astronomical tomb paintings, like the Middle Kingdom fragment shown above, provide a glimpse of the Egyptian understanding of time. The gods capped with bright red disks symbolize specific days or months, while the large circles represent the feast days—divided into hours—of the 12 months of the year. Such paintings served an important religious function, since offerings to the dead had to be made on certain occasions that were calculated by the lunar calendar.

To measure the passage of time during daylight hours, the Egyptians had sun clocks, similar to a sundial. Some Middle Kingdom coffins were decorated with star clocks—a list of stars known as *decans* that were identified with different hours of the night at various times of the year.

During the reign of the New Kingdom pharaoh Amenhotep I, clocks that kept time without reliance on the sun or stars made their appearance. These clocks consisted of a water-filled vase with a very small perforation in the bottom. The inside of the vase was inscribed at different levels to mark the hours. These water clocks were often carved in the shape of a baboon, an animal representing the god Thoth, who was associated with the measurement of time. It is interesting to note that except for the abstract concept of *at,* or "moment," the Egyptians—for all their skill as timekeepers—had no name for a unit of time shorter than an hour.

his second wife, Iutenheb, who was being mistreated by other members of his household. He suspected that his children, still grieving for their deceased mother and resentful of his new wife, were the chief instigators of the offenses against Iutenheb, but evidently a woman named Senen had been particularly disrespectful. He instructed Merisu to "turn the housemaid Senen out of my house" as soon as he received the letter. Hekanakht did not, however, let Merisu off without a reprimand: "It is you who let her do evil to my wife," he charged.

The domestic wrangling was not halted simply by getting rid of Senen, Hekanakht discovered. A few weeks later, he dictated another letter, this time addressed to his mother, Ipi, and the rest of his family, in which he chided them for a series of transgressions against one another. For example, their female relative Hetepet had recently reported that she had not been allowed to see her hairdresser and certain other of her attendants. In his letter, Hekanakht appeared to feel that depriving a woman of her hairdresser was a gross insult. And it was true that almost as soon as a woman of high social standing woke up, she would call for this important attendant to begin the time-consuming job of shaping her long hair or wig into many tiny braids or ringlets.

As for Hekanakht's darling son Snefru, the spoiled young man had refused to visit his father. Yet Hekanakht indulged this child in a manner opposite to his harsh treatment of Merisu. To the youngest and weakest members of his household he was kind and protective. If Snefru didn't want to join his brothers in cultivating the land, that was all right, and "if Snefru wants to be in charge of those bulls, you should put him in charge of them," he asserted. "Whatever else he wants, let him enjoy what he wants."

In the meantime, however, the problem with Iutenheb,

instead of being resolved, took a turn for the worse. One of Hekanakht's dependents apparently had become enamored of Iutenheb and had taken advantage of his master's absence from the household. "Whoever shall make any sexual advance against my new wife, he is against me and I am against him," Hekanakht warned. He then lashed out plaintively at his family: "You will not respect my wife for my sake!" For all his anger, Hekanakht's heart must have lifted a bit as he thought of Iutenheb, for he at last decided on a course of action to ensure that his wife would no longer be harassed by the family. "Send Iutenheb to me," he dictated to the scribe.

While his business trip might be brightened by Iutenheb's presence, Hekanakht surely yearned to be back home, working in his comfortable quarters, or relaxing in his bathroom, where his servants would bring cool water to pour over him while he stood in the shallow bathtub, essentially a stone slab with a low-slanting surface that allowed the water to drain into a hole. Like many Egyptians who washed several times a day, Hekanakht was probably fastidious about his person and his clothes. Of course he bathed daily while on his trip, and was shaved and combed by barbers as always, but while he was away from home he probably missed the deference he received in his own household.

From his boat of tightly bound papyrus *(right)*, a lightly clad but well-outfitted angler prepares to club the catfish fighting his hook and line. Other Nile fishermen netted schools of mullet and harpooned massive Nile perch so large that one fish, from mouth to tail, reached to a man's shoulder. The river's deep waterways and dense papyrus thickets sheltered an abundance of wildlife, offering ancient Egyptians both sustenance and sport. Lurking in the canebrake, hippos were known for violent tempers when provoked, although the faience miniature at left displays as much charm as ferocity.

There was little time for such musing, however, for the flooding was now more advanced, and its level was becoming a source of concern. At the peak of the inundation in a normal year, flood basins in the valley and delta were covered to an average depth of about five feet, with the water remaining in them for many weeks. Yet the country did not become one vast lake. A considerable amount of land lay beyond the flood's usual reach, particularly in the valley, and even the delta had many patches of high ground. The extent of the Nile's rise was unpredictable, and at times the normally beneficent river became a devouring monster, bursting through banks and dikes, sweeping away villages, drowning livestock, and lingering so long in the basins that the plant-

he read and then discarded them. They were swept, along with other trash, into a hole in the tomb's floor. In addition to these first two letters, there were six more documents that Hekanakht sent to Merisu. The additional communications dealt exclusively with business matters. Perhaps, by that time, Hekanakht had sorted out his family problems, or perhaps he postponed their resolution until his return. His further messages offer no clues.

Egypt's agrarian economy was controlled by the pharaoh, together with his bureaucrats and priests, from a few great religious and administrative centers. Apart from these cities, urban life in Egypt was modest, conducted in market towns where trade and manufacturing

"The whole land is perished, while you are not hungry."

ing for the next year was thrown off schedule. In other years—and sometimes many years in succession—the flood was inadequate, and large segments of the population were in danger of starvation, the rich as well as the poor.

By the time of Hekanakht's second letter, it had become clear that the flood was low and the harvest would be inadequate that year. Hekanakht gave instructions for grain to be doled out from the reserves on his estate. He listed each of his dependents and the amount they should receive. "The whole land is perished, while you are not hungry," he reminded his family. Perhaps he exaggerated the hardship of others so that his relatives would be more grateful for their grain allotments, for he also alleged, quite improbably, that "they are beginning to eat men here."

When Merisu received Hekanakht's letters, he took them to an empty tomb that was located near Hekanakht's estate, where

were the prime occupations of the residents. The towns hummed with activity. Here craftsmen produced a wide range of utilitarian articles and luxury items: linen and wool clothing; leather bags and sandals; jugs and basins; jewelry, furniture, copper pots, and utensils; glass amulets and figures; and weapons. Merchants offered salt, dried fish, oils, ox hides, tools, rolls of paper made from the papyrus reed, and cosmetics. Business was typically done in the form of barter. Among the more prosperous artisans were those directly employed by the pharaoh. Such a man was Paneb, who started out in life working at his father's stoneworking craft. At an early age, however, he was tapped by fortune for a significant rise in status.

Paneb lived in a walled village located beyond the cultivated area, on the west bank of the Nile, near Thebes, at a site known today as Deir el-Medina. The desert ridges on which it

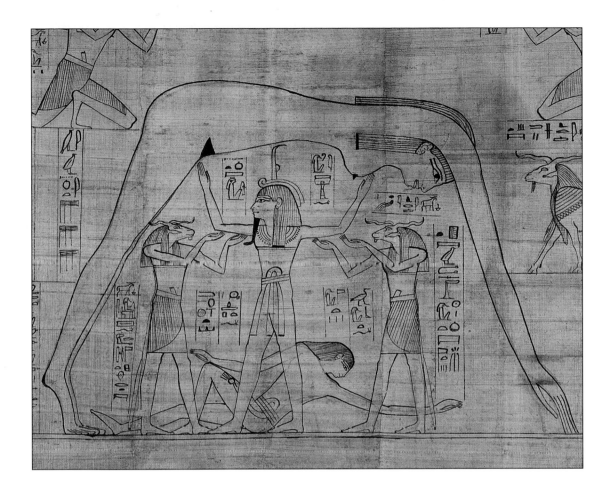

had been built bordered the Valley of the Kings, where the pharaohs of the New Kingdom were buried in underground tombs. Founded by Tuthmosis I in the late 16th century BC, the hamlet served as home to as many as 120 construction workers, artisans, and artists, and their families. These were the men who built and decorated the tombs and their furnishings. The village still housed these kinds of laborers when Paneb lived there during the last years of the 13th century and the beginning of the 12th century BC. At this time Egyptians were seeing an end to the stability that had been brought about by the 67-year reign of Ramses II, a great warrior and builder. Pharaohs now followed one another in rapid succession, each beset by rival factions and civil strife, which was often mirrored in the lives of ordinary citizens including those at Deir el-Medina.

The workers of Deir el-Medina lived in circumstances somewhat different from those of other Egyptian laborers. Although at the bottom of the ladder, they were attached to the pharaoh's bureaucracy. The scribes who directed their labor were also their neighbors, and these men reported directly to the king's top official, the vizier. Under royal patronage, the standard of living in Deir el-Medina was higher and more secure than in the agricultural villages along the Nile. Its artisans were paid in fish, grain, and vegetables, with an occasional bonus of sesame oil or salt, in the form of cones, to be scraped into food as needed. The grain was distributed monthly, and a typical laborer's ration would feed as many as 10 persons; foremen were allotted

IN THE BEGINNING

By raising his daughter—the sky goddess Nut—above her brother and earth god Geb, the air god Shu gives form to the world. The mythical separation of sky and earth represented but one explanation of divine creation. From Memphis came quite a different creation story, one similar to that in Genesis: The first god, Ptah, created the world simply by naming all things in it. Such stories about the creation of the world and mythical descriptions of the cosmos helped to form a frame of reference for the ancient Egyptians' world-view, and all Egyptian creation stories shared the common theme of an orderly, balanced process, moving in stages and ensuring a coherent and stable world.

EGYPT'S DIVINE HOST

From birth to death and beyond, religious ideals permeated every aspect of ancient Egyptian life. Everyone, from pharaoh to peasant, depended on an array of gods and goddesses to maintain balance and harmony in the world, produce a bountiful harvest, bring victory in war, keep loved ones safe from harm, and accompany them on their journey to life everlasting.

Although hundreds of deities occupied the Egyptian pantheon, only a few were prominent at any one time. Generally, these included the gods of creation and the underworld, a host of lesser guardian spirits and evil demons, as well as a specific local god. For everyday favor and good fortune, Egyptians most often prayed and made offerings to the local god and a few household spirits. The national gods were honored on major holidays and at special events.

Typically, the reigning pharaoh elevated his local god to national status. To increase a deity's influence, the king and his priests embellished the god's history and strengths. Gods took on new traits, assumed different roles, and even saw their identities merged with those of other gods. This flexibility in Egyptian religious belief gave one god a dominant role during the New Kingdom. After the shift of political power to Thebes, Amun, a local Theban god, rose to prominence. Instead of attempting to unseat the powerful sun god Re, the Thebans arranged for Amun to take on both Re's name and his attributes, and the new composite god, known as Amun-Re *(left),* ultimately became the New Kingdom's supreme state deity.

Hathor, represented as a woman with cow's horns and a solar disk, was the most widely revered Egyptian goddess. Her symbolic association with the highly valued animal the cow connects Hathor with love, fertility, motherhood, and the fullness of life.

Her hands raised protectively, Hathor sits behind Re-Harakhty, a falcon-headed composite of the sun god Re and Horus, god of living kings. Hathor's posture reflects her dual roles as mother of Re and consort of Horus.

Personifying truth, justice, and ethical conduct, the goddess Maat *(left)* maintained order in the universe and harmony in the natural world. Her emblem, the ostrich feather, was the weight against which a person's heart was measured after death. The divine scribe of the gods, ibis-headed Thoth *(below),* then recorded the results of the weighing of the heart for posterity. Thoth was regarded as a patron of learning and wisdom.

Rendered in gold, a likeness of King Osorkon II takes the enviable form of Osiris, king of the land of the dead *(center).* Osiris crouches on a pillar between his son Horus *(left)* and his sister and wife, Isis *(right),* who raise their hands in a gesture of protection.

The jackal-headed Anubis *(right),* divine patron of embalming and the mummified dead, figures prominently in the Book of the Dead as the god who sets the balance in the weighing of hearts.

PRIDE OF CRAFTSMANSHIP

With simple tools and skilled hands, ancient artisans turned out furniture that has stood the test of time. In the painting shown below, a craftsman bores a hole in the seat of a chair remarkably like the ivory-inlaid ebony example on the facing page, preserved intact after 3,500 years. The lion's-foot leg design—once exclusively reserved for royal furnishings—symbolized the owner's power and invincibility. An Egyptian drill *(left)* employed a curved wooden bow and a length of strong twine to spin the sharp copper or bronze bit anchored in a wooden shaft. Axes, chisels, scrapers, saws, and adzes like the one at the craftsman's feet rounded out his array of tools.

about one-third more, leaving them with a greater surplus to barter for other goods.

The royal administration tried to compensate to some extent for what the workers lacked because they lived in the desert. Since they, for example, could not go to the river each day and wash their clothes, laundry service was provided. The government also supplied servants to help in domestic tasks such as grinding grain for the daily bread. Teams of donkeys delivered fresh water daily to the village, and their drivers brought news and gossip from other towns.

The villagers could get their gossip firsthand, however, by hiking to the bustling market, about two and a half miles away on the west bank of the Nile. There traders, many of whom were women selling goods they had made, sat beside large baskets that held their cakes, fish, foodstuffs, fabric, clothing, and other articles. Artisans, weavers, sailors, farmers, and fishermen crowded around the peddlers to exchange part of what they earned or produced for these items.

In the community of highly skilled artisans at Deir el-Medina, Paneb and other youngsters were taught painting, drafting, reading, and writing, an education that was available to many of the villagers' children, not merely to the sons of the scribes. Some women as well as men were at least minimally literate. As a consequence, residents of the little village sketched and scribbled messages, letters, receipts, work records, and laundry lists on limestone flakes that had been salvaged from tomb excavations, as well as on shards of pottery known as ostraca, both of which were used like scrap paper. For almost a century, scholars from many different countries have been working with these shards, with graffiti and inscriptions carved into stone, and most important of all, with several archives of papyrus, including a famous court document containing allegations that reveal much

of the story of Paneb. From this labor has emerged a set of vignettes that describe the lives of some of the individual villagers.

The families of Deir el-Medina occupied approximately 70 houses, aligned in two rows along the major street that bisected the village and the various alleys feeding into this main road. These routes were probably kept relatively clean. Most of the trash was periodically collected and taken to a large rubbish heap located south of the hamlet, outside its walls. Inside the homes, chamber pots served for wastes, for even Egypt's wealthiest people had no running water.

Paneb's house was most likely typical of the mud-brick four-room houses that made up Deir el-Medina. Upon entering his home, he would pass through an antechamber and arrive at the central living-sleeping-dining area. Behind this room were another chamber, sometimes used for sleeping, and a small back room with stairs leading up to the roof and down to an underground storeroom where perishables could be kept cool. The only seats in the main room were mud-brick benches cushioned with reed mats that were sometimes used as both sofa and bed. Cooking was generally done in the kitchen, located in a courtyard in the back of the house and equipped with an oven, bricked on three sides, for baking bread.

Like most Egyptians, Paneb lived on bread and beer, both made from barley and wheat. They also ate chickpeas, lentils, and vegetables such as lettuce, cucumbers, garlic, and onions. To the daily bread his family added dried fish such as catfish and mullet, caught by one of the multitude of fishermen casting hooks, nets, or harpoons into the Nile from papyrus canoes. The fishermen then hung gutted fish on strings in the sun until they were thoroughly dry; such food was, like grain, very cheap.

To make beer, Paneb's mother mixed crushed grain with water; this mash was allowed to ferment for a few days, then it was strained and poured into jars. Beer could also be made from stale bread loaves, which were crumbled to serve as the basis of the mash.

Paneb belonged to one of the two crews of artisans in the town; each of these groups was led by a foreman and a scribe. Paneb's boss was a foreman named Neferhotep, a middle-aged, childless man, worried about who would take over his duties when he could no longer perform them. Although he lived with his brothers and their children, he longed for a son of his own to whom he could teach his skills and who would succeed him in his office. He had his choice of eager, talented youths, and Neferhotep selected Paneb. But without the permission of Paneb's father, the adoption would have been impossible.

Upon learning of Neferhotep's intent, Paneb's father must have immediately recognized the material advantages for his son. He probably examined with new interest the foreman's heavy woolen cloak, made of 14 yards of wool, quite adequate to keep him warm on a windy wintry day. He might well have gazed with satisfaction on Neferhotep's red leather slippers and the colored weavings and embroidery that decorated Neferhotep's fine, pleated linen robe, a long, loose garment tied at the neck with tassels. These clothes were far grander than his own rough leather sandals and coarsely woven kilt, although the foreman was similarly attired when he was working.

Well aware that there would be a considerable improvement in his son's status, Paneb's father gave his consent. After Neferhotep made a public announcement of the adoption before the village authorities, Paneb went to live with the foreman, his wife Wabkhet, and his huge clan. They inhabited a cluster of houses at the end of the main street, where Neferhotep lived in one house while his

THE QUEST FOR HEALTH AND BEAUTY

In the Nile Valley, beauty and personal adornment were important to rich and poor alike, and not just for vanity's sake. Needing protection from sun, dust, and wind, the Egyptians developed formulas for countless unguents and oils. Concoct-ed from plant extracts—and using cat, hippo, or crocodile fat as a base—these ointments smoothed and softened the skin. In addition, when augmented with aromatic essences blended from flowers, fruits, or herbs, they helped mask body odor. Such scented oils and ointments were considered so necessary that tomb workers at Deir el-Medina went on strike when an expected shipment did not arrive.

Those who could afford more than necessities strove to live in an elegantly sensuous manner, as portrayed in the painting at left. There, the prominent sculptor Ipuy, second from left, and his family enjoy a sumptuous banquet. Ipuy's wife, Duwameres *(far left),* raises her hand in greeting to her son and daughter-in-law *(right).* The white linen garments of all except the young man, who is draped in priestly leopard skin, are accented by colorful jewelry, decorative diadems, and

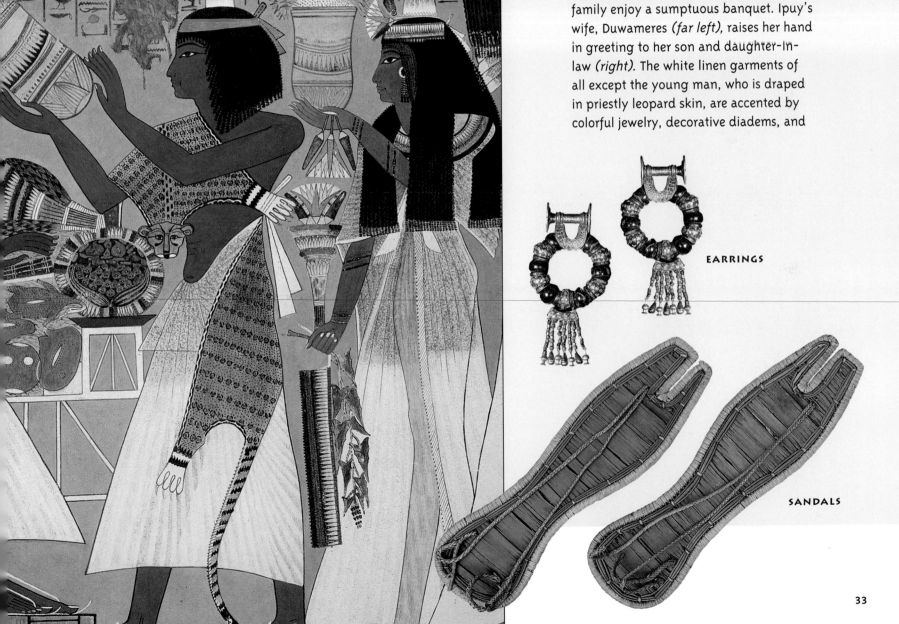

EARRINGS

SANDALS

33

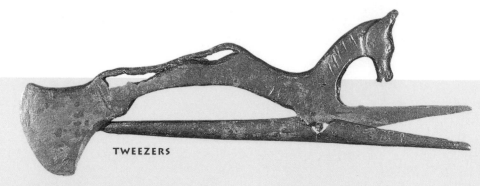

TWEEZERS

vibrant beaded collars at their throats. Only the men wear sandals, but everyone sports plaited wigs that support perfumed cones of ox tallow scented with myrrh. As the evening progresses, the cones will melt, allowing the fragrant pomade to drip over wigs, faces, and clothing.

Wigs, typically woven from human hair and padded underneath with vegetable fibers, served several purposes. Care of one's own hair was complicated by the persistent problem of head lice, so many Egyptians cut their hair very short or shaved their heads with hooked bronze razors (below). Wigs, sitting away from a bald head on their padding, felt cooler

than hair. And wigs looked uniformly attractive; graying hair and natural baldness were considered highly unbecoming. Those who kept their own hair may have tried one Egyptian formula for restoring natural color to fading hair. The recipe involved using the boiled blood of a black cat or black bull, blended in oil—with the appropriate magical incantation.

Similarly, the wearing of kohl, or eye paint, was considered both attractive and pleasing to the gods and also offered pro-

tection from the sun's glare and disease-bearing insects. Egyptian men, women, and even children used cosmetics to accentuate their eyes. A favorite effect was dark gray on the eyebrows and upper eyelids—using galena, or lead ore—and green on the lower lids—using malachite. The minerals were ground fine, mixed with animal fat or vegetable oil, and applied with a wooden or ivory stick. To finish the look, powdered hematite, a red ocher, lent a blush to cheeks and color to lips.

COSMETIC BOX

RAZOR

As in use, the top tray of an elaborately painted cedar cosmetic box holds lustrous alabaster and brightly colored glass jars filled with unguents and oils, including a blue eye paint container with a wooden kohl applicator (center of tray). The box belonged to Merit, a noblewoman and wife of Kha, supervisor of public works at Deir el-Medina under Tuthmosis III. When she had finished making up and perfuming herself, Merit would replace the precious jars in the drawer and store the box under her bed.

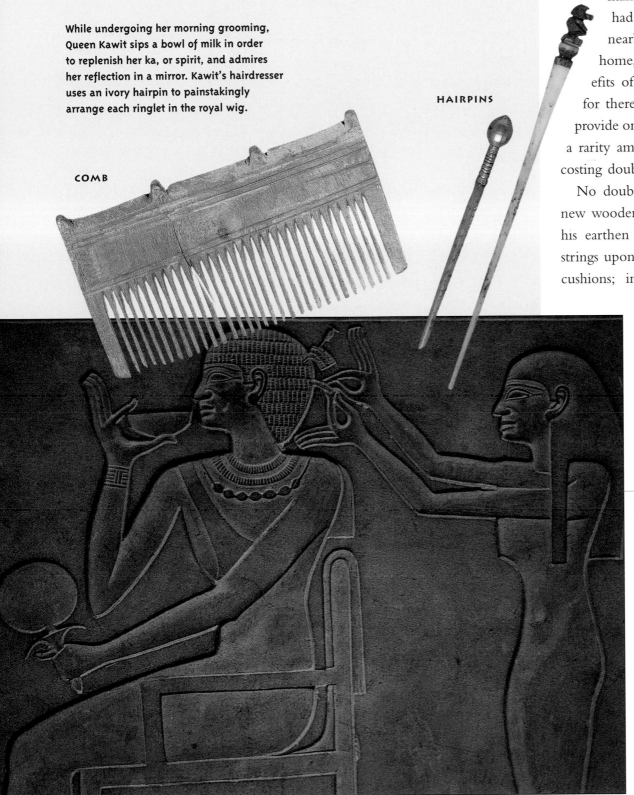

While undergoing her morning grooming, Queen Kawit sips a bowl of milk in order to replenish her ka, or spirit, and admires her reflection in a mirror. Kawit's hairdresser uses an ivory hairpin to painstakingly arrange each ringlet in the royal wig.

HAIRPINS

COMB

many brothers, each of whom had a large family, occupied nearby dwellings. In his new home, Paneb experienced the benefits of a foreman's compensation, for there his benefactor was able to provide on occasion the meat of an ox, a rarity among the workers, and wine costing double the price of barley beer. No doubt Paneb slept better on his new wooden bed than he had done on his earthen cot. Its frame held plaited strings upon which rested large, woolen cushions; in winter he enjoyed the warmth of woolen blankets, woven like shag rugs with long, loose pile that retained the heat of his body. In the summer Paneb used a cool wooden headrest, as he slumbered on light sheets of fine linen. He probably enjoyed the comfortable footstools as well, and cast a delighted eye upon the handsome pots whose traditional designs had been applied with consummate skill.

Instead of luxuriating in his newfound wealth, however, Paneb grew sullen and aggressive. Perhaps the good wine that Paneb now drank affected him adversely. Or maybe it was the heady feeling that accompanied the sudden elevation of his status, or the pressures of living in a household of newly acquired relatives who were jealous of his sudden good fortune and considered him an interloper. Whatever the reason, Paneb, in the household of Neferhotep, proved a difficult lad, belligerent, prone to heavy drinking and prolonged rages that often led to fights.

Despite his behavior, Paneb's luck held, for his adoptive father went on regarding Paneb as his successor. It may in fact have been early signs of Paneb's aggressiveness that led Neferhotep to believe that Paneb would make, if not a willing follower, then a good foreman, able to keep the other men in check.

The second of the two work gangs of Deir el-Medina was under the direction of a foreman by the name of Hay, who had inherited the job from his father. Paneb married one of Hay's relatives, a young woman named Wabet. The marriage might have been arranged to establish ties with the family of Hay, who would one day be his coforeman. But it is also possible that Paneb and Wabet themselves decided to marry, or at least were pleased to agree to their parents' scheme.

It may be that Paneb happened upon Wabet at the end of an afternoon, while strolling among the tombs in the Valley of the Kings during one of the religious festivals. Dressed for the special occasion, Wabet was probably wearing a long, tightfitting, pleated white linen sheath with short billowy sleeves, her long dark hair plaited in masses of tiny braids. Her sandals, made from papyrus leaves, were no doubt drawn up in front in the shape of a ship's prow, a style that had recently become fashionable.

To win Wabet, Paneb may have sought a love spell, as did one of his fellow villagers who used a magic chant that would induce the woman of his dreams to "run after me like a cow after grass, like a servant after her children, like a drover after his herd." Wabet in turn may have been inspired to express herself in terms similar to a young woman in a love poem, who said, "My heart thought of my love of you when half of my hair was braided. I came at a run to find you and neglected my hairdo."

Such emotional openness often continued far beyond courtship, as husbands and wives took pains to portray their handholding and affectionate embraces in the reliefs and paintings they ordered for their tombs. These portraits reflected the close ties of the nuclear family—a husband, his wife, and their children living in their own home—which was the norm. Premarital sex was permissible and men were allowed multiple wives, yet monogamy was standard, perhaps partly for economic reasons; few except the rich could afford more than one wife.

The marriage of Paneb and Wabet involved few formalities. According to custom, simply deciding to live together was sufficient to join a couple; no religious ceremony was necessary. The young couple soon added several offspring

THE STAFF OF LIFE
Pottery bread molds like the one at left are common artifacts surviving from ancient Egypt—for good reason: The Egyptian diet depended largely on bread. Flour for the bread, made from emmer wheat or barley, was ground daily by women using rollers on stones called saddle querns. Just as is done today, bakers kneaded together flour, yeast, and water—sometimes enriching the mix with milk or flavoring it with spices, honey, or fruit—and left the dough to rise. Then, as shown in the scene at upper right, they filled two-piece clay pots with the dough and set them over glowing coals. At precisely the right moment, the baker pulled the pots from the fire and freed the loaves with a few deft strokes of his stick.

to the busy household of Neferhotep, and at last the growing family moved to a home of their own.

Paneb arranged for workmen to build a brick wall, separating his family's living space from a room he designated as his workshop. He began to buy goods for his new house, such as chests and baskets woven of reeds and rushes, and a bed. Eventually, as foreman, he would be in a position to acquire more expensive goods, wooden furniture, for instance, and large copper cooking pots. Wabet probably added to the family income, as did many of the village wives, by weaving cloth and making clothes beyond the needs of her immediate family, so that she could barter them for other valuable items.

Despite his increasing family obligations, Paneb's contentious behavior continued, and eventually an incident occurred that tried Neferhotep's patience beyond endurance. While the source of this infamous quarrel between Paneb and his stepfather is not known, the results were apparent to all the villagers as they watched one night about 12 years after Paneb had left his stepfather's house. Paneb, consumed with fury, chased Neferhotep through the village and into his house.

"I will kill him in the night!" Paneb cried, pounding on the door as a group of village men tried to restrain him. "He took a stone and broke the door," one of Neferhotep's brothers later reported, and a band of men had to stand guard through the night at Neferhotep's house to protect him. Paneb then turned his fury against other villagers and according to Neferhotep's brother, "he beat nine men that night."

This time Paneb had gone too far. Instead of complaining to the village assembly, made up of the two foremen, the scribes, and other town notables, Neferhotep took the exceptional step of reporting Paneb to the pharaoh's vizier. In order to avoid the vizier's sentence, a severe beating or a term at hard labor, Paneb mounted a daring counterattack: As the king's top official was considering Neferhotep's charges, Paneb brought a complaint against the vizier.

Fortune once again favored Paneb. Around 1197 BC, palace intrigue had set the stage for the reception of Paneb's petition: Five years earlier, Amenmesse had usurped the throne from the crown prince, a young man who would eventually become Seti II. Now Amenmesse had died, and Seti II had at last taken his rightful place as pharaoh. The vizier in question had been appointed by Amenmesse. The new king undoubtedly had in his

THE HEALING ARTS

Some of the health problems that plagued the early residents of the Nile Valley have changed little since ancient times. Papyrus texts from 1500 BC list among common complaints ear infections, indigestion, headache, hernia, gallstones, and "smarting in the anus"—probably hemorrhoids. Abnormalities observed in mummies suggest tuberculosis, pneumonia, and polio. The average life expectancy for a man was about 35 years, for a woman, 30. The infant mortality rate was very high, while people who beat the odds and lived to an old age faced such ailments as arthritis and bone tumors.

In those days, many thought that internal disorders originated in the bowels as a result of faulty digestion and that other illnesses were carried on the wind or caused by supernatural agents—spirits, demons, or the malevolent dead. In reality, poor health was due largely to poor hygiene. For example, viral trachoma, a common source of blindness, was transmitted hand to hand by humans and eye to eye by the Nile's plentiful flies. Parasitic tapeworms came from contact with infected dogs, cattle, and other animals. Soil fouled by animal feces carried hookworm and roundworm, while the standing water in a farmer's irrigation ditches could harbor blood flukes that caused intestinal pain and kidney failure.

To prevent and combat disease, a combination of magical and medical

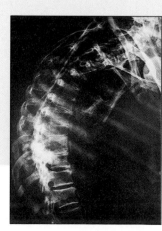

The curved back of an overburdened water carrier graphically depicts the effects of the hard physical labor that made up most Egyptians' everyday lives. The result could be permanent disability, as shown in the x-ray of a mummy's contorted spine.

A blind harpist's fingers caress the strings of his instrument *(below)*. Music was one of the few avenues open to the blind; those who could not work often became beggars. A diet of gritty bread—and the sand that found its way into all food— wore down the teeth of this man *(right)*, who died in his twenties. Even the pharaohs were susceptible to cavities, inflamed gums, and dental abscesses.

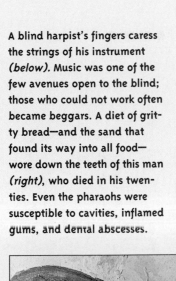

Unable to stand on his withered right leg, a man leans on a staff for balance. Some scholars believe that this carved image from the 14th century BC may be one of the earliest illustrations of the effects of polio.

resources were brought to bear. People could seek relief from their aches and pains by visiting various kinds of healers, conjurers, or priests. The more mainstream medical practitioner, or *swnw*—pronounced "soo-noo"—studied in a House of Life located at one of the major cult temples. There he would read treatises on topics ranging from wounds to gynecology. The medical students learned that a patient's pulse was associated with the heart—"it speaks out of the vessels of every limb"—but also that blood, along with breath, tears, mucus, urine, and semen, circulated through the body in a network of interconnected channels. Anatomical hieroglyphs showing human figures with the internal organs of animals suggest that an Egyptian doctor's knowledge of anatomy did not come from embalmers—who never dissected bodies—but from studying the work of temple butchers who sacrificed cattle and other animals.

A physician's bedside manner included interviewing patients, palpating abnormalities, examining secretions, and even smelling wounds. Along with aloe, garlic, and honey, his medicine chest might contain such items as lead, sandal leather, soot, semen, cow bile, and excrement—both animal and human. Salves and poultices prepared with these distasteful ingredients were intended to make the patient's body so repugnant that the disease—or the demon—would be compelled to find a more suitable host. At best this treatment had a limited effect; at worst it hastened the inevitable results.

One of history's first physicians, Hesire *(left)*, held the title Chief of Tooth-doctors and Doctors at the court of the Old Kingdom pharaoh Djoser. During that same period, the fractured forearm bones pictured below were wrapped in palm-fiber lint and set with tree-bark splints.

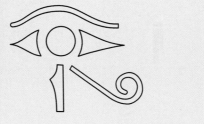

$^1/_2$ $^1/_4$ $^1/_8$ $^1/_{16}$ $^1/_{32}$ $^1/_{64}$

A New Kingdom headache remedy *(above)* recommends uttering a prayer "over a clay crocodile with grain in its mouth, a faience eye set in its head." When writing prescriptions, doctors used the individual parts of the eye of Horus symbol *(above, right)* to denote fractional measurements for the ingredients.

Requests for divine intercession were basic to the healing arts. The magical power of the votive inscription on a New Kingdom temple stele was enhanced by adding images of ears *(lower left)* to make it easier for the intended god to hear the petitioner's plea.

entourage powerful aspirants to the vizier's position, ready to seize on any pretense to depose the former pharaoh's chief officer. Then too, Paneb's charge against the vizier was probably a serious one suggesting some laxity in the vizier's oversight of the royal tombs. Whatever the case, Paneb the stonemason managed to obtain the discharge of the highest official in the land from his lofty post before he could act against Paneb.

How Paneb must have strutted and crowed to the wonder and admiration of the villagers! Perhaps even Neferhotep was proud of him. For in spite of all Paneb's foibles, his adoptive father did not abandon him, not even when Neferhotep was ill and surrounded by blood kin who entreated him to do so. After Neferhotep's death, Paneb became foreman, and the relatives of his adoptive father alleged that he had bribed the new vizier with the gift of five slaves belonging to Neferhotep. Any such gifts, however, would have paled beside the service Paneb had already done the new vizier by getting rid of his predecessor.

Another person who never left Paneb was his wife, Wabet, who might easily have done so, for divorce was an uncomplicated matter. Much could go wrong in a marriage; divorces probably occurred most frequently for adultery or infertility, but also for many other reasons, including strong personal dislike. Either partner could initiate the dissolution of a marriage simply by releasing the other from the marriage bonds. Had she divorced Paneb, Wabet would have been required to leave the household and return to the home of her parents. She could take with her any possessions she had brought to the marriage, and she would also receive a portion of the familial property and be free to remarry.

Wabet had other alternatives besides divorce. If Paneb had taken out his temper tantrums upon Wabet, she could have brought him before a local judge. While a man had the right to beat his wife, if she was injured he could be punished by receiving 100 lashes and forfeiting a portion of his possessions.

It is possible that Paneb adopted techniques for maintaining marital harmony, though, such as those recommended in a New Kingdom wisdom text: "Do not control your wife in her house when you know she is efficient. Do not say to her: 'Where is it? Get it!' when she has put it in the right place. Let your eye observe in silence; then you will recognize her skill."

Even so, Paneb was the kind of husband who would try any woman's loyalty. He may have loved Wabet, but after marrying her he found himself attracted to other women, and he pursued a series of affairs with a number of village wives. At one point his own eldest son, Aapehty, denounced him in a public declaration, listing the women with whom he had had liaisons. Adultery was regarded as a serious matter, although more so if the wife was the unfaithful partner. In such a case, besides a likely divorce ensuing, the culprits were sometimes punished by flogging. But throughout most of his life, Paneb seemed to get away with everything.

Among Paneb's lovers was a woman named Hunro, a weaver in the workshops of the temple of Ramses II. She was married to a tomb painter named Pendua, whom she divorced during her affair with Paneb. She then married Paneb's stepbrother, Hesysunebef, who also had been adopted by Neferhotep many years after Paneb's adoption. Hunro and Hesysunebef had a baby girl.

Throughout this period, Paneb remained Hunro's lover, and so it hardly seems surprising that three years after their marriage, Hesysunebef divorced his wife. Each of them made a public declaration of the contributions he or she had made to the family's accumulated wealth: "I gave her during three years, in every single month, 28 pounds of wheat, making nine sacks,"

MEASURE FOR MEASURE

"Give over your goods for my sweet syc-amore figs," cries a fruit vendor *(above, left)*, as a woman offers the contents of her bowl in exchange. Behind them, a vigilant market attendant and his leashed baboon nab a would-be thief in the act.

Bartering was the norm in the Egyptian marketplace, since money was unknown. If the seller didn't want what the buyer offered, silver coils and copper weights served as a medium of determining value. A commodity such as livestock or property, for example, might be assigned a value based on the weight of copper or silver, then swapped for something of equal worth. Shown at left *(clockwise from right)* are silver—in the form of a ta-pered ingot, shards of ore, and polished coils—and three spherical copper weights.

Hesysunebef asserted. Hunro, for her part, had provided the family with a large amount of cloth, and there ensued a debate over its value. A local merchant dispar-aged the fabric, declaring it a "bad" piece of work. After a bit more dickering, how-ever, they ultimately agreed on the division of goods, and the marriage was over.

For all his faults, Paneb served as a competent foreman for 15 years, apparently justi-fying his benefactor's choice. When he was not drunk or angry, he must have been charming, perhaps even charismatic. Besides being attractive to the village women, Paneb retained the loyalty and respect of his workers.

Paneb's luck, however, ran out before his boldness subsided: There came a day when one of his bitterest enemies, Amennakht, Neferhotep's brother, who had hoped to succeed his sibling as foreman, submitted to the authorities a long list of charges against Paneb that he had been compiling for years. They included stealing, assault, rape, adultery, and even murder. Some of the allegations were probably based on hearsay, distortions, or outright lies, but others were undoubtedly true.

Among these transgressions was the theft of a golden goose from the tomb of a queen, one of the wives of Ramses II. "He took an oath by the lord concerning it, saying 'it is not in my possession.' But they found it in his house," asserted Amennakht. Caught red-handed robbing a tomb and then swearing falsely, Paneb was removed from his foremanship and may have been executed in 1175 BC, as is suggested by a shard of pottery bearing the phrase "the killing of the chief."

Upward mobility in Deir el-Medina was not limited to males, and a young girl might, like Paneb, rise above the state in life to which she was born, usually through a good marriage. After Paneb and Wabet were mar-

When Naunakht reached her 78th year, she went to the village court to declare her will and have the document properly recorded: "I am a free woman," she began, signaling at once that no one could take her for granted. She then said that she had brought up eight children "and gave them everything that is proper to their station."

Apparently Naunakht felt that not all of them had appreciated and returned the care and consideration she had expended on them, for she continued: "I have grown old and they do not look after me in their

"I have grown old and they do not look after me in their turn."

ried, Naunakht, a 12-year-old village girl, wed the scribe Kenherkhepeshef, a childless man who had just turned 70.

The unusual union may have done them both good. Suddenly becoming rich and taking on adult responsibilities at such a tender age could have played a part in the development of Naunakht's independent spirit. And having a young wife may have kept Kenherkhepeshef lively for the next 16 years as he continued his scribal work, his health further safeguarded by a magic charm to keep away the demons that were thought to bring disease. Folded into a small square, the charm bore the admonition "Get back, Shehakek, who came out of heaven and earth" and hung by means of a flax string around his neck.

Upon the death of her heirless husband, Naunakht received the bulk of his property, more than the one-third normally due a widow, and soon afterward she married one of the village workmen. She lived with him for 30 years and raised eight children. The eldest she named Kenherkhepeshef, after her first husband, surely a sign of her affection for the elderly gentleman.

turn. Whoever has aided me, to them I will give of my property; he who has not aided me, I will not give of my property."

Following the death of Naunakht, four of her eight children lost out on the inheritance, but Kenherkhepeshef, the eldest, in addition to his one-fourth of the property, received, "as a reward, a washing bowl of bronze, over and above its fellows."

The people of ancient Egypt have long been known by the manner in which they memorialized themselves. Fantastic amounts of time and effort went into their many monuments of stone, each specifically designed to present an individual's most appealing face to the gods in order to attain the happiest life everlasting. But these images, while very revealing, still represented only their public faces. Through careful sifting of a few scattered remains, however, such as the ostraca and papyri and ruins of Deir el-Medina, it is possible to catch a glimpse of the rich, full, and compelling lives of people such as Hekanakht and Paneb, ancient dwellers in the valley of the Nile.

A Woman's Place

Of all the people he encountered in his journeys throughout the ancient world, perhaps none surprised the fifth-century-BC Greek historian Herodotus more than those he met in Egypt. "The Egyptians themselves in their manners and customs seem to have reversed the ordinary practices of mankind. For instance, women attend market and are employed in trade, while men stay at home and do the weaving," he wrote incredulously. Though a widely traveled and highly educated man of Greece's Golden Age, Herodotus was used to seeing the women of his homeland confined to their residences with virtually no rights or influence in society.

In contrast, women in Egypt could be seen in the marketplace bartering goods, working in the fields, or participating in the celebration of festival days. The art and literature of ancient Egypt give some indication of the place of women in society. The statue at left, for example, portrays a woman in one of her roles—bearing offerings to the dead consisting of a duck and a basket containing jars of beer. And when women appeared in Egyptian literature, scribes used the silhouetted shape of a seated woman shown in the background to express the idea of *female* in hieroglyphs.

Egyptian women from all walks of life possessed rights, responsibilities, and privileges not seen anywhere else in that era. By Herodotus's time, four women, including the powerful Hatshepsut, had led Egypt as god-kings, and a number of queens, most notably Nefertiti, wife of Akhenaten, and Nefertari, consort of Ramses the Great, had served with their husbands as partners in power. And while most women could not hope to attain the prestige of Hatshepsut or Nefertiti—political power, bureaucratic position, and even literacy remained inaccessible to those outside elite circles—they still played vital roles in the Egyptian world.

The legal status of Egyptian women, in particular, was appreciably higher than that of women elsewhere in the world. Although laws in Egypt were based on custom rather than on code, women had rights comparable to those of men. Representing themselves—without a male guardian—women wrote their own wills and could bear witness and testify in court. They also owned and controlled their own property. One court document records that a wife loaned some of her silver to her own husband but required that it be repaid over three years at a 30 percent interest rate.

Egyptians viewed marriage as a personal matter requiring only the consent of both partners. In the event of a divorce, which the couple also handled themselves and either spouse could request, the former wife usually kept what was hers as well as one-third of the joint property. But during Egypt's Late Period, some couples left nothing to chance and prepared the equivalent of a prenuptial agreement. After a divorce, both partners were free to remarry.

Women shared with men the same expectations for eternal life on the Nile's west bank. A wife usually joined her husband in his tomb, but she might have her own dedicatory markers to pave the way to her afterlife. In death, a woman's family provided her with mummification and all the funerary offerings worthy of anyone—man or woman—of her class.

Garbed in a panther skin, Princess Nefertiabet reaches for loaves of bread to ease her hunger in the afterlife in this dedicatory stele dating from the Old Kingdom. The food and other necessary articles portrayed on the stele represent the funerary provisions made on behalf of the deceased.

"I shall lay down offerings for you when the sun's light has risen."

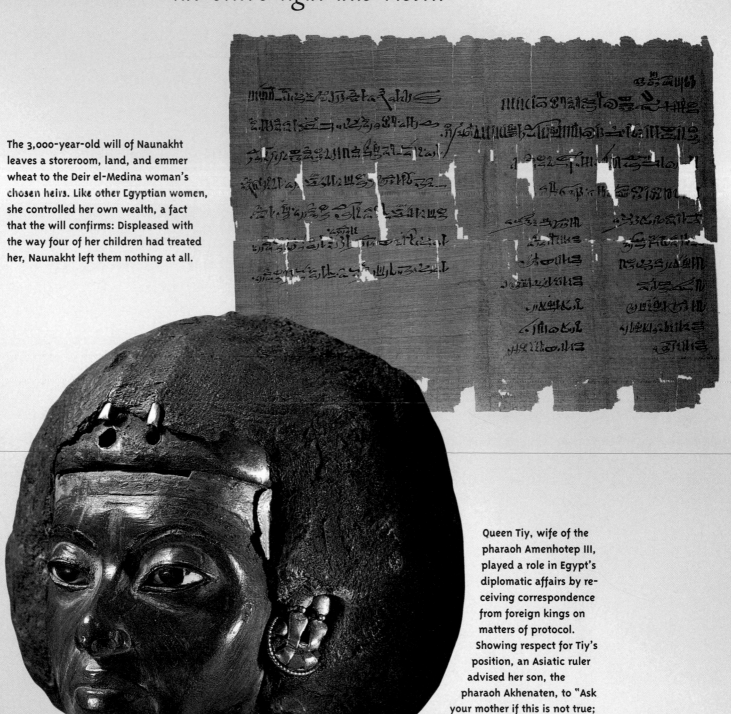

The 3,000-year-old will of Naunakht leaves a storeroom, land, and emmer wheat to the Deir el-Medina woman's chosen heirs. Like other Egyptian women, she controlled her own wealth, a fact that the will confirms: Displeased with the way four of her children had treated her, Naunakht left them nothing at all.

Queen Tiy, wife of the pharaoh Amenhotep III, played a role in Egypt's diplomatic affairs by receiving correspondence from foreign kings on matters of protocol. Showing respect for Tiy's position, an Asiatic ruler advised her son, the pharaoh Akhenaten, to "Ask your mother if this is not true; she knows all about it."

Women's Work

Whether at home, in the marketplace, or in a workshop, women in the ancient Nile Valley shouldered the responsibilities of daily life right along with the men. By itself, managing a household was an enormous task that included preparing food, caring for children, and making everything from clothing to baskets and other home furnishings by hand.

In addition, the mistress of the household controlled her family's wealth by bartering her homemade goods at the various markets that formed the backbone of the Egyptian economy. On larger estates, wives had their own servants and oversaw the farms and workshops whose produce and goods added to the family's assets.

Outside the home, male and female workers toiled together in the fields and in the bakeries and breweries that supplied the bread and beer central to the Egyptian diet. And although many jobs were open only to men, such as those within the Egyptian bureaucracy, resourceful women still found employment as millers, musicians, beauticians, florists, and doctors.

Ironically, weaving, the occupation of men that so startled Herodotus, once was the sole domain of women. Weaving was important work, second only to farming. Egyptians needed great quantities of linen for clothing and for wrapping their dead—a single mummy required as much as 400 yards of cloth. Until the New Kingdom, it was mostly women who spun and wove the cloth, supervised other weavers, and delivered the woven textiles for payment.

"Do not check on your wife
in her house when
you know that she is competent."

A female brewer strains beer from a fermented loaf of barley bread through a sieve into a holding vessel. Women and men shared the task of making the beer that was the thick, staple drink of the Egyptian diet.

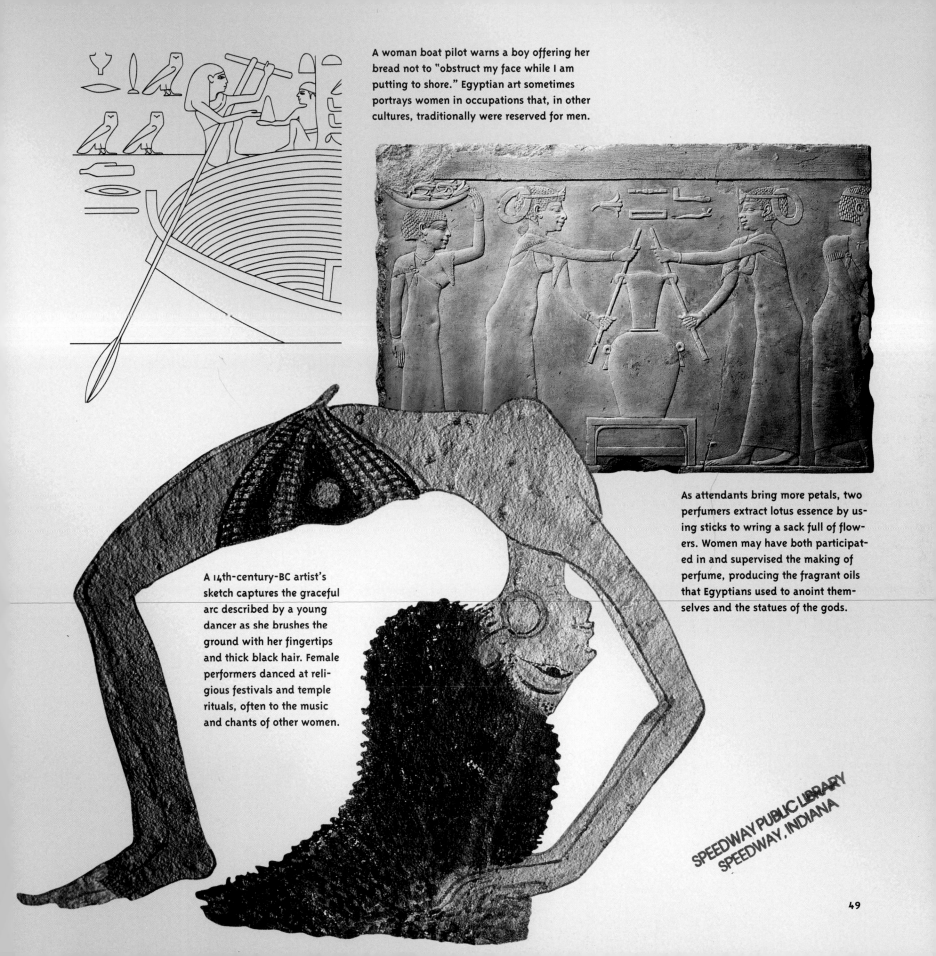

A woman boat pilot warns a boy offering her bread not to "obstruct my face while I am putting to shore." Egyptian art sometimes portrays women in occupations that, in other cultures, traditionally were reserved for men.

As attendants bring more petals, two perfumers extract lotus essence by using sticks to wring a sack full of flowers. Women may have both participated in and supervised the making of perfume, producing the fragrant oils that Egyptians used to anoint themselves and the statues of the gods.

A 14th-century-BC artist's sketch captures the graceful arc described by a young dancer as she brushes the ground with her fingertips and thick black hair. Female performers danced at religious festivals and temple rituals, often to the music and chants of other women.

Love and Marriage

Romantic love and the prospect of a happy marriage figured prominently in an Egyptian woman's life, as the words from an ancient love song attest: "Little does he know how I long to embrace him, and for him to send word to my mother." A woman's relatively independent status provided some opportunity for socializing and even premarital relations with the opposite sex.

But the ideal in Egypt for both men and women was marriage, for that was the best setting for the ultimate goal: having children. Young men, with longer reproductive spans, may have tended to put off commitment. So-called wisdom texts, guidebooks for proper conduct, often exhorted their male readers to "Take a wife while you're young, that she may make a son for you; happy the man whose people are many, he is saluted on account of his progeny."

Girls were considered ready for marriage when they attained sexual maturity, and it appears that many wed between the ages of 12 and 14. Marriage between cousins and other close relatives took place reg-

ularly, but the joining of brother and sister occurred only within the royal family, where the purity of bloodlines was paramount. Family and guests celebrated a marriage with feasting and entertainment; no ceremony, religious or civil, was required. Afterward, a woman customarily went to live with her new husband in his or his family's home, where she assumed her role of mistress of the household.

In an ideal Egyptian marriage, spouses treated each other with affection and respect. Tomb art reflects such harmony, often portraying couples in the most tender poses—holding hands or with one's arm resting on the other's neck or shoulder. In some cases, husband and wife embrace each other tightly, and many inscriptions accompanying the images of wives read "his beloved."

A young girl on the cusp of adulthood carries lotuses and ducks gathered during a hunting expedition with her father. Though her figure is womanly, the girl's face still resembles that of a child.

Sennefer, mayor of Thebes, and his wife Meryt, a musician in the temple of Amun, greet each other fondly in a painting from Sennefer's tomb. Intended to portray the couple's reunion in their next life, the scene evokes the deep affection that was shared by husbands and wives in the ancient Nile Valley.

"*The sight of her makes me well!*
When she opens her eyes, my body is young;
her speaking makes me strong;
embracing her expels my malady."

Pregnancy and Childbirth

Cradling her child's head in one hand, a mother tenderly suckles her baby. In ancient Egypt, this special bond between mother and child lasted up to three years—longer than in many other cultures—and acted as a form of birth control.

Fertility was highly prized in ancient Egypt, and most women wanted and expected to bear children. Newly wed young women often gave birth within the first year or two. If a woman experienced difficulty becoming pregnant, the medical knowledge of the day offered a number of regimens to aid conception; one recommended squatting over a steaming mixture of frankincense, oil, dates, and beer.

When a woman suspected that she had conceived, she might conduct a test by urinating over seeds to see if they germinated. Although the ancient Egyptians had no understanding of hormones, it is now known that these substances in a pregnant woman's urine can cause grain to sprout.

Egyptian women probably continued their daily chores right up until the time of delivery. Once labor had begun, female family and friends—and perhaps a midwife—gathered to assist. Charms and prescriptions hastened the birth: One such prescription, "to loosen a child in the body of a woman," called for a plaster of sea salt, emmer wheat, and rushes to be applied to the woman's abdomen. The gathered women invoked the goddesses Isis, Hathor, and Taweret to protect the birth, as the mother strained, kneeling or squatting, sometimes on bricks to allow the midwife room to catch the baby in the final moments of delivery.

Despite family, magic, and the gods, childbirth had its risks: Maternal mortality rates undoubtedly were quite high. Queen Mutnodjmet of the 18th Dynasty, for one, probably died in childbirth; the body of a fully formed fetus was found with her body. In addition, as many as 50 percent of all children may have died before reaching the age of five.

For those who wished to avoid maternity, early attempts at contraception included sponges made of plant fibers coated with a mixture of crocodile dung and sour milk, and suspensions of honey and natron, a salt. These efforts may have been successful occasionally, because the lactic acid in milk and alkaline substances like natron can slow the movement of sperm.

Seated on a *meskhenet,* or confinement chair, a woman braces herself for the rigors of birth. Two manifestations of the cow-horned goddess Hathor support the mother-to-be's elbows and impart, by their presence, a safe and easy delivery.

Pregnant women guarded against miscarriage by wearing amulets to keep evil spirits from entering the womb. The shape of the Isis-knot amulet at left followed the design of a vaginal plug that Isis was said to have used to protect her unborn son Horus from his uncle Seth.

Guardian of pregnant women, the obviously fertile goddess Taweret drew from the fiercest elements of Nile life: a hippo's head, the legs and paws of a lion, and a crocodile-tail headdress.

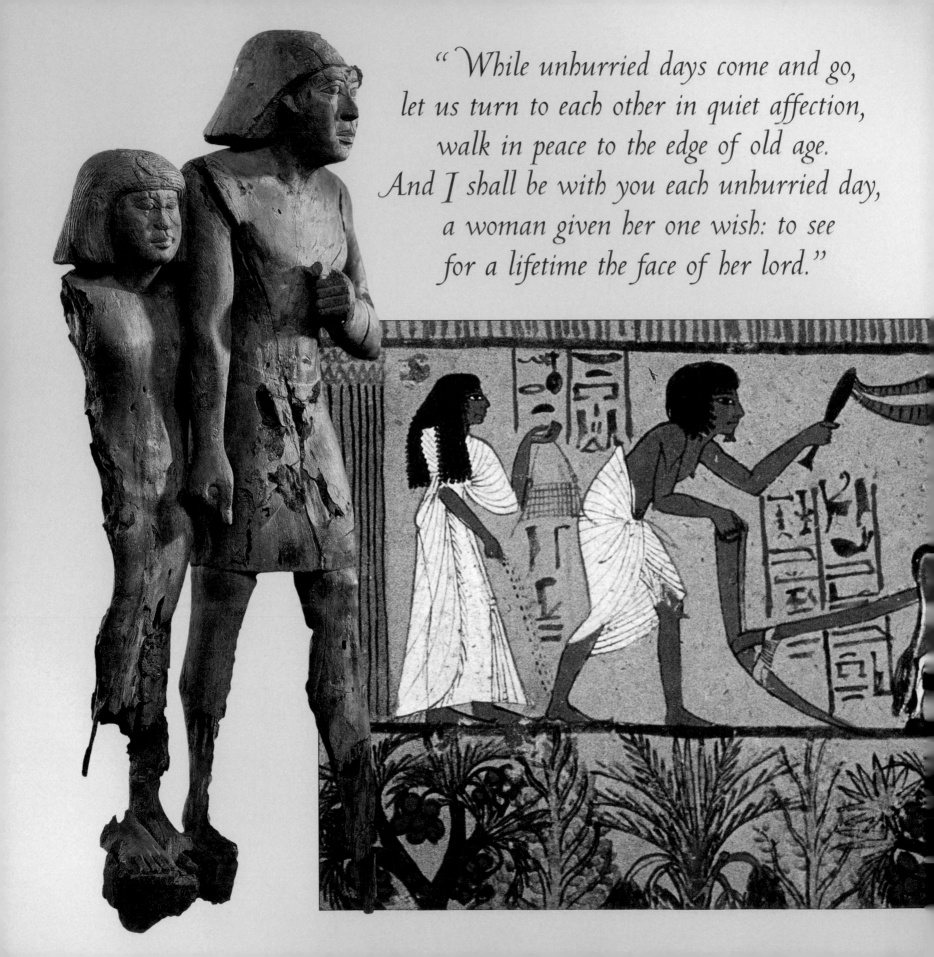

"While unhurried days come and go,
let us turn to each other in quiet affection,
walk in peace to the edge of old age.
And I shall be with you each unhurried day,
a woman given her one wish: to see
for a lifetime the face of her lord."

Into the Next World

When some couples in ancient Egypt spoke of their eternal love for each other, they may have meant it quite literally. These husbands and wives expected to be companions in death as they had been in life, so they tried to forge bonds of love and affection that would endure into the next world. Many also commissioned works of funerary art—tomb paintings and sculptures—that showed themselves as young and vital, to help ensure that their afterlife together would be a happy one.

During the period of time that a spouse awaited that posthumous reunion with the deceased partner, he or she maintained contact by writing letters. Some of these letters seem merely conversational, asking advice about daily problems. Others beseech and implore, requesting assistance with family illnesses or financial issues. But many of the messages capture the universal sentiments of grief and pain felt by anyone who has lost a mate. One bereaved husband lamented at length in a note left at his wife's tomb: "And when this condition had come to pass with you, I spent this total of eight months without eating or drinking like a human being. And now, behold, I have passed three years dwelling alone, though it be not right that one like me should be caused to do it. And behold, I have done it on your account."

Sennedjem, a Theban tomb builder, and his wife Iyneferet (*left*) pictured themselves in the afterlife harvesting the fields of Iaru, or paradise. By commissioning the life-size sculpture at far left, another couple hoped to provide an alternate repository for their souls if their mummies were damaged or destroyed.

Children of the Nile

"Aneksi!" or "She belongs to me!" cried an Egyptian mother at the birth of her baby. Subsequently that exclamation of delight became her new daughter's name. In ancient Egypt, a child's birth brought great joy, and parents frequently chose names that reflected their excitement: "Welcome to you" or "This boy I wanted." Some names, such as "Amun has proved gracious," paid grateful tribute to a god. Often children acquired nicknames that revealed the tenderness felt by parents for their little ones. A favorite for girls was Miw, a word that sounds its meaning: "little cat."

Egypt's youths remained close to their mothers, breastfeeding until the age of three. Mother's milk provided some immunity to illness, but once weaned, children were more susceptible to infection and disease. For protection, parents sought the help of the gods, tying amulets and pendants around their babies' necks. Some pendant cases contained tiny papyrus scrolls inscribed with chants and spells to drive away maladies. If a child did get sick, medical intervention especially tested a parent's devotion: The remedy to draw away one illness from a baby required a nursing mother to eat a mouse.

57

At Play

"Your arm is much stronger than his. Don't give in to him," exhorts the hieroglyphic caption on a Sixth Dynasty tomb drawing. Beneath the inscription stand two lines of boys engaged in a game easily recognizable today: tug of war. In this version, the opposing captains grasp each other by the wrists and pull fiercely while two chains of teammates hold on to the leaders from behind.

Many games that were enjoyed by the ancient Egyptians continue to enchant children thousands of years later. Boys and girls living along the Nile played at leapfrog, wrestling, and a donkey game in which players balanced one another on their backs. They loved whirling games that made them dizzy, and they also liked to throw and juggle balls.

Playthings, also, were remarkably similar to their modern counterparts. Egyptian children played with basic objects such as sticks and mud as well as with elaborate animals with jointed legs and mouths that moved. Tugging on the string of one of the most ingenious toys made its four carved-ivory figurines dance and twirl.

As might be expected in the punishing Egyptian heat, swimming was a favorite pastime for youths. Racing and wrestling figured among popular athletic activities. In addition, boys of the upper classes received instruction in archery and horsemanship in order to prepare them for their future roles as warriors and rulers.

A young girl's parents chose to portray her for posterity with her treasured pet kitten in this statue carved in the 14th century BC. Ancient Egyptians kept cats, dogs, birds, and even monkeys as domestic animals.

Toys ran the gamut from simple leather, reed, linen, or wood balls to more complicated works, such as a carved wooden mouse with a moving tail and a cat with a working jaw *(below)*, whose parts were set in motion when a child pulled a string. Dolls varied in design from painted wooden paddles, some with beaded hair and painted decorations, to sophisticated figures with lifelike bodies and movable limbs *(left)*.

At right, four girls test their balance and accuracy in a piggyback game of catch. Although the original rules for the contest are lost, experts believe that teammates switched positions when a player dropped a ball.

Coming of Age

An apprentice, carrying a papyrus roll and a writing tablet, follows his mentor, a high official. Pupils learned to write on wooden tablets covered in plaster, such as this one *(above, right)* inscribed with hieroglyphs in black ink.

"You shall not spare your body when you are young; food comes about by the hands, provision by the feet," advised a New Kingdom proverb. For most Egyptians, education began early and was largely vocational: Boys learned a trade from their fathers, going to work with them as farmers or laborers; girls helped at home and pitched in when needed in the fields, harvesting and gleaning.

Children of the ruling class received a more formal education in writing, literature, and arithmetic. Some pupils proved as reluctant to study as their modern counterparts: One declared over his copy tablet, "Lesson-time endured forever, like the mountains!" Teachers were quick to punish such laziness: An Egyptian proverb held that "A boy's ears are on his back; he hears when he is beaten."

Most young scholars were male, studying to become scribes, draftsmen, and bureaucrats. But an excavated portrayal of a princess holding a writing tablet indicates that some daughters of the nobility also attended classes. Almost certainly, these girls did not learn to read and write to prepare themselves for employment, however, but for the social and cultural benefits that literacy offered.

Two young boys assist a pair of government bureaucrats during the inspection of a field of wheat for tax assessment purposes. The official at right carries a line to measure the government's quota.

"As for writing, it is profitable to him who knows it . . .
pleasanter than bread and beer. . . .
It is more precious than a heritage in Egypt,
than a tomb in the West."

A boy of 10 or 12 undergoes circumcision, a procedure that
may have marked the transition to manhood. At
right, a priest applies ointment to ease the pain, indicated by
the hieroglyphic caption, "I will make it comfortable."
On the left, a helper grasps the boy from behind
during the procedure. A caption instructs the assistant to
"Hold him firmly. Don't let him swoon."

CHAPTER TWO

Lords of the Two Lands

Hatshepsut, one of the few women ever to rule Egypt, appears in the traditional manly guise of a pharaoh, complete with a ceremonial beard, on the wall of a chapel she built at the Karnak temple in Thebes. Wearing the bulbous White Crown of Upper Egypt and holding a flail, she takes part in a ritual designed to honor the god Amun and appeal to him for prosperity and fertility, symbolized by the bull at her side.

The people of Egypt were perplexed. Tradition dictated that a man should preside over them as pharaoh and god-king. But the ruler they were now being asked to revere and obey was indisputably a woman.

Her name was Hatshepsut, and she had taken charge of the affairs of state in the year 1503 BC, following the death of her husband and half-brother, Tuthmosis II. Such royal marriages between relatives were not uncommon in ancient Egypt, for they united two people of the highest origins—descendants of god-kings—and produced heirs whose divine right to rule was beyond question.

Alas, Hatshepsut had provided her husband with a daughter but no son. When Tuthmosis II died, he left as heir a boy he had fathered by one of the secondary wives in his harem—a secluded quarter of his household occupied by honored Egyptian women and princesses from foreign lands sent as diplomatic offerings to the king. Officially, Hatshepsut was just serving as regent for that youthful heir, Tuthmosis III, until he grew up. But now his boyish locks had been shorn as a mark of maturity, and Hatshepsut was still very much in command.

Sovereignty suited her well. Faced with the prospect of having to yield to the half-royal stripling in whose name she ruled, she rebelled.

All that impeded her was the fact that she was a woman, and Hatshepsut was not one to let mere gender hold her back.

So she proclaimed herself pharaoh and god-king in her own right. Being aware of the cautious and conservative temper of her subjects, however, she was careful to reassure them by honoring the customs of kingship. She adopted all the pharaoh's time-honored titles as her own, with the sole exception of the overly masculine Mighty Bull. Statues portrayed her as a man, even to the extent of showing her wearing the false beard that was one of the pharaoh's ancient emblems of power.

Yet such formalities could never satisfy the deeper concerns of her people. What they really wanted to know was whether her rule was sanctioned by the gods, without whose approval the kingdom could not hope to flourish. The wives and daughters of pharaohs had long been women of great influence, and a few had even held power for a while in the absence of male heirs. But could Hatshepsut show that she had the god-given right to rule now that Tuthmosis III had come of age?

Hatshepsut was not alone in seeking such legitimacy. Supporting her were priests and officials who were loyal to her and want-

A bearded Hatshepsut exudes a timeless serenity in this fragment from an 18-foot-high limestone statue portraying her as Osiris, a god who rose from the dead and inspired pharaohs in their quest for immortality. The statue graced Hatshepsut's spectacular mortuary temple (lower left), hewn out of the cliffs west of Thebes at the site known today as Deir el-Bahri. Hatshepsut dedicated the temple to "my father Amun," and inscribed on its walls the story of how Amun fathered her and granted her the right to preside over Egypt as pharaoh.

ed her to remain in power. Schooled as scribes and steeped in religious texts, they knew that words had power to command reverence and devotion. Their task was to compose an account of Hatshepsut's divine ancestry that dispelled any doubt—on earth or in heaven—that she had a sacred claim to her position.

When Hatshepsut was satisfied with their efforts, she commissioned workers to inscribe that account on the facade of her great mortuary temple, whose limestone terraces descended in stairstep fashion from the steep cliffs bordering the west bank of the Nile, across from the ceremonial center of Thebes. Following her death, priests would make offerings in that temple to ensure that the greatest of Egypt's gods would embrace Hatshepsut as one of their own. Even while she lived and prospered, however, the sanctuary and its inscriptions publicly proclaimed her majesty. Each day at dawn, the sun rising over Thebes set the temple walls aglow and illuminated the hieroglyphs that told of Hatshepsut's miraculous conception.

According to the inscription, her sire was none other than Egypt's supreme god, Amun—the mysterious Hidden One who had given birth to himself at the dawn of time and engendered all the other deities. During the reign of Hatshepsut's father, Tuthmosis I, a great warrior king, Amun set out to produce a child who could carry on in the glorious tradition of that pharaoh. Amun began by consulting Thoth, the ibis-headed god of wisdom and patron deity of scribes, who advised him to take the human form of Tuthmosis I and impregnate the king's principal wife, Ahmose.

Amun did as he was counseled by Thoth and crept up on the queen while she lay sleeping in the palace, rousing her with his divine fragrance. In the words of the inscription: "He went to her immediately, desiring her. He caused that she see him in the form of a god." Queen Ahmose knew him in all his splendor, and "his love passed into her limbs." Having done "all that he desired of her," Amun told the queen that she would bear him a daughter and that she should name the child Khenemetamen Hatshepsut, or She Whom Amun Embraces, Foremost of Noble Women.

When Hatshepsut came into the world, the people of Egypt assumed that she was the king's natural child and that she would be content to serve her father and his male successors in the traditional manner, as a daughter, wife, and mother. In time, however, she realized her divine nature and fulfilled her destiny as pharaoh. As her name foretold, she was embraced by Amun and brought forth blessings for the people of Egypt—regular floods, bountiful harvests, and the reassuring knowledge that their ruler was beloved of the gods.

The story inscribed on Hatshepsut's temple was exceptional because it justified the royal ambitions of a woman. But similar accounts were put forth by the men who reigned before and after her to show that they too were divinely destined to rule. Although more than a few of Egypt's rulers reached the pinnacle of power by means of sheer human effort and intrigue, they all claimed divine descent and stood before their subjects as god-kings.

In theory, pharaohs lived on after death as gods and were to be revered as such by the living. In practice, however, dead kings often suffered indignities. Thieves plundered their tombs, priests neglected their rites in favor of more pressing duties, and

THE TEMPLE ECONOMY

Three times a day—at dawn, midday, and dusk—the high priest of the god Amun disturbed the still waters of the sacred lake at Karnak to wash and purify himself before entering Amun's innermost sanctuary. Then, intoning prayers, the priest and his retinue would bathe and dress the god's statue and leave offerings of bread, meat, beer, and wine. These time-honored rituals secured the god's favor toward the people of Egypt and held back the forces of chaos for another day.

To support such simple acts of reverence, Karnak and other temple complexes grew into thriving enterprises. They were not only integral parts of the Egyptian government but also engines that drove the local economy. Temples had granaries to supply their own breweries and bakeries. Skilled weavers produced the god's linen in temple shops.

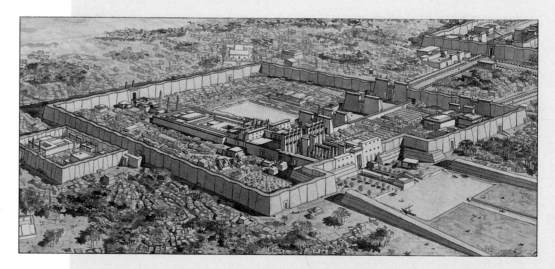

Over the course of 3,000 years, Karnak grew from a small shrine to a sprawling community, shown here about 370 BC, surrounded by high walls.

A breath of wind ruffles the waters of the sacred lake at Karnak, once a bustling religious complex where kings erected chapels and obelisks to honor the god Amun.

Goldsmiths and jewelers labored to create the god's necklaces and other adornments. Karnak even had its own seagoing trading ships to bring back from foreign lands such necessities as myrrh for incense and cedar for the bark the god was carried in on sacred occasions.

Such busy concerns required ample sources of income. Temples owned significant tracts of land—often bequeathed by wealthy citizens in return for a day or two of memorial prayers—and collected up to one-third of the grain harvested on that land as rent, to be stored in temple granaries. Other revenue came from gold and silver mines and gifts of precious stones.

Overseeing it all was a veritable army of priests. The high priest, who was appointed by the pharaoh, carried out the daily rituals on the king's behalf. His deputy, or "second prophet," was responsible for the temple property, staff, and businesses. Under them were part-time priests who served in the temples at regular intervals as porters, sacrificers, head gardeners, painters, or scribes and monitored the work of various functionaries, including carpenters, vintners, and bakers.

The pharaoh as god-king had both a spiritual and a worldly inter-est in contributing to these holy enterprises. Part of the spoils of war brought home by the king's army went to the temple. In exchange, the temple served as a kind of reserve bank for the pharaoh, who supplemented what he collected in taxes from the country at large by drawing on surpluses in temple granaries to feed the men building royal tombs and monuments.

Payment to the priests came in a form known as the reversion of offerings. Once Amun had taken his fill of the spiritual essence of the food and beverages placed before him, the temple staff consumed the solid remainder. Priests also served occasionally as judges, dispensing justice to the citizenry at the temple gates. For the Egyptians, the temple of Amun—and its bureaucracy—was an inescapable presence, providing justice for some, income for many more, and a spiritual focal point for all.

The priest Penmaat, portrayed at left holding incense, served Amun at Karnak about 950 BC as head archivist, supervising the scribes who recorded the commodities flowing into and out of the treasury. As a priest, he was allowed to marry and raise a family outside the temple, but he had to abstain from sexual activity for several days before entering the sacred precinct.

Plying the Nile to collect rents for the temple granaries, barges like this one could hold about 650 sacks of grain—the yield from 72 acres of farmland. Temples provided insurance by returning surpluses collected during bountiful years to help feed the populace in times of want.

In this view of activities at Karnak in the 13th century BC, the priestly scribe Neferenpet *(seated, below)* keeps a careful tally as assistants weigh offerings to the temple. Elsewhere, workers carry baskets into one of the temple's storerooms *(below, left)*. Other chambers hold jars of oil and bolts of fine linen *(upper left)*.

ambitious successors defaced their monuments. Such was the fate of Hatshepsut. After holding power for roughly two decades, she either died or was deposed by Tuthmosis III. In time, he erased all public references to her as pharaoh. Her statues were mutilated, and her name was chiseled from royal inscriptions.

Even when pharaohs were at the height of their worldly powers, they depended mightily on others. As Lord of the Two Lands—Upper and Lower Egypt—the god-king professed to be the master of all things seen and unseen. But to administer the state, he needed the help of mere mortals, many thousands of them, organized in an elaborate bureaucratic pyramid. At its base were the common scribes, who served in various capacities as clerks and recordkeepers. Some scribes collected taxes from farmers in the fields; others doled out supplies to soldiers in their camps or forts. In the busy temples, with their workshops and storehouses, priestly scribes tallied the goods and balanced the books.

Above them in the pyramid were dignitaries such as high priests, army officers, mayors, and provincial governors. The most gifted and powerful of those officials might be chosen by the pharaoh to serve as his central administrators, who boasted such impressive titles as Master of the King's Largess. Higher up, just below the pharaoh himself, stood his two viziers, or deputies, one for Upper Egypt and one for Lower Egypt (originally, there was just one vizier, but the enormousness of the task led to a division of responsibilities). The vizier

dured another such crisis when Asiatics known as the Hyksos came to power in the delta at the end of the Middle Kingdom. In ousting the Hyksos, Ahmose I of Thebes founded the 18th Dynasty—to which Hatshepsut belonged—and inaugurated the golden age of Egyptian might known as the New Kingdom. Rulers of the New Kingdom revealed themselves to posterity in rich detail. Hatshepsut and her successors told of their dreams and deeds on the walls

"No one rebels against me. All foreign lands are my subjects."

served as the king's eyes and ears—the overseer who, in the words of one inscription, was duly informed of "all that is and is not."

The lofty pharaoh was not just the supreme judge and ruler of the people and the commander in chief of the army but also the sole representative of the gods on earth. As divine delegate, the king ensured that the gods would continue to favor Egypt by keeping her secure. "No one rebels against me," declared Hatshepsut in an inscription praising her father Amun. "All foreign lands are my subjects."

Rulers who could maintain such strength and stability earned the gratitude of their people. The Egyptians had a word for this happy state of affairs—*maat,* or the order and harmony that prevailed when authority was respected and traditions were honored. In truth, there were periods of violent unrest in Egyptian history. One such nightmare had occurred centuries before Hatshepsut's time, when the Old Kingdom of the pyramid builders fragmented into warring factions. "I shall show you a son as a foe, a brother as an enemy, a man killing his own father," recalled one text written after order had been restored. "Every mouth is full of 'I want,' all goodness has fled." More recently, Egypt had en-

of their monuments and corresponded with royalty abroad, affording future generations telling glimpses of the flesh-and-blood figures who assumed the idealized role of god-king. Among the vivid characters who wore the crown during this period were Amenhotep III, who took a commoner as his principal wife and placed her in a setting of unparalleled grandeur; the sun king Akhenaten, who turned his back on Thebes and the Great Temple of Amun and founded a new cult at his own capital, only to be denounced as a heretic by his successors; and the formidable Ramses II, who outdid the most extravagant of his predecessors when it came to amassing wealth and wives and erecting stupendous images of himself. Like all rulers, these kings were fallible. But the continuing strength and prosperity of Egypt confirmed people in their belief that even the most imperfect of

The vizier Ramose, who served in that powerful post for two kings of the 18th Dynasty—Amenhotep III and his son Akhenaten—wears the finery of a nobleman, including a heavy gold disk collar and a heart amulet around his neck, in this scene carved on the wall of his tomb. Viziers prided themselves on being well informed, and they advised pharaohs on spiritual as well as worldly matters. One vizier boasted that there was nothing he was "ignorant of in heaven, on earth, or in any hidden place of the underworld."

pharaohs served divine purposes and conferred greatness on Egypt.

In Thebes citizens celebrated the fruitful link between their pharaoh and almighty Amun during the boisterous festival of Opet, held annually at the time of inundation, when the silt-laden waters of the Nile overspread the flood plain and lapped at the city walls. In that season of expectation, when work in the fields was suspended, the people joined with their pharaoh in a grand procession that began at the Karnak temple, dedicated to Amun, and ended at the Luxor temple at the south end of the city.

At Karnak on the appointed day, priests in Amun's sanctuary lovingly bathed the image of the god, dressed him in fine linen of many colors, and draped him with jewelry. Then they placed the god in his enclosed shrine atop a ceremonial boat, or bark, supported on poles. Ranks of priests hoisted the bark onto their shoulders and carried it out through the pillared halls and courtyards of Karnak and into the noisy streets, where the common people jostled

A servant pours wine for a seated woman during the Beautiful Feast of the Valley, which allowed the living to commune with their loved ones in the afterworld. The woman and her companion hold lotus blossoms, symbols of rejuvenation, whose fragrance pleased both the living and the dead. Wine was offered liberally to all family members, alive and deceased.

FESTIVITIES IN A ROYAL CITY

Among the acrobats and musicians performing above in honor of Amun during a festival in Thebes are women shaking sistrums like the one at right. The instrument produced a soft jangling sound resembling a breeze blowing through papyrus reeds that was said to soothe gods and goddesses such as Hathor, who when angry took the form of a lioness.

The ancient Egyptians found a welcome respite from their daily routine in the stirring religious festivals that highlighted their calendar. Two such events were unique to the royal city of Thebes: the Opet Festival and the Beautiful Feast of the Valley.

Celebrated annually in late May or June, the Beautiful Feast of the Valley provided an opportunity for all Thebans to honor the dead, and the gods who watched over them, by joining in a colorful procession on the west side of the Nile, site of the city's necropolis and the royal tombs and mortuary temples. Festivities began at Karnak on the east bank, where the sacred image of the god Amun was placed in an enclosed shrine atop a ceremonial bark, or boat, which was mounted on poles and carried by priests down to the Nile. Originally, Amun alone was so honored, but later the god was joined by images of his wife, Mut, and their child, Khons, set in their own portable vessels. At the riverside, the holy family and their shrines were loaded onto barges and towed across the Nile to visit the pharaoh's mortuary temple and the temples of other gods. The public procession ended at the necropolis, filled with tomb chapels where citizens housed the remains of their dead relatives and performed rituals for them.

Every family wealthy enough to have a tomb chapel entered that chamber and laid out offerings of food and drink for the dead. The celebrants feasted heartily themselves and drank wine until they passed out and entered a twilight state between life and death that brought them closer to their departed loved ones. The Valley Feast thus gave people the chance to express their deepest concerns—their love of family, their reverence for the gods, and their preoccupation with the afterlife.

Later in the year, when the Nile flooded, Thebans joined in another dramatic ceremony, the festival of Opet. On that occasion, the people accompanied the pharaoh and the enshrined image of Amun in a

VALLEY OF THE QUEENS

VALLEY OF THE KINGS

DEIR EL-MEDINA

HATSHEPSUT'S MORTUARY TEMPLE
(DEIR EL-BAHRI)

N E C R O P O L I S

WESTERN
THEBES

NILE RIVER

LUXOR
TEMPLE

KARNAK

TEMPLE
OF MUT

TEMPLE OF
KHONS

THEBES

GREAT TEMPLE
OF AMUN

one another to catch a glimpse of the sacred vessel. The king himself was there to greet Amun and conduct him to the Luxor temple. Soldiers beat drums, while men from Nubia danced to songs of devotion.

Luxor lay a mile and a half from Karnak, and in Hatshepsut's time, the procession was made entirely on foot, with the priests stopping at way stations to rest. In later days, the bark was carried to the Nile and placed on a larger vessel, which was towed upriver to Luxor by oarsmen in tugboats and gangs of men on the riverbank pulling at ropes. This was no task for common laborers: High government officials vied for the strenuous duty.

Thebes (*left*) hosted the Valley Feast and the Opet Festival, both of which began at Karnak. The Valley Feast culminated at the necropolis, west of the Nile. The Opet procession led to Luxor on the east bank. During these and other festivals, the king—Hatshepsut in the scene above, wearing a crown adorned with the ram's horns of Amun—attended Amun's bark, which was carried by priests.

procession that began at the Karnak temple and concluded at the Luxor temple at the south end of Thebes. There the pharaoh took part in a mysterious ritual that confirmed his powers. Afterward, priests carried Amun in his bark back to Karnak, and Thebans had a chance to ask the god questions that could be answered yes or no. A man might inquire if his brother in the army was in good health. If the bark dipped forward toward the questioner, the god's answer was yes; if it backed away, the reply was no. On such occasions, the populace also enjoyed the largess of the gods. During one Opet Festival in the 12th century BC, temple officials distributed to citizens 11,341 loaves of bread and 385 jars of beer.

After reaching Luxor, the pharaoh and priests left the crowd behind in the forecourt and accompanied the bark into the dark, incense-laden recesses of the temple, where they communed with another holy image representing Amun in a different guise—the potent Amun-Min, who inseminated the earth and brought abundant harvests. That sacred encounter put the pharaoh in touch with the royal ka, or the immortal essence of kingship. When he emerged from the sanctuary, clothed in fresh linen and reinvested with godliness, the citizens greeted him with praises. For whatever errors he had committed

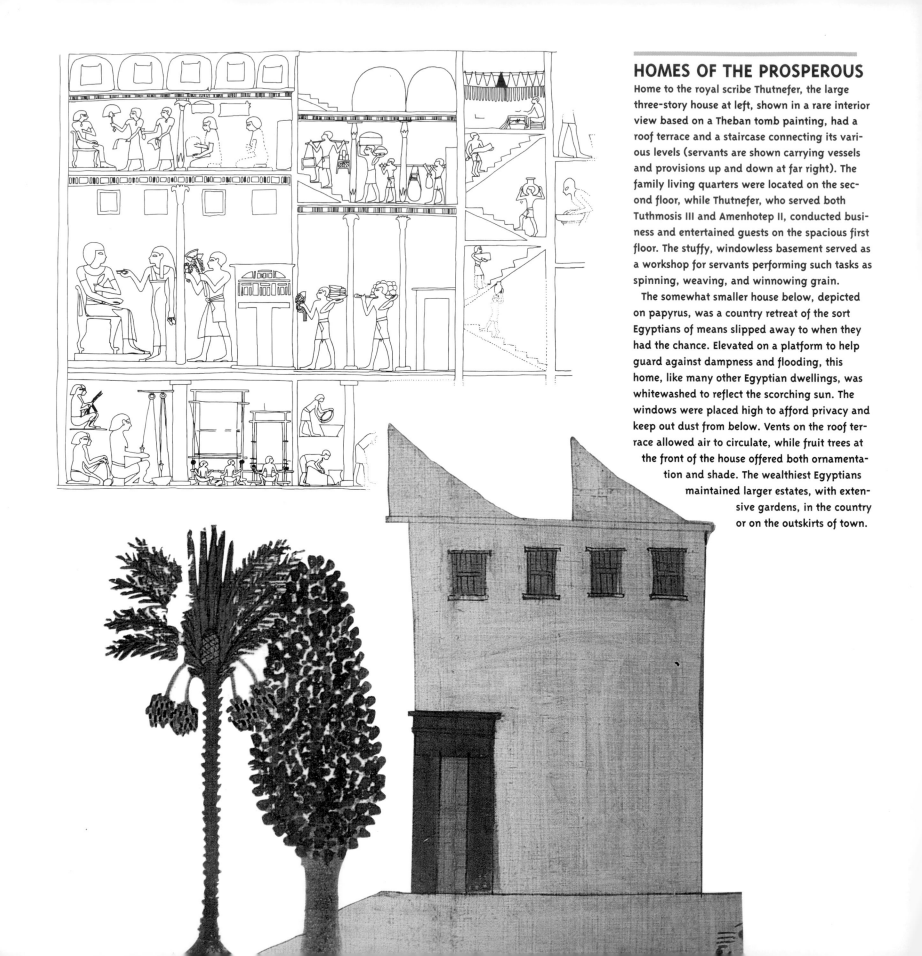

HOMES OF THE PROSPEROUS

Home to the royal scribe Thutnefer, the large three-story house at left, shown in a rare interior view based on a Theban tomb painting, had a roof terrace and a staircase connecting its various levels (servants are shown carrying vessels and provisions up and down at far right). The family living quarters were located on the second floor, while Thutnefer, who served both Tuthmosis III and Amenhotep II, conducted business and entertained guests on the spacious first floor. The stuffy, windowless basement served as a workshop for servants performing such tasks as spinning, weaving, and winnowing grain.

The somewhat smaller house below, depicted on papyrus, was a country retreat of the sort Egyptians of means slipped away to when they had the chance. Elevated on a platform to help guard against dampness and flooding, this home, like many other Egyptian dwellings, was whitewashed to reflect the scorching sun. The windows were placed high to afford privacy and keep out dust from below. Vents on the roof terrace allowed air to circulate, while fruit trees at the front of the house offered both ornamentation and shade. The wealthiest Egyptians maintained larger estates, with extensive gardens, in the country or on the outskirts of town.

in the past, he was once more the embodiment of divine strength and generosity, the source of bounty and well-being for Egypt.

If any one reign could be said to epitomize the glory days of the New Kingdom, it was that of the luxury-loving Amenhotep III. When he came to power as an adolescent about 1386 BC, he inherited an empire of unprecedented scope. To the north, the princes of Syria and Palestine bowed to his command; to the south, Nubia rendered him lavish tribute in gold. Indeed, wealth poured in from every direction—turquoise and other precious stones to adorn members of the royal family in this life as well as the next; perfumes and panther skins for the priests and their fragrant temples; and ebony and ivory to grace the homes of the pharaoh's privileged followers. Other rulers could only look on in envy. "Gold is as common as dust in your country," a Babylonian king would write.

The world must have seemed a place of infinite possibility to young Amenhotep. The battles that had helped forge the Egyptian empire had been fought and won by his predecessors. Apart from some minor actions in Nubia, which were duly proclaimed as great victories, his long reign was to be largely peaceful.

Freed from military exertion, Amenhotep devoted himself to sport and sumptuous display. One traditional royal pastime was hunting, and he pursued it on an epic scale. Under the burning African sun, he set out in the company of selected courtiers in light, two-horse chariots to target antelope and ibex on the desert fringes of the Nile flood plain. A sure-armed charioteer handled the reins for the king, who strained to keep his balance while the cart careered over the sandy scrubland. As the driver closed in, Amenhotep drew his bow and loosed an arrow at the panting, panic-stricken beast in his path, adding one more number to the grand tally kept by scribes of all the royal kills.

Amenhotep also tested his skills against bigger game reserved for him alone, although his attendants carefully arranged matters so as not to put the royal person at risk. Wild bulls, for example, were corralled before he came to slaughter them. So too, no doubt, was the most dangerous quarry Amenhotep took on—the lion. An official tally for the first 10 years of his reign put the number of "fierce lions" that His Majesty bagged "with his own arrows" at 102.

"A monument of eternity and everlastingness, of fine sandstone worked with gold throughout."

All the arts flourished under Amenhotep, and none more so than architecture. Not since the days of the pyramids more than 1,000 years before had Egypt seen such a frenzy of construction. Like the pyramid builders, New Kingdom monument builders probably conscripted Egyptians for the task, although perhaps in smaller numbers. Thanks to recent imperial conquests, they had a fresh source of labor for their works—foreign slaves.

Thus Amenhotep was able to afford several massive building projects. He commissioned magnificent new shrines at Karnak and Luxor. Across the river from Thebes rose the pharaoh's own mortuary temple, guarded by two 60-foot-high statues of the king (known as the Colossi of Memnon). Amenhotep dedicated that temple to "his father Amun," in the hope that the greatest of gods would grant him life and dominion without end. The structure was a "monument of eternity and everlastingness," Amenhotep declared, built "of fine sandstone worked with gold

Ducks, geese, and fish swim among lotus petals in the pool of this lush garden on an aristocratic New Kingdom estate, shaded by acacias, date palms, and fig trees laden with fruit. Well-to-do Egyptians loved their gardens, which served as oases amid the pervasive heat and dust.

throughout." Like other great temple complexes of the day, it was a world unto itself, with fishponds, flocks of fowl, and a workshop, "filled with male and female slaves."

Credit for this and other projects went to the king himself. The task of designing the monuments and overseeing the construction, however, was shouldered by his trusted aides—most notably a celebrated builder and administrator who bore the king's own name: Amenhotep, Son of Hapu. A man of common origin, he rose to become one of the leading figures in the land. He boasted in writing that he was "promoted because of the soundness of his counsels, elevated by the king over his peers." Like other officials, he owed much to his early training as a scribe, which allowed him to master the "tools of Thoth," or hieroglyphs. "I was well schooled in their secrets," he declared, "and my advice was sought on all their points."

Of all the royal building projects, the one that most absorbed the king and his aides was his palace complex on the west bank of the Nile, across from the heart of Thebes—a cluster of gaily decorated chambers, courtyards, and pleasure gardens covering more than 50 acres. Here, as in humbler settings, the basic building material was mud brick (stone was reserved for temples and other monuments that were meant to last for eternity). Gangs of masons clad in rough loincloths toiled from dawn to dusk on the palace grounds, mixing moistened clay with chopped straw and shaping the bricks in molds before drying them in the sun. The brick walls erected at such pains were then plastered over and painted with floral designs and other motifs to delight the king and his courtiers.

The pharaoh's privileged followers lived like wealthy landowners elsewhere in Egypt but had even larger houses and more servants. Guests arriving for dinner at the walled estate of a prominent official would be admitted to a well-tended garden, where date palms and fig trees shaded a long rectangular pool. There children too young to join in the evening's festivities could paddle a papyrus skiff amid the lotus blossoms while their elder siblings relaxed beneath awnings, nibbling fruit retrieved from the treetops by trained monkeys. The mother of the house could enjoy herself without fretting over her youngsters because wealthy families often entrusted their children to nurses.

Flanking the pool were sheds where the servants crafted pots, tended domestic animals, and prepared meat, bread, beer, and other fare for the forthcoming banquet. Guests entered the master's house at the far end of the garden, through a portico graced

A floor painting from the palace of Amenhotep III at Thebes conjures up the beauty of the garden indoors by portraying waterfowl amid lotus blossoms and other aquatic plants in the naturalistic style of the period.

with tall wooden columns, and took their seats in a spacious central hall, where a serving girl wearing only a waistband poured water over their hands before they feasted from bowls made of silver and alabaster.

The king lived in even grander surroundings and spent nearly all his waking hours in the presence of servants and aides. Each morning, trusted retainers bathed the king in water mixed with soda or some other cleansing agent, plucked him with tweezers, shaved him with a razor of bronze or gold, and rubbed him down with unguents such as hippopotamus oil that kept his skin supple in the hot, dry climate. Like other men and women of his circle, he commonly wore a wig, lined his eyes with kohl kept in a beautifully crafted cosmetic chest, and wore golden bracelets as well as a splendid collar, made of multicolored glass beads or other alluring materials.

Once properly attired, Amenhotep might go for a stroll in the royal gardens and admire his exotic plants and animals (in earlier days, Hatshepsut stocked her grounds with baboons and giraffes imported from central Africa, and later pharaohs kept pet lions). Afterward, the king might visit the women of his harem at their lavish quarters. He needed plenty of room at the palace to accommodate his growing company of wives and their many personal retainers. One of the princesses in his harem arrived from the distant kingdom of Mitanni (a powerful realm in eastern Syria) to seal an alliance with Egypt, accompanied by 317 female attendants. Amenhotep was required to support them all and pay court to the princess in the manner to which she was accustomed.

Amenhotep III, portrayed here in polished red granite, wears the tall crown of Upper Egypt, adorned in front with the uraeus—a rearing cobra symbolizing his power as king. Ascending the throne when Egypt was at the height of its imperial strength, Amenhotep III had little need to lash out at enemies abroad and concentrated his attention instead on architectural projects.

If he failed to treat her or other princesses in his harem with due respect, he stirred up hostility abroad. He once sent a message to the king of Babylon, asking that ruler for his daughter in marriage. The king replied angrily that his sister had already been received as a wife by Amenhotep and had since become a virtual nonentity at the palace. "No one has seen her," her brother complained, "or knows whether she is dead or alive." Amenhotep offered written assurances that the princess was still among the living, but she was clearly not one of his favorites. Nor would he ever consider appeasing the king of Babylon or any other foreign ruler by offering one of his daughters as a bride in return. "From old," he declared proudly, "the daughter of an Egyptian king has not been given in marriage to anyone."

No princess meant as much to Amenhotep as his principal wife, Tiy, whom he married in his early teens around the time he came to power. She was nonroyal by birth, the daughter of Ay, a prominent Egyptian army officer who served as a master of horses and charioteers. Throughout Amenhotep's long reign, Tiy retained his public devotion. As an avid hunter, he may have felt more respect for the child of a horseman than for the pampered daughters of kings. Or perhaps he simply prized Tiy's beauty and wit above those of any royal woman in his circle. Over the years, she bore him two sons and four daughters and took on official responsibilities, issuing decrees in her own name and corresponding with foreign rulers. Her power and grace were memorialized in a statue at Amenhotep's mortuary temple. There she sat beside her husband on the throne, arm in arm with him, clad in a long, tight linen gown that displayed her hips and breasts to advantage and wearing an imposing crown that combined the queen's traditional vulture headdress with the uraeus, or cobra emblem, denoting kingship.

Amenhotep honored her with other conspicuous displays of respect and affection. To celebrate his 11th anniversary in power, he constructed a pleasure lake for her along the Nile. Such was the labor force at his command that only 15 days after he gave the order, he was able to escort Tiy across the lake in the royal barge. Crewmen strained at the oars, and courtiers gathered around to salute their majesties. But the fond young

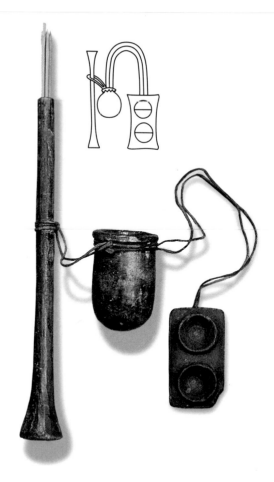

Amenhotep, Son of Hapu, architect for Amenhotep III, sits with a sheaf of papyrus in his lap in the cross-legged pose of a scribe, an occupation he mastered before being summoned to serve the king. A palette containing his dried ink dangles over his left shoulder. The typical palette (bottom, right) held two disks of pigment, one red and one black, across which the scribe brushed his reed pen (left) after moistening it with water. Together, the pen, the jar, and the palette formed a hieroglyph denoting the term scribe (below).

couple seemed oblivious to distractions.

Tiy had little reason to regard the women of the harem as rivals in the romantic sense. Secure in her position as Great Royal Wife, she worried about the secondary wives only to the extent that they bore the king sons to challenge the claims of her own offspring. As it happened, Tiy's elder son by Amenhotep died young. Later, she may well have worried about the health of the surviving boy, for she sanctioned the marriage of her daughter Sitamun to Amenhotep, with the apparent purpose of providing the king with additional male heirs and ensuring that the succession remained within the family. Such a match between father and child would have been unthinkable for ordinary Egyptians, but god-kings could freely wed a daughter or a sister if that would help furnish Egypt with a worthy successor.

For Amenhotep, who was now in his forties, the vexing issue of succession was one more reminder of his mortality. As he approached the 30th anniversary of his reign, he laid plans for a ceremony that would signal to his followers that he still had the god-given strength to rule. He drew inspiration from the past, when pharaohs of long tenure staged a

THE SCRIBE'S SKILLS

In ancient Egypt, the mysteries of writing could be deciphered by only a select few. Perhaps one in a hundred Egyptians could read and write, a fact that endowed scribes with prestige and power. Theirs was the most impor-tant of all occupations, claimed one text written during the Middle Kingdom to encourage young scribes: "There is no job without an overseer except the scribe's." In fact, many scribes performed clerical tasks for high priests and officials. But knowledge of writing was essential for all who aspired to leadership.

The training for scribes was rigorous because the written language was complex. Students had to master more than 700 hieroglyphs, some of them representing objects or ideas and others representing sounds. Beginners practiced writing on ostraca—flat stones or broken pieces of clay pottery that could be found anywhere. As the student progressed, he copied out texts dictated by the instructor. Some were amusing animal tales, and others were stern moral tracts that had less

Sheets of papyrus, such as this example from the 13th century BC, were made by cutting long slices from the inner white pith of papyrus reed stalks and laying them out crosswise to form a mat, which was then pounded with a mallet into a sticky sheet and left to dry under a weight. Once the plant's juices had evaporated, the sheet was light and pliable. The scribe had only to burnish the papyrus surface with a piece of wood or ivory, then he could begin to write.

At left, laborers scoop grain into standardized measures, as a scribe seated on a mound keeps count on his fingers and standing scribes (far left) record the tally, using their palettes as writing boards. Scribes kept notes on narrow scraps of papyrus affixed to palettes like the one at right, equipped with a slot to hold pens.

effect on unruly youngsters than the teacher's stick. The curriculum included not only reading and writing but also mathematics so that the would-be scribe could serve as a tax collector, treasurer, quartermaster, or architect.

Successful graduates enjoyed a life free of manual labor. Their soft hands and clean white linen kilts were signs of their privileged status. And they earned the respect of posterity as well, for it was through their writings that the genius of ancient Egypt endured.

The chart at right shows 25 of the phonetic symbols used by Egyptian scribes to represent sounds in the spoken language. (In addition to such phonograms, there were hundreds of ideograms, representing objects or concepts.) The hieroglyphs in the first column denote sounds associated with the objects symbolized—a vulture represents a sound roughly approximated by the vowel *a*, for example, and a basket stands for the sound *k*. Because hieroglyphs were originally carved in stone, they tended to be angular. Scribes working with reed pens on papyrus developed a rounded, flowing script known as hieratic (*second column*), which later evolved into a plainer script called demotic (*third column*).

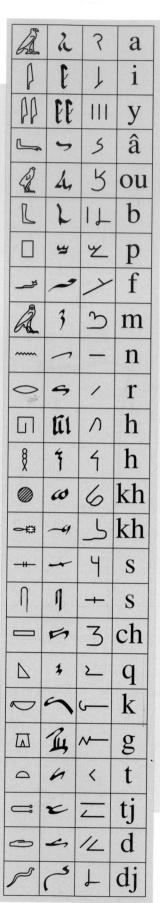

			a
			i
			y
			â
			ou
			b
			p
			f
			m
			n
			r
			h
			h
			kh
			kh
			s
			s
			ch
			q
			k
			g
			t
			tj
			d
			dj

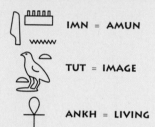

1		
5		
10		
100		
1000		

5,285 =

Calculations for everything from the number of wine jars to the weight of an obelisk were denoted by the hieroglyphic numerals in the second column and their hieratic equivalents in the third column.

Cartouches from the panel at right spell out various titles of King Tutankhamun, as defined below. The name Tutankhamun consists of phonograms for the sounds *tut* and *amun* and the ankh sign for the concept *living*.

LIVING IMAGE OF AMUN

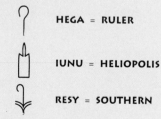

IMN = AMUN

TUT = IMAGE

ANKH = LIVING

RULER OF SOUTHERN HELIOPOLIS

HEGA = RULER

IUNU = HELIOPOLIS

RESY = SOUTHERN

LORD OF THE MANIFESTATIONS OF RE

RE = SUN GOD

KHEPERU = MANIFESTATIONS

NEB = LORD

The cartouches on this panel from the back of a cedar-wood chair discovered in Tutankhamun's tomb are flanked by ancient symbols of royalty, including the Mighty Bull and the falcon god Horus, shown wearing the double crown of Upper and Lower Egypt.

jubilee called the Heb-Sed which was intended to replenish the king's power.

Priests combed the temple archives for ancient references to the Heb-Sed that would help make Amenhotep's jubilee more authentic. In the meantime, laborers toiled near the palace grounds to build a temple to Amun and a colonnaded pavilion for the occasion. Messengers fanned out across the land to summon representatives from all the administrative districts of Egypt, who were instructed to bring with them sacred images from their local temples so that those gods too could witness and confirm the forthcoming rite of renewal. Dignitaries arrived from abroad as well, fully expecting to be received by the king, in accordance with diplomatic protocol. Amenhotep had much on his mind, however, and left at least one royal visitor feeling slighted. "My chariots were ranged in the midst of your mayors' chariots," complained the king of Babylon to Amenhotep, "and you never gave them a glance."

None of those who were on hand would soon forget the royal entertainment that opened the festivities—the sweet fragrance of the perfume cones that crowned

the heads of the guests and the fresh garlands that servants draped about their necks; the intoxicating sight of dancers from distant lands in their scant tunics, leaping and twirling by torchlight; the haunting strains of pipers and harpers, whose songs urged the revelers to make merry.

When the Heb-Sed ritual itself commenced, all eyes were on Amenhotep, who arrived at the pavilion with Tiy by boat, rowed by his leading courtiers. In times past, pharaohs had celebrated the Heb-Sed by running a brisk circuit around markers that symbolized the boundaries of the kingdom. There is no evidence that Amenhotep revived that old custom, but he most likely toured the grounds in grand fashion, visiting the various gods in attendance and demonstrating with his every gesture that he was still in command, still fit to rule.

The onlookers may have been reassured for the moment, but the king could not long disguise the fact that he was past his prime. For too many evenings, he had feasted on rich fare—beef from the royal herds, washed down with wine from vineyards in the delta, sweetened with honey. Egyptian sculptors reveling in the new artistic freedoms of his reign were not afraid to portray him as a potbellied figure, slumping on the throne. And now when he dined, he felt the sharp pangs of abscessed teeth, an affliction that would plague him to the grave.

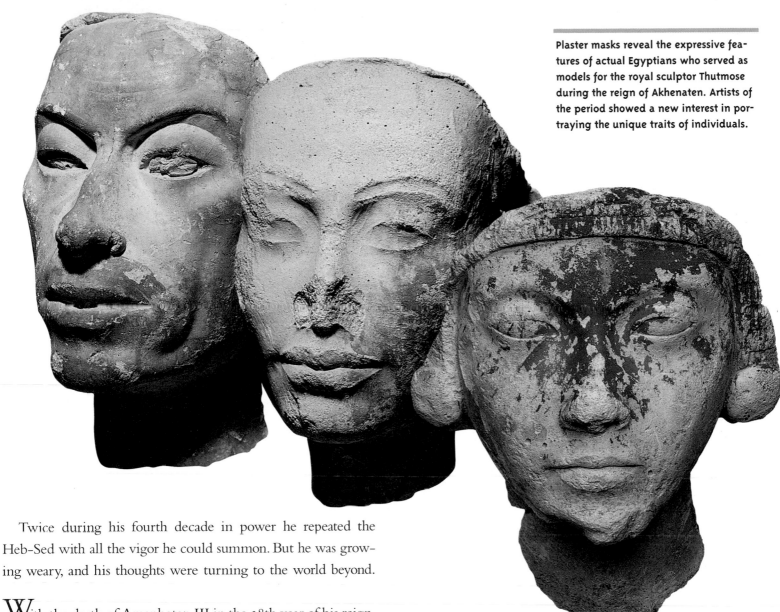

Plaster masks reveal the expressive features of actual Egyptians who served as models for the royal sculptor Thutmose during the reign of Akhenaten. Artists of the period showed a new interest in portraying the unique traits of individuals.

Twice during his fourth decade in power he repeated the Heb-Sed with all the vigor he could summon. But he was growing weary, and his thoughts were turning to the world beyond.

With the death of Amenhotep III in the 38th year of his reign, power passed to his sole surviving son by Tiy. The young king was crowned Amenhotep IV, but he bore little resemblance to his father, either in body or in spirit. In his prime, Amenhotep III had lived up to the physical ideal of the pharaoh as a strong man, capable of laying waste to lions and bulls if not to legions of foreigners. But his successor, as portrayed by court artists, was an awkward-looking youngster with a protruding jaw and broad thighs that were almost feminine in appearance. His curious condition did not prevent him from perpetuating his royal line: He wed the beautiful Nefertiti and raised six daughters. But his looks may well have set him apart from others at court at an early age and encouraged him to live by his own standards.

Much that had given pleasure to his father proved hateful to the young king. He grew disenchanted with Thebes and its brooding monuments. Above all, he disdained the sanctuaries of Amun, the Hidden One, who seemed to shrink from the light as if he feared exposure. During his fifth year in power, the king sig-

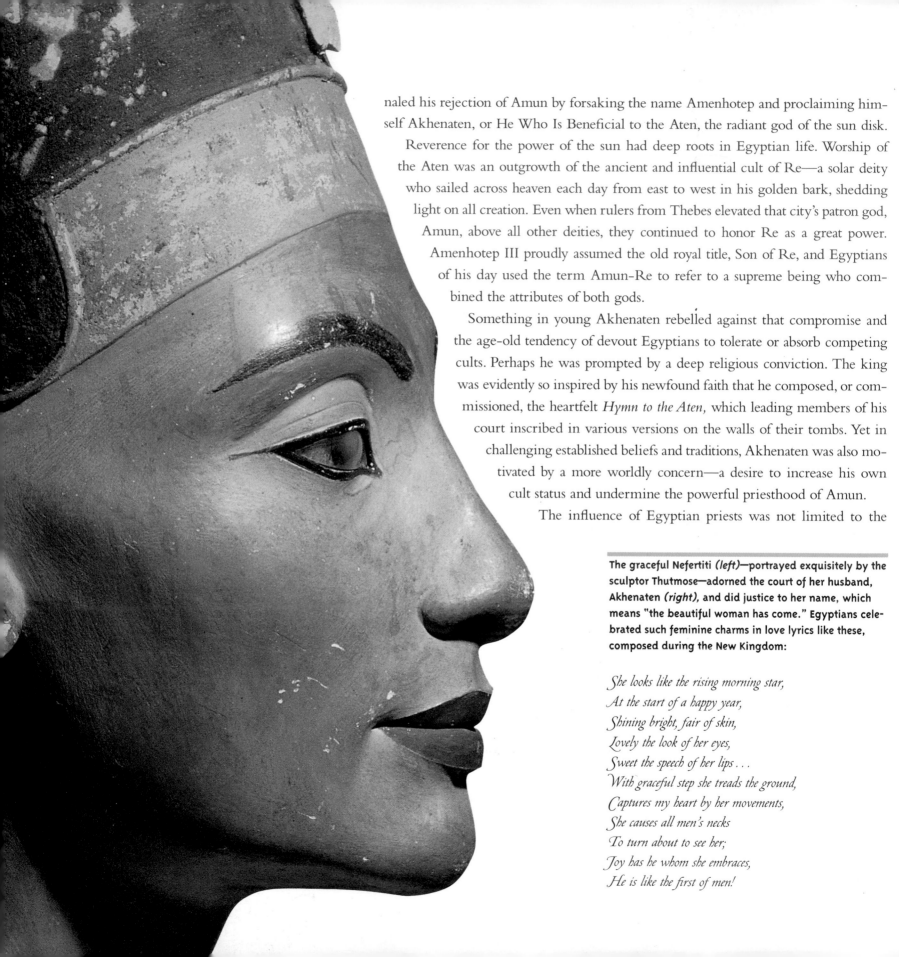

naled his rejection of Amun by forsaking the name Amenhotep and proclaiming himself Akhenaten, or He Who Is Beneficial to the Aten, the radiant god of the sun disk. Reverence for the power of the sun had deep roots in Egyptian life. Worship of the Aten was an outgrowth of the ancient and influential cult of Re—a solar deity who sailed across heaven each day from east to west in his golden bark, shedding light on all creation. Even when rulers from Thebes elevated that city's patron god, Amun, above all other deities, they continued to honor Re as a great power. Amenhotep III proudly assumed the old royal title, Son of Re, and Egyptians of his day used the term Amun-Re to refer to a supreme being who combined the attributes of both gods.

Something in young Akhenaten rebelled against that compromise and the age-old tendency of devout Egyptians to tolerate or absorb competing cults. Perhaps he was prompted by a deep religious conviction. The king was evidently so inspired by his newfound faith that he composed, or commissioned, the heartfelt *Hymn to the Aten,* which leading members of his court inscribed in various versions on the walls of their tombs. Yet in challenging established beliefs and traditions, Akhenaten was also motivated by a more worldly concern—a desire to increase his own cult status and undermine the powerful priesthood of Amun.

The influence of Egyptian priests was not limited to the

The graceful Nefertiti *(left)*—portrayed exquisitely by the sculptor Thutmose—adorned the court of her husband, Akhenaten *(right),* and did justice to her name, which means "the beautiful woman has come." Egyptians celebrated such feminine charms in love lyrics like these, composed during the New Kingdom:

She looks like the rising morning star,
At the start of a happy year,
Shining bright, fair of skin,
Lovely the look of her eyes,
Sweet the speech of her lips . . .
With graceful step she treads the ground,
Captures my heart by her movements,
She causes all men's necks
To turn about to see her;
Joy has he whom she embraces,
He is like the first of men!

temple grounds. Most priests had families and duties outside the holy precincts and reported to the sanctuaries periodically to serve their god and look after his image. While in service, they practiced ritual cleanliness, washing four times a day in cold water and shaving their entire body every few days. They had to avoid certain foods and abstain from sex for several days before entering the god's presence. But nothing in their code obliged them to forsake the world. Among their ranks were shrewd administrators, who ran the sprawling temple complexes with a firm hand and served as close advisers to the king. When Akhenaten came to power, he confronted high priests of Amun who had enjoyed great influence and prosperity under his father and who no doubt expected the awkward new king to defer to their wisdom and holiness.

Proud and supremely ambitious, Akhenaten would do nothing of the sort. He distanced himself from the traditionalists at court and promoted officials who shared his views, or at least paid lip service to them. And after five restless years at Thebes, he determined to abandon the city altogether for a new capital he planned to build from scratch, where he and his faithful followers could worship the Aten without opposition. The site he chose for his grand project lay on the east bank of the Nile 240 miles north of Thebes, where the limestone cliffs receded to form a natural amphitheater. He called the new capital Akhetaten, or Horizon of the Aten. At the dedication ceremony there, army officers and other proud men had to abase themselves before the king, who claimed to be the god's son. "They were on their bellies before him, kissing the earth in his presence," related one inscription; "Said His Majesty to them: See Akhetaten, which the Sun Disk wishes to have built for himself as a memorial in his own name."

So eager was Akhenaten to put Thebes behind him that he moved to his new capital before the buildings had been completed. He and his retinue evidently camped out in tents while workmen put the finishing touches to the palace. His family joined him in his new home, for he enjoyed the support of his loved ones. The almond-eyed Nefertiti, his elegant consort, was an avid partisan of the new religion. And in time, Tiy, the royal mother, also made the journey downstream to the desert capital, although she may well have looked back wistfully on her days in Thebes.

Akhenaten was not content simply to distance himself from rival gods and their followers. In his most radical act, he outlawed the worship of other deities and

closed their temples. The cult of Amun was his prime target. Akhenaten's agents destroyed images of that god and removed his name from shrines and monuments. In their zeal, they even defaced references to Akhenaten's father, Amenhotep III, because the king's name incorporated the hated term Amun.

Soon Akhenaten could look around his kingdom with satisfaction, knowing that his sweeping reforms were well under way. In his new capital, he made offerings to his heavenly father in the Great Aten Temple—an airy, sunlit sanctuary that presented a stark contrast to the dark and mysterious precincts of Amun. There was a spaciousness about the rest of the city too. The ambitious young nobles who had followed the king from Thebes moved into lavish new villas with pools and gardens. The rooms were brightly painted, often with lifelike scenes of flowers, animals, or birds. A broad avenue linked Akhenaten's residence and the nearby estates of his top aides with the administrative heart of the city to the south. Among the shops there were breweries and bakeries that provided offerings for the Aten as well as sustenance for his priests, who consumed what the god left untouched. Wells furnished fresh water for the citizens, and ample greenery offered them shade and solace in the heat of the day.

Guards patrolled the avenues on foot and in chariots to keep the peace. Not that the residents were much inclined to cause trouble. They owed their livelihood to Akhenaten, and when he stood before them in the Window of Appearance—a balcony at the palace expressly designed for royal displays—decked out in the gleaming ornaments of kingship, they knew that he was their sun, the radiant source of their good fortune.

In this flattering setting, Akhenaten ceased to be ungainly and became beautiful in the eyes of his beholders. Court artists, who had begun depicting the individual peculiarities of the king and his retinue during the reign of Amenhotep III, did so even more freely now. With Akhenaten's blessing, they portrayed the oddly shaped king not as a conqueror, riding in a war chariot and trampling his enemies, but as a family man, relaxing with Nefertiti and his daughters.

Away from the capital, some Egyptians took a dimmer view of Akhenaten and his works. Priests of the forbidden gods found themselves without a role to play. For the mass of the population laboring in the fields along the Nile, the changes were no doubt unsettling, but most discreetly retained their loyalty to the old gods. Even in the capital, people in the poorer sections held on to their statues of the dwarfish but benevolent household god Bes.

The sun king was soon to be eclipsed. His cult never took root in Egyptian society at large, and it wilted following his death in the 17th year of his reign. His successors renounced him and reverted to the old ways. The once thriving capital devoted to the Aten was abandoned, and Akhenaten's very name was excised from the official King List. One scribe later referred to his unspeakable tenure as the "reign of that damned one."

For generations to come, Egyptian kings would seek to live up to the grand example of Amenhotep III while avoiding anything that smacked of his son's radicalism. The 18th Dynasty ended some 40 years after the death of Akhenaten with the demise of King Horemhab, who left no heir and bequeathed power to his trusted aide and vizier, Ramses I. Ramses and his successors traced their origins to the delta, far from Thebes. But they carried on in the proud tradition of the 18th Dynasty by maintaining Egypt's military might and the flow of tribute and trade goods from foreign lands.

The pharaoh who came to personify this last, triumphant phase of New Kingdom glory was Ramses II, or Ramses the Great. His father, Seti I, son of the first Ramses, prepared the boy well for the commanding role he was destined to play. From his early teens, he was involved in governing the country under Seti's guidance. Unlike Akhenaten, Ramses heartily endorsed the values of his forefathers. He simply wanted to outshine them.

WORSHIPING THE ATEN

Bearing offerings in their upturned palms, Akhenaten, Nefertiti, and one of their daughters *(far left)* pay homage to their god, the sun disk Aten, whose rays reach out with lifelike hands to accept the offerings and bless the worshipers. The faith of the king and his followers was eloquently expressed in the *Hymn to the Aten,* attributed to Akhenaten:

Splendid you rise in heaven's lightland,
O living Aten, creator of life!
When you have dawned in
eastern lightland,
You fill every land with your beauty,
You are beauteous, great, radiant,
High over every land;
Your rays embrace the lands
To the limits of all that you made. . . .
All eyes are on your beauty until you set,
All labor ceases
when you rest in the west;
When you rise you
stir everyone for the King,
Every leg is on the move since
you founded the earth.
You rouse them for your son who came
from your body,
The King who lives by Maat,
the Lord of the Two Lands.

Endowed with a piercing gaze and hawklike nose, he was quick to swoop down on Egypt's enemies. In one of his many campaigns, he clashed in Syria with the Hittites. He later made peace with them and devoted the rest of his long reign to other forms of self-aggrandizement. As a builder of royal monuments, he surpassed even Amenhotep III, completing a great pillared hall at Karnak and erecting a new capital in his ancestral delta homeland that one text described as "beauteous of balconies, dazzling with halls of lapis and turquoise." It may have been there that the Israelites labored for the pharaoh, as described in the Book of Exodus: "The Egyptians forced the sons of Israel into slavery, and made their lives unbearable with hard labor, work with clay and with brick, all kinds of work in the fields."

Another consuming project of Ramses was to enlarge his household to monumental proportions by collecting wives and fathering children. Seti had kindly given him a head start. "He equipped me with women, a royal harem, as beautiful as those of the palace," Ramses wrote of his father. Thus endowed, Ramses sired as many as 20 children by the age of 25, when Seti died and he took sole charge of the kingdom. By the end of his life, he had fathered dozens of daughters and about 50 sons, ensuring that death would never rob him of legitimate heirs—and outstripping the reproductive feats of many a potent predecessor.

His principal wife, Nefertari, died after bearing him at least four sons and two daughters. Among Nefertari's many successors in later years was a daughter of the Hittite king, sent from distant Anatolia to seal the peace that had recently blossomed between the two powers. As part of the bargain, Ramses was promised a dowry that included jewels, horses, and slaves. When the bride and gifts were slow in coming, he complained in writing to her parents, and the Hittite queen answered him in kind. "My brother possesses nothing?" she wrote sarcastically of his concern for the dowry. "That you, my brother, should wish to enrich yourself from me is neither friendly nor honorable!" At length, the Hittite princess and prizes set out for Egypt by caravan through the mountain passes of Syria in the dead of winter. Ramses later claimed credit for keeping the approaching wedding party safe from the elements by praying to the gods, "May you not send rain, icy blast or snow, until the marvel you have decreed for me shall reach me!"

Four colossal images of Ramses II, carved of sandstone and measuring 66 feet from head to toe, guard the entrance to the great temple built for Ramses at Abu Simbel in the Nubian desert. Nestled between his feet are smaller figures of his wives and relatives. The temple, dedicated to Amun-Re, was oriented so that sunlight flooded through the entrance into the cavernous interior twice a year at dawn on the spring and fall equinoxes.

However much Ramses looked forward to her arrival, she was just another jewel in his coffer. Other gems arrived over the years to dazzle the aging pharaoh, including a second Hittite princess, a sister of the first. Among the women who served him either as principal wife or as leading members of his harem were royal brides from Syria and Babylon as well as several of his close relatives, including at least one

kill him and put her own son on the throne in place of his designated heir. Among those she drew into her plot were other women of the harem, men assigned to keep an eye on them, and close confidants of the king. They used all the weapons at their disposal, including witchcraft. One conspirator allegedly made wax models of the pharaoh and his loyal aides with the aim of injuring them magically.

"May you not send rain, icy blast or snow, until the marvel you have decreed for me shall reach me!"

of his sisters and three of his daughters. Many of Ramses' children died before he did and were consigned to burial chambers west of Thebes, either in the Valley of the Queens or in the nearby Valley of the Kings. His would-be successors must have wondered if the old man would ever take his place there. He died at last in his early nineties, having held power for 67 years.

Although Ramses gloried in his many wives and children, harems in fact posed a risk to kings and their chosen heirs. The pharaoh could sequester his secondary wives behind walls and appoint aides to watch over them. But he could not keep the women from nurturing grand hopes for the children they bore—ambitions that sometimes conflicted with the king's own plans. Within their gracious quarters, women of the harem whiled away the hours by singing and weaving. On at least one occasion, during the reign of Ramses III, they spun out something daring and sinister—a plot aimed at the god-king himself.

Coming to the throne 30 years after the death of Ramses the Great, Ramses III did credit to his name by repeatedly beating back foreign forces that were threatening Egypt. At the end of his 32-year reign, however, this conqueror was nearly undone by forces close to home. One of his secondary wives conspired to

By one means or another, the plotters may indeed have harmed Ramses III. He died just weeks after the conspiracy was uncovered, of an unrevealed cause. Before his demise, he set the wheels of justice in motion against the conspirators. Such was the commitment of Egyptians to the principle of law that even those accused of this gravest of crimes—an assault on the god-king—received a full hearing. More than 30 defendants stood trial before a panel of 12 judges. Most of them were found guilty and paid with their lives. Afterward, several of the judges were themselves accused of compromising their integrity by consorting indecently with defendants, including women of the harem. One judge was acquitted, but three others had their noses and ears severed in punishment, and one was forced to commit suicide.

In the end, Ramses IV, the late king's intended heir, assumed the throne. Those who had remained loyal to the royal family gave thanks that order had been restored. But if somehow the plot had succeeded, the adaptable Egyptians would surely have come to terms with that reality and acknowledged the usurper as the legitimate representative of the gods on earth—a ruler worthy of reverence, so long as the Nile rose and fell, and the fields flourished, and the enemies of Egypt remained at bay.

A Joy for Living

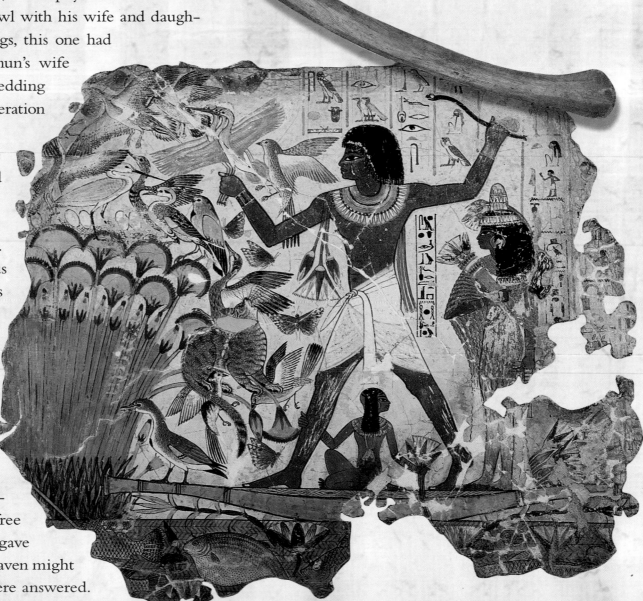

For Egyptians, the good life was summed up by this scene, showing Nebamun, chief physician to Amenhotep II, hunting waterfowl with his wife and daughter. Like all tomb paintings, this one had spiritual meaning. Nebamun's wife was pictured in her wedding dress, symbolizing regeneration in the afterlife. But the scene also revealed the worldly pleasures enjoyed by Nebamun and his family, who went on outings like this in real life. The girl might pick lotus blossoms from the papyrus raft while her father prepared to stun fowl with a snake-shaped throwing stick like the one shown above. Even the family cat might accompany them. Such trips were one of many diversions of the well-to-do, who filled their free hours with delights that gave them a glimpse of what heaven might be like, if their prayers were answered.

A Flair for Games and Storytelling

All Egyptians enjoyed contests and stories, but the wealthy pursued those pastimes with an elegant flourish. Royalty such as Nefertari *(right)*, wife of Ramses II, were portrayed on the walls of their tombs playing the game senet, which reenacted the quest for eternal fulfillment after death. In real life, Nefertari and her kind played senet on beautiful boards crafted of ebony, ivory, and other rare materials. Another game with royal associations was called mehen, played on a circular board resembling a coiled snake *(left)*. The playing pieces—shaped like marbles or reclining lions—were occasionally inscribed with the names of Egypt's early kings, and contestants moved them from slot to slot in an inward spiral toward the goal at cen-

ter, where they escaped through the snake's mouth.

In storytelling as in game playing, wealthy Egyptians had certain advantages. Like the common folk, they liked to recite tales from memory. But the educated elite also delighted in stories and poems penned on papyrus, which were often recited or sung for the enjoyment of others. Love lyrics told of young people who pined away when they were separated from their sweethearts, regardless of the efforts of their doctors. "When the physicians come to me, my heart rejects their remedies," one lovesick poet wrote. "To tell me 'She is here' would revive me! Her name would make me rise."

Egyptian writers and artists were not afraid to poke fun at the proud and powerful members of their society. A scene from the so-called Satirical Papyrus *(above)*, dating from the 20th Dynasty, made light of the tomb paintings of worthies like Nebamun by showing foxes and cats leading goats and geese as offerings to the deceased and a lion with a gloating look on his face playing senet with an antelope. Well-to-do Egyptians probably enjoyed such wry humor, even if it came at their own expense.

At left, Nefertari plays senet on a board much like the ebony-and-ivory one below, from the tomb of Tutankhamun, with a sliding compartment for its wooden pieces. Players threw sticks to determine each move. Another popular game was hounds and jackals (below, left), whose pegs were moved from slot to slot on the board—in this instance, the back of a hippopotamus.

"With a beaming face celebrate the joyful day and rest not therein. For no one can take away his goods with him. Yea, no one returns again, who has gone hence."

Inspiring Festivities

Wealthy Egyptians liked nothing better than to throw lavish banquets for their friends and kin on solemn occasions as well as lighthearted ones. Only someone of means, with plenty of food and drink and a sizable retinue of servants, could host a get-together like the one at left, depicted on the walls of Nebamun's tomb.

Although the gathering portrayed in this painting was a funerary banquet—held following a funeral and every year thereafter in memory of the deceased—it resembled the parties that Egyptians staged on other occasions. They believed that the passage of a loved one to the next life was as much to be celebrated as a marriage or any other turning point in one's earthly existence.

Each guest was warmly welcomed to the festivities and draped in blossoms and fragrant wreaths of flowers, whose bouquet mingled with the scent of the perfume cones atop the guests' heads. Barely clad servant girls

Guests at Egyptian banquets feasted from handsome implements such as the matching plate and cup at left, decorated with a lotus design and made of blue faience, consisting of a base of stone or clay, glazed over to produce a lustrous glasslike finish.

99

served rich dishes concocted of butter, cheese, fattened fowl, and beef, flavored with spices such as rosemary, cumin, garlic, parsley, cinnamon, and mustard, and sweetened with honey, figs, and other fruits. The diners sat on mats or stools and ate heartily from platters with their fingers after dipping them in water.

At funerary feasts, guests were expected to drink freely until they reached a state of intoxication that put them in touch with the deceased. The purpose was serious, but Egyptians were not too pious to see humor in it. In one tomb inscription, a woman at a banquet calls to a servant: "Bring me 18 more goblets of wine! Can't you see I am trying to get drunk! My throat is dry as dust."

Music filled the air as the feast continued. Among the instruments used to serenade the guests were the harp, lute, lyre, tambourine, single flute, and double flute. Trained singers offered up sacred lyrics to suit the occasion, but the beat was lively. Bejeweled dancing girls in slender waistbands twisted and turned, rattling castanets, while guests snapped their fingers, clapped their hands, or knocked together ivory clappers shaped like hands *(right)*.

The pleasures of the moment did not blind guests to the fact that death brought a conclusion to earthly delights. No one passing from this world to the next could take "his goods with him," counseled one tomb inscription. By adorning their grave sites with scenes like these, however, dignitaries such as Nebamun expressed their hope of being able to commune with their loved ones after death. They trusted that with the assistance of the gods and the prayers of their surviving kin, they would "traverse eternity in joy" and remain rich in spirit, if not in substance.

"You waken gladly every day,
All afflictions are expelled. You traverse eternity in joy."

Above, in a banquet scene from the tomb of Nebamun, a musician plays a double flute, while her companions clap their hands and dancers sway to and fro beside jars of wine. At right, an Old Kingdom musician plays a single flute to the beat provided by his partner.

CHAPTER THREE

"I Fought Bravely in His Majesty's Presence"

Ramses III sat on a golden throne resplendent in his full-dress uniform as the regiments marched into the broad square fronting the storehouses. Officers barked orders at the sweating men and hustled about keeping the lines in perfect order for such an august occasion. When all were assembled in their ranks, the pharaoh rose from his seat and a solemn hush fell over the throng. "Bring forth the weapons! Send out the troops to destroy the rebellious foreign lands that know not Egypt through the potency of my father Amun."

The troops in charge of the supply depot quickly moved forward lugging equipment of every sort: visored helmets, short-sleeved coats of bronze mail, leather shields, bows and quivers, javelins, spears, and a type of sword with a sickle blade known as a *khopesh*. They stacked the items in huge piles in front of the drawn-up formations.

At that time, the soldiers, wearing nothing but kilts, advanced in single file to collect their battle gear under the pharaoh's watchful eye. All the while, army scribes hovered over the proceedings, carefully making detailed entries on their papyrus ledgers of the names, units, and the various items of equipment issued to the troops.

Once all the supplies were drawn, the army prepared to move out. The formations crossed the bridge at the border outpost of Sile with suitable pomp and ceremony, leaving behind the lush delta lands and heading into the sandy wastes of the Sinai. In the forefront was an infantry regiment aligned in columns eight ranks deep. Behind them marched the army's heralds with their polished silver-and-copper trumpets. Next in line came the pharaoh's staff, accompanying the standard of the ram-headed god Amun. Then came the pharaoh himself, driving his own chariot with two parasol-wielding aides trotting alongside to shield him from the broiling sun.

Behind the pharaoh's entourage marched the remainder of the army: first the infantry, then the chariotry, and finally the supply train, a miles-long column of ox-driven wagons and heavily laden donkeys. Through the oppressive heat and choking dust cloud raised by the tramp of thousands of feet and hoofs, the army set forth to battle Egypt's enemies in distant lands.

The description above is drawn from scenes carved on the walls of the funerary temple of Ramses III. He reigned during the New Kingdom—Egypt's golden age—when military campaigning against one foe or another was practically an annual event. Often, as recounted here, the enemy was met in battle in far-off Canaan or Syria. Other campaigns would require a march westward from the delta against the tribes of Libya or a long voyage by ship up the Nile to fight the ever troublesome Nubians. Egypt in those days was a superpower, and its spheres of influence extended outward in all directions from the Nile.

By the time of the New Kingdom, the pyramids were already 1,000 years old, and the glories of Egypt's founding dynasties—the Old Kingdom—were ancient history. Since then, the country had gone through periods of greatness and decline, but Egyptian civilization and its social and political foundations—including the military—had survived it all.

In the far-off days of the pyramid builders, the army had been made up of amateur militia units. During peacetime, the army provided labor for public works projects such as quarrying stone and digging canals. Citizens were also called to duty to deal with immediate crises, for instance, raids by nomadic desert dwellers from the fringes of the Nile Valley.

Combat between these poorly trained mobs of armed men involved no grand strategy and only rudimentary tactics. The two sides would approach to within arrow range and begin loosing volleys at each other. This was seldom enough to decide the issue, so foot soldiers would advance until the opposing lines were at arm's length. Then the battle would turn into a confused struggle, with soldiers stabbing, clubbing, and hacking one another until one side broke and ran away.

After centuries of unchallenged dominance, the central authority of the Old Kingdom pharaohs gradually withered away, leading to a chaotic time known as the First Intermediate Period. For close to a century, the flames of civil war blackened the banks of the Nile, as Egyptians slaughtered Egyptians for the greater glory of ambitious local rulers.

Eventually the princes of Thebes gained the upper hand and reunited the country under a strong monarchy. This period, known as the Middle Kingdom, brought great change and improvement to Egyptian society. Through irrigation, thousands of new acres were put under cultivation. Art and culture flourished; contact and trade with countries that lay beyond the desert increased. The military developed into an institution with a complex organization and a well-defined command structure.

Recruits were drafted by army scribes on a regional quota basis and served for a fixed period of time. This system gave soldiers the chance to train together and develop a sense of esprit de corps. Most conscripts served their tours and went back to their civilian lives, but the idea of professional career soldiers seems to have taken hold in Egypt during the Middle Kingdom.

Each infantryman (below) carries a copper-bladed spear and
a shield that bears his personal
design, perhaps to make it more
readily identifiable when the call
to action demanded quick re-
trieval from the weapons cache.
These carved and painted wood-
en figures found in a Middle
Kingdom tomb offer a rare and
detailed portrait of the common
Egyptian soldier of that time.

There must have been incentives to lure young Egyptian men into devoting their lives to the army. With the country once again unified, campaigns would have been fought against foreign enemies such as Nubia, offering the possibility of booty or slaves as reward for bravery in combat. In addition, common soldiers were now given the opportunity for advancement through the ranks: An elite, handpicked unit known as the "retainers" enjoyed the privilege of accompanying the pharaoh himself into battle, where personal acts of valor were sure to be noticed and rewarded.

Weapons of war had changed little since the Old Kingdom. Archers with simple bows still fired wooden arrows with stone or copper arrowheads. For close-in fighting, infantrymen carried spears, copper axes, or daggers. There was no body armor, and everyone still fought on foot.

All that was about to change, however. The reasons for the collapse of the Middle Kingdom are lost to history, but after 400 years of dominance, it crumbled. For the first time, Egypt lay open to foreign occupation. Taking advantage of the turmoil, the Hyksos, a technologically advanced people, crossed the Sinai and wrested control of the delta from the Egyptian nobility. Their success was due in no small measure to radically superior weaponry, including bronze blades and the horse-drawn chariot.

For almost 100 years—a time that was known as the Second Intermediate Period—the Hyksos were the strongest power in the Nile Valley, but that too would eventually change. Fortunately, many records from this period have remained intact over the centuries. Included among them is a detailed first-person account inscribed on the tomb walls of an Egyptian soldier named Ahmose, who participated in many military campaigns.

Like little boys all over Egypt, Ahmose had been reared on folk stories of mighty battles, villainous foreign invaders, and courageous Egyptian heroes. Growing up in the Upper Egyptian town of el-Kab, Ahmose had a special connection to the legends: His father,

Baba, a professional army officer, had actually fought in some of these battles and could relate them blow by blow to the wide-eyed child. The villains of these tales were the dreaded Hyksos, a Semitic people whose homeland was across the Sinai in Asia. Their name derives from an Egyptian term meaning roughly "rulers of foreign lands." In some respects the Hyksos were as advanced as the Egyptians. And in at least one way—making war—they were far superior.

The Hyksos brought with them new and powerful weapons unknown to the Egyptians. Their spearpoints, arrowheads, and

The life story of Ahmose, the much-traveled and highly decorated soldier, was carved into the limestone walls of his tomb outside his hometown of el-Kab. Staff in hand, Ahmose wears a soldier's tunic and kilt; he is depicted much larger than the figure of his adult grandson to reflect his prominence.

THE STORY OF SINUHE

The broad range of foreign relations—diplomacy, commerce, and military duty—often took Egyptians abroad for long periods. Yet if ambassadors, traders, or soldiers had to spend a large percentage of their lives outside Egypt, they nevertheless expected to end their days in the familiar surroundings of the Nile Valley. The Egyptians' deeply rooted fear of dying in a foreign land is well reflected in a Middle Kingdom composition entitled *The Story of Sinuhe*. This extremely popular work served as a standard educational text for scribes well into the time of the New Kingdom.

Sinuhe, unlike his countrymen sent abroad temporarily to serve the pharaoh, voluntarily chooses exile, though under ambiguous circumstances: He is a palace official who fears he might be implicated in a conspiracy against his king, Amenemhat I. He flees into the land of Retjenu, where he prospers and eventually becomes a powerful chieftain. But still he looks upon his adopted land as little more than a wilderness. The older Sinuhe grows, the greater his longing for Egypt: "My arms are weak, and my legs have slackened. My heart is weary; I am near to departure."

Learning of Sinuhe's plight, King Senusret I takes pity on the homesick expatriate. "You must not die in a foreign land!" he writes to Sinuhe, granting his request for a royal pardon. "The Asiatics shall not escort you to burial. You shall not be put in a sheepskin and a mound made over you! This is too long to tread the earth. Be mindful of illness, and come back!"

Rejoicing at this invitation, Sinuhe returns home to enjoy lavish royal favor in the few years remaining to him. When death finally comes, he is content in the knowledge that his body will be embalmed, wrapped in linen, and placed in a well-furnished tomb with his achievements inscribed upon the walls—all the requisites for ensuring a peaceful journey into eternity.

battle-axes were forged from bronze, an alloy of copper and tin that gave a harder, more lethal edge than copper alone. Hyksos archers, moreover, carried composite bows made of laminated strips of wood, horn, and sinew that could fling their bronze-tipped missiles twice as far as wooden bows. Even more intimidating, the Hyksos wielded their weapons from mobile platforms—horse-drawn chariots that darted swiftly in and around enemy soldiers fighting on foot.

With these advantages, it is not surprising that the Hyksos expanded their territory and eventually took over all of Lower Egypt. The Hyksos also cut off Egypt's source of gold by concluding an alliance with Kush, the Nubian kingdom far up the Nile that had long been considered Egypt's domain. What a humiliating turn of events this must have been for such a proud people, to be reduced from the pinnacle of the ancient world to a weakened realm only a few miles wide stretching from Thebes south to Aswan.

In all truth, the Hyksos turned out to be relatively benign occupiers—and were eventually accepted as legitimate rulers by many Egyptians. They took pains not to disturb the cultural status quo of Egypt and, in fact, adopted local ways themselves, such as hieroglyphic writing and traditional Egyptian titles in their royal court. Upriver in Thebes, however, resentment continued to grow while the foreign intruders, those "vile Asiatics," remained on Egyptian soil.

From their stronghold at Avaris in the Nile Delta, the Hyksos rulers heaped indignities on poor Egypt—or so it was described in the stories told the young Ahmose. He had certainly heard the tale of the greatest insult of all. According to this story, the Hyksos king Apophis decided to taunt the Egyptians in Thebes. He demanded that Seqenenre Tao II, the Egyptian prince at Thebes, do away with the royal hippopotamus pool because the noise of the animals disturbed his sleep. Left unsaid was the fact that the hippo pool was hundreds of miles from Apophis's royal bedchamber.

Although the story was probably untrue, this or some similar outrage proved the last straw for Thebes. The city finally erupted in open revolt. Seqenenre became the first of a new breed of Egyptian warrior kings whose courage fueled the nationalistic fires of young Ahmose's generation. The boy's father, Baba, fought alongside Seqenenre in the first battles of the rebellion. Then, in about 1576 BC, the brave Seqenenre was killed in action, his skull shattered by one of the newfangled bronze Hyksos battle-axes.

The slain king's son, Kamose, took up the fight with patriotic fervor, vowing to his royal ministers, "I will grapple with him and rip open his belly, for my desire is to deliver Egypt and to smite the Asiatics." True to his word, Kamose attacked down the Nile and destroyed Hyksos power in middle Egypt. It is possible that he was killed in one of these engagements; all that is known for sure is that he reigned for a very short time. His widowed mother, Ahhotep, kept up pressure on the Hyksos for more than a decade until Kamose's younger brother was old enough to ascend the throne.

By this time, Ahmose had grown into a young man. He enlisted in the army according to the time-honored practice of taking his father's place. His first assignment as a soldier illustrated the new strength and versatility of the Egyptian army. Ahmose was posted aboard *The Wild Bull,* a ship rigged with rectangular flaxen sails and manned by a crew of up to 30 rowers to propel it when the wind failed. Vessels like *The Wild Bull* patrolled the Nile and transported troops, supplies, and weapons. Crew-

The mummified head of Seqenenre Tao II, the Egyptian king who led the revolt against the Hyksos, bears witness to the horrors of hand-to-hand combat. A modern diagnosis of the wounds revealed that his skull was pierced in several places by an ax blade, a mace, and a spear.

men had to be able to fight either on water or on land, leaping off their ships when necessary to go into combat as bowmen or spear-carrying infantry. Ahmose and his brothers-in-arms were, in effect, one of the earliest examples of that elite fighting force known today as marines.

To prepare for the coming showdown with the Hyksos, Ahmose and his fellow recruits underwent rigorous training. They practiced advancing under archery fire against specially constructed "enemy fortifications." They learned how the various components of the army could work together most effectively, with bowmen providing

jackets provided the rank and file with some protection over their traditional combat garb of short kilt and breechcloth. They also borrowed from the Hyksos the idea of wearing leather helmets instead of the customary shoulder-length wigs.

About 1560 BC, the climactic campaign against the Hyksos began. Ahmose I and the army pushed northward along the Nile, landing periodically to fight and burn enemy property. They captured Memphis, Egypt's largest city, and then turned eastward to besiege the Hyksos capital. In his tomb autobiography, Ahmose the common soldier states: "I followed the sovereign on foot when he rode

> ## "I sailed downstream to beat back the Asiatics, with my valiant army going before me like a flame of fire."
> ~Kamose

covering fire while assault teams rushed forward with ladders to scale the walls and battering rams to splinter the gates.

By chance, the first king Ahmose served had the same name—a familiar one in those days meaning "the moon is born." This was Ahmose I, the son of Seqenenre Tao II and Ahhotep and younger brother of Kamose. King Ahmose I was a young adult when he took the field, and his army likewise was coming of age. The ranks now included increasing numbers of career soldiers like Ahmose as well as units of mercenaries like the Medjay, crack Nubian archers whom the Egyptians had recruited from the desert east of the Nile.

Just as important, Egyptian troops now possessed bronze-tipped weapons, composite bows, and even a few chariots—all copied from Hyksos gear captured in battle. Body armor in the form of overlapping scales stitched to linen or leather sleeveless

in his chariot. When the town of Avaris was besieged, I fought bravely on foot in His Majesty's presence."

The weapons of Ahmose's day, with their bronze tips and blades, were more lethal than those soldiers had employed previously, but tactics hadn't changed a great deal since the time of the Old Kingdom. The Egyptians first bombarded the Hyksos army with long-range archery, then the infantry charged in to grapple hand to hand with the foe. Neither side gave nor expected any quarter in this kind of fighting. Soldiers who fell wounded and could not crawl to safety would be dispatched without mercy by the enemy, for wounded prisoners were of no use either as conscripts or as slaves.

In the close-quarters fighting near Avaris, Ahmose "carried off a hand," meaning he killed an opponent and then severed his hand to bring before the scribes who compiled the body count.

He also leaped into the Nile, captured an enemy soldier, and towed him to shore. For both of these acts he was awarded Gold of Valor—the golden ornaments customarily bestowed for bravery in combat.

The Battle of Avaris was a smashing victory; the Egyptians sacked the city, then chased the surviving Hyksos eastward across the Sinai into Palestine. After a three-year siege, the Hyksos' last stronghold fell to King Ahmose's army. "Now when His Majesty had slain the nomads of Asia," Ahmose's autobiography reads, "he sailed south to destroy the Nubian Bowmen."

For most of the journey up the Nile, Ahmose and his fellow crewmen could rest on their oars while the prevailing wind from the north moved them along, even against the current. The difficult part of the passage to Nubia began south of Aswan at the so-called First Cataract—a stretch of swift, unnavigable rapids. The crew had to jump out and, under the grueling desert sun, haul the boats by hand through and around six miles of *mu bin*, the Egyptian term for "bad water."

Two hundred miles upstream, the river-borne army reached the Second Cataract, site of the great fort at Buhen, built five centuries earlier during the Middle Kingdom. They easily recaptured it from the Kushite defenders. "His Majesty made a great slaughter among them," Ahmose recorded enthusiastically. "His Majesty journeyed north, his heart rejoicing in valor and victory. He had conquered southerners, northerners."

Egypt was fully liberated by 1546 BC, when Ahmose I died at about the age of 35, but the other Ahmose soldiered on to help create an empire. His ship carried King Amenhotep I, son of Ahmose I, into battle against the Kushites south of the Second Cataract. "I was at the head of our army; I fought really well," bragged Ahmose. He took two hands during this fighting and presented them to the king, and was named to the highly honored rank of Warrior of the Ruler.

In one of his final campaigns about 1520 BC, Ahmose again sailed southward beyond the Second Cataract. The new pharaoh, Tuthmosis I, felt the need to teach the ever rebellious Kushites another lesson. Ahmose's bravery in the king's presence—"in the bad water, in the towing of the ship over the cataract"—brought promotion to crew commander of the ship.

According to Ahmose's autobiography, King Tuthmosis killed the enemy ruler with his own arrow. Then, as a lesson to anyone who might be tempted to defy Egypt's new imperial power, Tuthmosis had the corpse tied to his royal ship and sailed home with, as Ahmose's inscription reads, "that wretched Nubian Bowman head downward at the bow."

Ahmose retired from the army not long afterward. He had soldiered for nearly a half-century, and his faithful service to the pharaohs had been well rewarded. Besides receiving Gold of Valor on seven separate occasions, he was also given slaves—nine males and 10 females who had been confiscated from the enemy—and substantial grants of land located near his hometown of el-Kab. In addition, his illustrious career paved the way for his own family's advancement: A son-in-law and grandson became tutors at the pharaoh's court, and the grandson was also appointed the mayor of el-Kab. Ahmose had his autobiography inscribed in painted relief covering the walls of his tomb in the limestone cliffs near el-Kab. It endures as the only surviving personal account by a common soldier from those turbulent days, and stands as a fitting conclusion to the exciting stories of villainy and heroism that he had first heard as a boy.

Ahmose I, Amenhotep I, and Tuthmosis I—the three sovereigns that Ahmose the soldier served—liberated Egypt and launched the era of empire that modern scholars call the New Kingdom. It was a time when Egyptian influence extended eastward to the Euphrates in Syria and 1,000 miles southward to the Fourth Cataract in Nubia. A new world-view on the part of the Egyptians emerged. Although they still saw the lands beyond their borders as alien and inferior, pharaohs and even ordinary citizens began to look abroad for new opportunities to enhance their wealth and glory.

One foreign land that the kings of Egypt had exploited long before the advent of the New Kingdom was the prosperous land of Nubia. To protect the lucrative copper and gold trade, the pharaohs had established a permanent presence in Lower Nubia during the Old Kingdom. The strong rulers of the Middle Kingdom reasserted this presence in a major way, building a chain of massive forts stretching from the First Cataract—the traditional border of Egypt proper—past Buhen all the way to Semna at the southern end of the Second Cataract.

Enclosed by deep ditches and mud-brick walls up to eight yards thick, these structures were among the most impressive fortifications in the ancient world. The forts not

Typical of the reward—the so-called Gold of Valor—given by the pharaoh for bravery on the battlefield, this necklace in the shape of three flies was sculpted from more than half a pound of finest gold and is shown here actual size. Queen Ahhotep, who led Theban troops into battle while acting as regent for her young son Ahmose, was awarded Gold of Valor on several occasions.

only watched over river trade and supported military and mining expeditions into the desert but also served, like the pyramids, as an inescapable reminder of Egyptian power and prestige. The haughty official Egyptian view of the Nubians was inscribed on a stone marking the southern frontier south of the Second Cataract and barring passage to all local residents except traders or envoys: "They are not people one respects; they are wretches, craven-hearted."

Egyptians who inhabited the forts generally subscribed to this biased—and, indeed, wholly inaccurate—view and mixed with the locals as little as possible. Each fort was a self-contained community complete with streets, temple, and even a cemetery. The barracks accommodated a garrison ranging from 50 to 300 soldiers. An arsenal for making weapons ensured that the archers would have plenty of arrows to shower upon the enemy through loopholes in the fortress walls. At first, soldiers rotated back home regularly, but eventually many of the garrisons became permanent. Some of the soldiers, most likely officers, brought their families from Egypt and lived in small modular houses of a few rooms.

The residents of these outposts ate well. Local inhabitants brought cattle for sale, and the forts had enormous grain storehouses sufficiently stocked to feed a much larger group if reinforcements were needed. It was a relatively easy life but insular and scarcely likely to yield many chances for excitement, promotion, or booty from battle. Life was apparently so humdrum that the arrival of a few Nubians to barter was news, duly recorded in the fort's dispatches, which then noted, "They sailed south to the place they had come from after they had been given bread and beer."

This observation comes from a batch of official correspondence known as the Semna Dispatches. Most of these documents were sent back to Thebes via river messenger from the southernmost fortress at Semna about 1840 BC. The reports kept headquarters apprised of everyday events in the field, especially the results of patrols and other surveillance. A recurrent topic concerned the comings and goings of the Medjay, the desert nomads who would later supply the new Egyptian army with expert bowmen. Medjay served as scouts and interpreters on desert patrols to help keep an eye

Built almost 4,000 years ago to repel threats from the Nubian kingdom of Kush, the great fortresses of Semna and Kumma near the Nile's Second Cataract have over the ages been eroded away to rocky stumps. In this aerial photograph, sand dunes drift against Semna's granite promontory, while Kumma lies in silence across the river. Although their walls were never breached by an enemy, in 1970 the legendary citadels disappeared beneath the waters of Lake Nasser, created by the Aswan High Dam.

on their fellow nomads. One Egyptian patrol commander reported, "We have found the track of 32 men and three donkeys." Another dispatch told of tracking down three Medjay and interrogating them about their origins. Other Medjay showed up at a fort on their own "to serve His Majesty," saying that "the desert is dying of hunger."

When the Middle Kingdom collapsed, the Upper Nubian kingdom of Kush moved in and took control of the fortresses. It was only after the Hyksos were expelled from the region a century later that Egypt could once again push beyond the First Cataract and reoccupy them. This formidable string of fortifications apparently continued to serve New Kingdom pharaohs like Tuthmosis III well by allowing them the freedom to look in other directions for conquest and commerce.

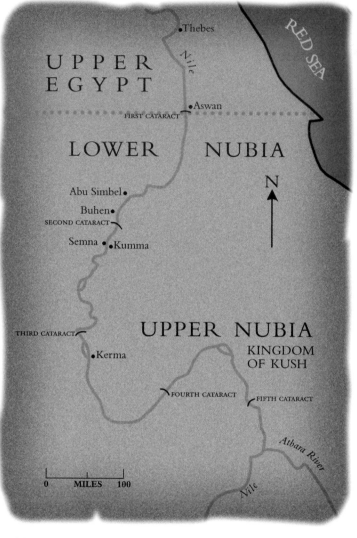

In a matter of weeks after becoming pharaoh in 1482 BC, Tuthmosis III confronted a crisis in the northeastern reaches of his empire—a rebellion that was headed by the ruler of Kadesh, a city-state on the upper Orontes River in Syria. The true power behind the revolt, however, was the king of Mitanni, who wanted to extend his control into central Syria south beyond the Euphrates. The coalition had moved its forces south and massed them at the strategically important city of Megiddo in modern-day Israel. Megiddo was the Armageddon referred to in the Bible, and it commanded a mountain passage on the old road that linked Egypt to the lands that lay farther to the north.

Tuthmosis could not abide this threat to his prestige. Although he was only in his early thirties, he was already a tested military leader and tactician as well as a strong and skilled archer, whose exploits with the bow and arrow are recorded on a stele discovered near Thebes. According to this inscription, he displayed his talent by shooting at a target erected on a pole. And even though the king's target "was a slab of beaten copper, three fingers thick," Tuthmosis's shot was so strong and sure

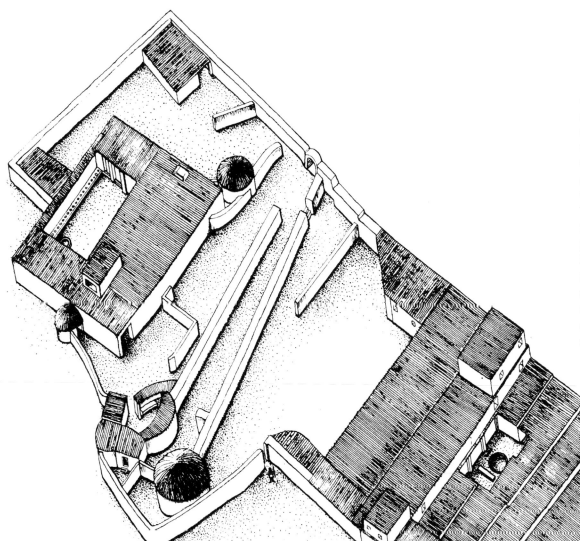

cattle and goats to be penned at night. The officers and their wives and children resided in the complex, each family occupying a pair of rooms that opened onto a small courtyard. While monitoring Nile river traffic, the troops also kept a sharp lookout for raiders from nomadic Nubian tribes who remained beyond Egyptian control.

From their various forts and garrisons, the Egyptians nervously watched the rise of a powerful rival—the Upper Nubian kingdom they called Kush, centered on its capital city at Kerma. The Kushites had a thriving culture and were part of an extensive trade network that stretched from Punt to Minoan Crete. So hated was this new enemy that Egyptian commanders attempted to magically destroy the mounting power of Kush by smashing clay tablets inscribed with the words *Kush* and *Ruler of Kush*.

The armed might of the New Kingdom pharaohs—or perhaps magic—eventually brought the Kushites firmly under Egyptian rule. Nubians were sent north to Egypt to serve as soldiers in the pharaoh's army and as guards patrolling civil and religious structures. Tribute from Kushite princes and trade goods from other African communities farther to the south and west continued to flow downriver to the royal treasuries in Thebes. The list included such luxury items as ebony, ivory, amethyst, live animals and animal skins, and an average annual levy of vast amounts of gold.

The conquest of the kingdom of Kush extended Egypt's borders south to the Fourth Cataract and allowed Egyptian citizens to colonize Nubian settlements along the Nile. Nubian princes were sent to court in Egypt, where they adopted their conquerors' religion and writing system.

But the Kushites still had to be reckoned with: When Egyptian control over Nubia waned during the Third Intermediate Period, the Kushite king Piye invaded Egypt and declared himself pharaoh, thereby establishing a Kushite dynasty that would rule Egypt for nearly a century.

NUBIA, LAND OF THE BOW

As Egypt's closest neighbor, Nubia was at various times regarded by the pharaohs as a valuable colony and a feared enemy. Surviving Old Kingdom texts refer to Nubia as Ta Seti—the Land of the Bow—for the skilled Medjay archers the Egyptians encountered in border skirmishes, but Nubia had another, more peaceful face as well. In addition to having a prosperous life based on agriculture and cattle herding, Nubians were traders, craftsmen, and miners of gold.

Nubian gold was a primary target of the pharaohs of the Old and Middle Kingdoms. Their military victories over the inhabitants of the Nubian portion of the Nile Valley ensured the continued transshipment of gold and other precious minerals north to Egypt.

During the Middle Kingdom, Egypt tightened its hold on Lower Nubia (*the area between the First and Second Cataracts on the map at left*) by building a string of forts along the Nile. In addition to large forts at Buhen and Semna, smaller settlements such as the one at Areika (*above*) were home to Nubian troops under the command of Egyptian officers. This outpost had a granary, cooking hearths, an Egyptian-style brewery and bakery, and room for that his arrow hurtled through and stuck out "the other side by three handbreadths."

Now, as the king marched against "that wretched enemy," the ruler of Kadesh, he took with him a number of military scribes. They maintained an official diary of the expedition that would subsequently be incorporated into his temple inscriptions at Karnak. Along with the combatants, the army Tuthmosis led out of Egypt that spring included hundreds of donkeys and oxcarts laden with rations of bread, fruit, and jars of oil. A standard-bearer marched in front of each company of about 250 men carrying a painted wooden ensign that would serve as a rallying point in combat.

Tactics had become more sophisticated by Tuthmosis's time. No longer did masses of blade-wielding men simply rush headlong at each other and begin hacking away. When Tuthmosis and his generals deployed the army for battle, they would group their regiments into wings, a center, and reserves. And they would maneuver these elements in concert, hoping to turn the enemy's flank or pierce his line at a critical spot.

A new class of warriors, the chariot corps, was perhaps the greatest tactical innovation. The light, maneuverable vehicles of wood, leather, and wicker carried two soldiers: The charioteer handled the two-horse team and wielded a large wood-and-leather shield to protect the warrior standing beside him. The warrior supplied the firepower with his composite bow and bronze-tipped arrows that had an effective range of 300 to 400 yards. He also had available, in a container attached to the chariot, a dozen or so javelins to hurl from closer range.

Behind the chariots marched the long-suffering infantry. From this supporting position on the battlefield, the solid ranks of spearmen could exploit any breach that was made in the enemy's lines by a chariot charge or, if the charge should fail, provide a safe refuge behind which the horsemen could seek cover.

Respectful Nubians pay homage to the pharaoh by proffering baskets of local treasures and rings of gold in this wall painting from a Theban tomb. By Tuthmosis III's reign, Nubia had been culturally assimilated into the Egyptian empire.

Tuthmosis's army took a route along the northern coastline of the Sinai, covering about 15 miles a day. At night, the soldiers pitched their tents behind a rectangular wall of shields, where they could eat and sleep in relative security. Inside of the king's tent, a gold-paneled throne allowed Tuthmosis to repose in comfort while officers presented reports on the day's events.

The procession reached the coastal base of Gaza in 10 days. Eleven more days on the road brought the army to the city of Yehem, just four days' march from Megiddo. At Yehem, Tuthmosis called a conference with his top officers. They discussed three possible approaches to the enemy forces. All of the king's generals favored either of two roundabout routes—to the north or to the east—that would enable them to deploy their army on the open plain in safety prior to engaging the foe.

They pointed out to their leader that the direct route, northward by way of a town named Aruna, would take the army through a narrow mountain passage before reaching Megiddo. "What is it like to go on this road, which becomes so narrow? It is reported that the enemy is there, waiting at the other side, and gaining in

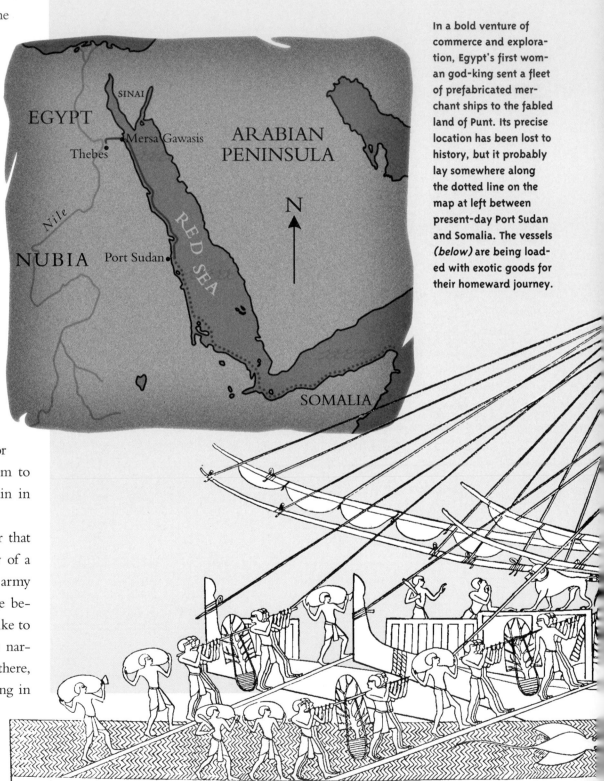

In a bold venture of commerce and exploration, Egypt's first woman god-king sent a fleet of prefabricated merchant ships to the fabled land of Punt. Its precise location has been lost to history, but it probably lay somewhere along the dotted line on the map at left between present-day Port Sudan and Somalia. The vessels (below) are being loaded with exotic goods for their homeward journey.

HATSHEPSUT'S EXPEDITION TO PUNT

Hatshepsut inherited a peaceful and prosperous empire. Her grandfather, Ahmose I, had expelled the Hyksos from Egypt. Her father, Tuthmosis I, conquered lands beyond the Fourth Cataract and eastward as far as the Euphrates. Now, serving as regent while awaiting the ascension of her young stepson to the throne, Hatshepsut cast an ambitious eye even farther afield.

Punt was a land that lay far beyond the empire, probably along the Red Sea in present-day Sudan near the northern Somali border. This land, which was so laden with exotic goods that the Egyptians referred to it as God's Land, had been visited by Egyptian traders, long ago, in the Old and Middle Kingdom times, but it had been some time since Egyptians had ventured there.

There was no denying the journey's dangers. It would require a combined effort by land and sea: five ships of the type named after the Lebanese port of Byblos, a small army of soldiers and workers, and a perilous trek across desert

and sea that would take nearly a year. In case anyone missed the point, Hatshepsut acted like any public-relations-conscious head of state. She commissioned a group of artists to depict the voyage in wall reliefs for her temple in the Theban hills at Deir el-Bahri.

The expedition left Thebes in the summer of the ninth year of her reign, around 1495 BC. The timing was crucial: A stiff current ran south in the Red Sea in summer, and the purest myrrh and frankincense resins were harvested in early fall. The five ships—unassembled for easy transport—were loaded onto oxcarts along with trade goods, such as clothing, mirrors, and weapons, for barter with the inhabitants of Punt. Then the caravan of men, donkeys, and oxcarts started eastward across the old desert trade route through the dry and dusty Wadi Hammamat or the Wadi Gasus to the Red Sea.

At the port of Mersa Gawasis, Hatshepsut's men assembled their vessels and set off southward on the 600-mile sea leg. The five ships were not that large by Egyptian standards, probably less than half the 200-foot length of the biggest vessels of the day, and each carried a crew of about 40, including 30 rowers. At those times when the wind failed, the oarsmen—facing the stern and equipped with a single curved, broad-bladed oar—rowed in time to a flute, gong, or rattle.

The ships hugged the western shore, making perhaps 30 miles a day with a following wind, much less under oar power. The sleek canoe-shaped hulls had a shallow draft of about five feet to negotiate the reefs near the shore. The captain stood in the bow with a long pole taking soundings to make certain they did not run aground. At night, the ships put ashore on the unfamiliar coast.

When the flotilla reached Punt, the Egyptians noted that the local population lived in beehive-shaped structures standing on high piles. And if the artists who decorated Hatshepsut's temple can be believed, the inhabitants shared a colorful tableau with all manner of creatures: panthers, giraffes,

apes, monkeys, and even a rhinoceros.

The expedition spent long months ashore filling the ships' holds and waiting for favorable conditions to sail back north. Only then could the heavily laden flotilla return in triumph to Thebes, bringing with them ebony, eye cosmetics, ivory, apes, monkeys, dogs, skins of the southern panther, and "all goodly fragrant woods of God's Land, heaps of myrrh-resin."

There were even several chieftains from Punt aboard to bring greetings to the great Hatshepsut. They offered the appropriate obeisance to the ruler of the Two Lands, and knelt with bowed heads before Amun, "who has set all the lands beneath her sandals, living forever!" What pleased Hatshepsut most were the living incense trees brought back from Punt—31 of them complete with roots and the soil in which they had grown. Citing the god Amun's command "to establish for him a Punt in his house," she ordered the trees planted in the garden in front of her funerary temple at Deir el-Bahri.

Superbly sculpted wall reliefs at Hatshepsut's funerary temple depict every stage of the great journey, here memorializing her prized potted incense trees, thatched huts beneath swaying palms, and a local queen, her arms extended in welcome. An endorsement from the god Amun also stands carved in stone: "I have given thee all Punt as far as the lands of the gods."

numbers. Will not horse have to go after horse, the army and the people of baggage camp likewise? Shall we risk having our advance guard fight while our rear guard is still standing here at Aruna, unable to join the battle? Let our victorious lord proceed upon any road he wishes; but do not make us go by that difficult road."

Tuthmosis replied that "he among you who wishes may go by these roads you have mentioned," meaning the longer, indirect routes, but he intended to take the route through Aruna. To choose the safer course, he said, would allow the enemy to think, "He is beginning to be afraid of us."

Lest any of his own officers question his courage, the scribe pointed out, "His Majesty had decided that he would go forth at the head of the army." After ushering the advance guard safely through the pass and into the Kina Valley beyond, he heeded the entreaties of his officers to "let our victorious lord listen to us this time, and let our lord await, for our sake, the rear guard of his army." The king and his army camped that night only a few hundred yards southwest of the Syrian troops deployed in front of Megiddo.

The battle began the next day when Tuthmosis sent the army's left wing northwest of Megiddo to cut off the Syrian line of retreat. He deployed his right wing to the south of the city and concentrated his force of chariots—probably more than 1,000 of them—in the center. At their head, riding "in a chariot of silvergold" and wearing the *khepresh*—the blue leather royal war crown—he personally led the assault. The chariots, with their arrows flying, smashed into the right flank of the surprised Syrians before they could get their vehicles into position. Then the Egyptian infantry came running up behind their charioteers to fling javelins and wade into the enemy lines with battle-axes and swords.

The Syrians, their lines crumbling, fled headlong to Megiddo, abandoning horses and chariots of gold and silver. They left on the battlefield 83 dead and 340 men to be taken captive. The city's inhabitants already had slammed the gates, so they had to lower ropes to haul their fleeing compatriots up over the stone walls. Among the fugitives saved in this humiliating manner were the rulers of Kadesh and Megiddo. The Egyptian

pursuit, meanwhile, bogged down in the greed for battlefield loot. "If only the army of His Majesty had not given their hearts to plundering the possessions of the enemy," lamented the scribe, "they would have captured Megiddo at this moment."

Tuthmosis, noting that "the capture of Megiddo is the capture of a thousand cities," ordered a siege. Megiddo finally fell seven months later. All the nobility except the leader of Kadesh, who had secretly

Such a situation loomed before Ramses II during the early years of his reign. By the onset of the 13th century BC, the kingdom of Hatti had succeeded Mitanni as the primary threat to Egyptian holdings in Syria. The Hittites, as they are known, were expanding southward into Syria from their homeland in present-day Turkey. During the reign of Ramses' father, Seti I, they had seized the city of Kadesh, the strategic stronghold that long had been a bone

"His Majesty slaughtered them in their places; they sprawled before his horses; and His Majesty was alone, no other was with him."

fled, swore an oath of allegiance and returned home. To make certain they stayed in line and provided fitting tribute in the form of gold and other riches, Tuthmosis III made a practice of leading expeditions into Palestine and Syria virtually every year for nearly two decades to demonstrate Egyptian military might.

Diplomacy was an important feature of New Kingdom foreign policy, since the potential for conflict with powerful neighbors was always present. Other major empires frequently challenged Egyptian dominance in Syria and Palestine, inciting rebellion among the local residents or occupying contested areas. While such challenges were often settled by negotiation, it was sometimes necessary to resort to other, more costly means.

Tuthmosis III smites his cowering Canaanite enemies with a battle-mace in this bas-relief from the temple of Amun at Karnak. While such scenes previously had been regarded as purely symbolic, there is now evidence to suggest that, on occasion, prisoners of war might actually have been sacrificed to the god.

of contention between Egypt and its rivals. Seti had ousted the Hittites from Kadesh, but after he departed, the city turned its allegiance once more to the Hittites. Northern and eastern Syria remained a very much contested land.

In the fourth year of his reign, Ramses escalated matters by campaigning in Syria, forcing vassals of Hatti to submit to Egypt. The Hittite king responded by assembling a large army at Kadesh to await Ramses' next move. Faced with this challenge, Ramses decided to march up to Kadesh for a showdown.

Although still young, Ramses already was demonstrating a penchant for doing things on a large scale. Before he set out for Kadesh, he made certain this would be the most thoroughly documented campaign ever. He commissioned royal scribes to recount the events in three different narrative styles—prose, poetry, and pictorial reliefs with captions—that would later be carved on temple walls at Abydos, Luxor, Karnak, Abu Simbel, and his own funerary temple, the Ramesseum. At least 15 versions of the battle narrative still exist, either inscribed in surviving temples or

written on papyrus. But Ramses was not interested in making a nonpartisan historical record when he set his scribes to work. The accounts would serve rather to perpetuate his own myth and add to the greater glory of Ramses.

It took a month for the Egyptians to cover the 490 miles to the vicinity of Kadesh. The ordinary soldier marched with pride but probably also with a sense of being swallowed up by the magnitude of the procession. Ramses' army included four divisions of about 5,000 men. Each division bore the name of a major Egyptian god: Amun, Re, Ptah, and Seth.

As the long column approached Kadesh, Egyptian soldiers came upon a pair of Bedouin stragglers who were hiding by the road and brought them before the king. They informed Ramses that they had deserted the Hittite camp in disgust and now wanted only to serve him. When Ramses demanded to know the whereabouts of the

SHIELD ME FROM MY ENEMIES

In an age when near-naked warriors clashed with sword and spear in hand-to-hand combat, a stout shield could mean the difference between life and death—victory and defeat. Like weapon makers in other early civilizations, Egyptians crafted tough wood-and-leather shields that could withstand all but the most powerful assault by keenly honed bronze blades and arrowheads.

These New Kingdom Theban tomb paintings show the process and the finished product: In an assembly-line workshop, a fresh hide is scraped, soaked, and sliced into pieces that are stretched and clamped over a series of wooden boards joined together side by side *(above)*. A leather strap attached to the shield let a soldier sling it over his back when on the march or to ward off a rain of arrows in combat.

Hittites, they replied that King Muwatallis had his forces concentrated more than 100 miles to the north at Aleppo "too fearful of pharaoh to come southward."

This was exactly what Ramses wanted—and expected—to hear, and he accepted the report without question. With himself at the head of the column and his four divisions strung out behind for many miles, Ramses proceeded toward Kadesh as if the army were on peacetime maneuvers back in Egypt. Accompanied by the Amun division as an advance guard, he blithely crossed the Orontes River and encamped northwest of Kadesh to prepare a siege. He neither sent out scouts to confirm the Bedouins' story nor did he wait for the rest of his divisions to come up so that they could support one another in case of attack.

But as Ramses took his seat on a throne of fine gold, his scouts picked up another pair of nomads. After a sound thrashing, they finally admitted that they were Hittite spies and made a startling confession. The enemy, reinforced by troops from more than a dozen allies—"more numerous than the sand of the shore," according to Ramses— was not at far-off Aleppo but poised in ambush just on the other side of Kadesh. The earlier captives had been spies planted by the canny Hittite king Muwatallis to lure the Egyptians northward into a trap, and Ramses had taken the bait.

Rather than place the blame where it belonged—squarely on his own shoulders— Ramses chewed out his generals for "failing to discover for themselves the Foe wherever he was." Then he quickly dispatched messengers to hasten the march of the Re division, which was at that time about five miles to the south.

It was too late. "Now while His Majesty sat speaking with the chiefs, the vile Foe came with his infantry and his chariotry and the many countries that were with him. Crossing the ford to the south of Kadesh they charged into His Majesty's army as it marched unaware." Unlike the light two-man vehicles of the Egyptians, the sturdy Hittite chariots were more akin to troop transports. Two spearmen rode behind the driver into the thick of the fray, then jumped off for hand-to-hand combat.

The Re division was strung out across the plain north of the river in columns—the worst formation for meeting an attack. The chariots smashed into the unsuspecting ranks with devastating effect. Horses trampled men underfoot, while Hittite spearmen impaled panic-stricken Egyptian infantry as they tried to flee. The division was quickly cut in two, half of the survivors running back the way they had come, and the rest fleeing north toward Ramses' camp. The Hittites reboarded their chariots and pursued these latter elements. Soon they had surrounded Ramses and the Amun division.

Made of some 450 bronze scales, this coat of mail is representative of what Egyptian chariot archers wore during the later New Kingdom. The scales were individually stitched in overlapping rows to a loose-fitting coat with a thick leather collar that protected the wearer's neck.

Even though Ramses may have been shocked by the surprise attack, he was still undaunted: "When His Majesty caught sight of them he rose quickly, enraged at them. Taking up weapons and donning his armor he was like Seth in the moment of his power. He started out quickly alone by himself. His eyes were savage as he beheld them; his power flared like fire against them. His Majesty charged into the force of the Foe and the many coun-

tries with him. His Majesty slew the entire force of the Foe. His Majesty slaughtered them in their places; they sprawled before his horses; and His Majesty was alone, no other was with him."

So goes the official, that is to say, Ramses', version. The truth was something else again. Ramses did in fact personally lead a bold and courageous counterattack against the Hittite chariots encircling his camp. But though he would later complain of cowardice by his men—"My numerous troops have deserted me, not one of my chariotry looks for me"—his personal guard battalion actually accompanied him in the charge.

What really saved the day was a combination of events. The Hittites, like the Egyptians at Megiddo two centuries before, stopped fighting and started a premature plunder of the king's camp. While they were preoccupied with loot, up marched the Nearuna, a special

Egyptian task force of chariots and infantry that had followed the coastal route to protect the army's left flank and were just now catching up with Ramses at a most fortuitous moment. Their lightweight chariots, outmaneuvering the heavy Hittite vehicles and firing fusillades of arrows, launched attack after attack directly into the enemy front.

Ramses' third division came up presently and struck the enemy rear, driving the Hittites back across the Orontes. One enemy commander, the prince of Aleppo, nearly drowned in the river. He swallowed so much water that his soldiers had to hold him upside down to clear his lungs—or so we are led to believe by an image of enemy embarrassment preserved for posterity in the Egyptian wall reliefs.

Although Ramses claimed a great victory, the battle was in truth a stalemate, as was clearly demonstrated by the fact that the Egyptian army turned around and went home, leaving Kadesh in the hands of the Hittites. Hostility simmered and more battles were fought over the next 16 years until about 1269 BC, when Ramses and his old adversary's brother and successor, Hattusilis III, concluded a remarkable treaty of "peace and brotherhood." The two kings cemented their alliance 13 years later when Hattusilis offered his eldest daughter as a bride for Ramses. She arrived in southern Syria at the border between the two empires accompanied by a dazzling dowry of "gold, silver, much bronze, slaves, spans of horses without limit," and a large honor guard of infantry and chariotry. The soldiers of both armies paraded before one another and then feasted together, "eating and drinking face to face," the wall inscriptions noted, "without fighting."

With the end of the New Kingdom two centuries later, Egypt's empire was lost forever. The fabled country's subsequent history was one of foreign invasion and domination: first the Kushites from the south, then later the Assyrians, the Persians, and eventually the Macedonians under Alexander the Great. With the founding of the Ptolemaic Dynasty in 312 BC, Egypt once again became the center of an extensive empire with a strong military base. But that story belongs more to Greek than to Egyptian history. ᐁᐅᐁ

Rows of spear-wielding infantrymen (*left*) march forward in perfect formation to do battle with Egypt's foes in this sandstone relief from the funerary temple of Ramses III. Boats like the one below carried Egyptian marines—who doubled as oarsmen—into battle up and down the Nile.

In the Service of the Pharaoh

"Come, I will relate to you the lot of the infantryman, the much tormented one. He is brought as a child and confined to a barrack. A painful blow is dealt to his body, a savage blow to his eye, and a splitting blow to his brow. He is laid down and beaten like a piece of papyrus. Come, I will relate to you his journey to the land of Kharu and his march over the hills. His bread and water are carried on his shoulders like a donkey's burden. He drinks foul-tasting water and halts to stand guard. When he reaches the enemy he is like a pinioned bird, with no strength in his limbs. If he succeeds in returning to Egypt he is like a stick that the wormwood has eaten—he is full of sickness. He is carried back in a state of paralysis on the back of a donkey."

This was one New Kingdom scribe's caustic view of the soldier's lot. Without question it was a rough life: hard, often brutal training, followed by long absences from home marching through foreign lands, perhaps to meet a gruesome death in battle. Yet the men of arms under the command of Egypt's pharaohs endured their hardships and soldiered on, in the process creating an empire that rivaled any in the ancient world.

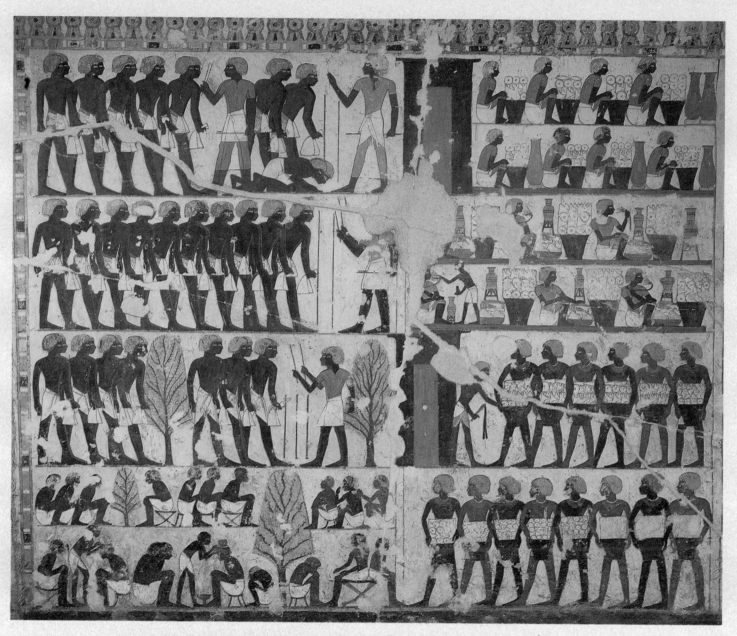

Drill instructors put columns of new recruits through
their paces *(upper left)* while others await their turn
in the barber's chair *(bottom left)* in this wall relief
from the tomb of a New Kingdom army officer. At
top right, eight junior officers sit with jars of beer—as
befitting their rank—while, below them, four senior
officers drink wine and fan themselves with lotus
flowers. The two columns of soldiers at bottom right
are carrying a variety of baked goods in baskets.

The future king Amenhotep
II receives personal archery
lessons in this reconstruction from a Theban tomb
painting. At far right, he
draws a simple bow. At
right, he is shown using
the much more powerful
composite bow while tak-
ing aim at a target already
pierced by several hits.

Training the Troops

During the New Kingdom period, the Egyptian army was composed of three branches: archery, infantry, and chariotry. Young recruits were schooled in one of these military skills with a blend of specialized training and physical intimidation meant to prepare them for the confusion and brutality of combat.

Egyptians were familiar with the simple bow as used for hunting. But the composite bow—made of a mixture of wood and animal horn and sinew—required much greater strength to operate. Novice archers performed specially designed exercises to develop their arm muscles, then instructors taught them the proper stance, bowstring tension, and how to judge the arrow's range by its angle of flight.

Foot soldiers, marching shoulder to shoulder, spent endless hours drilling on the parade ground while their officers bellowed commands—and sometimes applied the lash. But this grueling routine paid off in the thick of battle, where infantry units had to be able to maintain—and change—their formation under archery fire or in the face of a chariot charge.

The chariotry was the elite branch of the army and was associated with the upper class. It required long hours of practice to mount a mass charge. A driver had to learn how to maneuver his two-horse team at full gallop over uneven terrain while keeping pace with the other chariots and at the same time position his shield to protect himself and the bowman at his side.

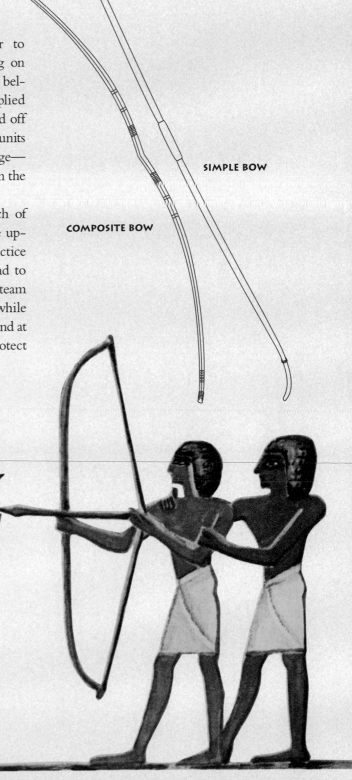

SIMPLE BOW

COMPOSITE BOW

The Weapons of War

The Hyksos conquest of the Nile Delta created a revolution in the technology of Egyptian warfare. To do battle with the invaders on an equal footing, the Egyptians had to copy the Hyksos inventory of weapons: bronze blades, composite bows, and, most important, the chariot.

Some ancient armies employed heavy chariots to transport troops into battle. But, not surprisingly, the Egyptians chose the battle-tested Hyksos style of a lightweight vehicle used as a mobile weapons platform.

The Egyptian military embraced the chariot wholeheartedly and tinkered with the design constantly in a search for the best combination of woods for the various parts as well as the proper placement of the

axle for maximum stability. These delicate vehicles required lots of maintenance. A 19th Dynasty papyrus describes a charioteer's visit to a repair facility:

"You are brought into the armory and workshops. They take care of your chariot so that it is no longer loose. Your pole is freshly trimmed and its attachments are fitted on. They put bindings on your collar piece and they fix up your yoke. They apply your ensign, engraved with a chisel, and they put a handle on your whip and attach a lash to it. You would then go quickly forth to fight at the pass and accomplish glorious deeds."

Early Egyptian chariots like the one shown here were direct copies of Hyksos models. More durable six-spoked wheels were introduced later in the 18th Dynasty and gained popularity throughout the New Kingdom.

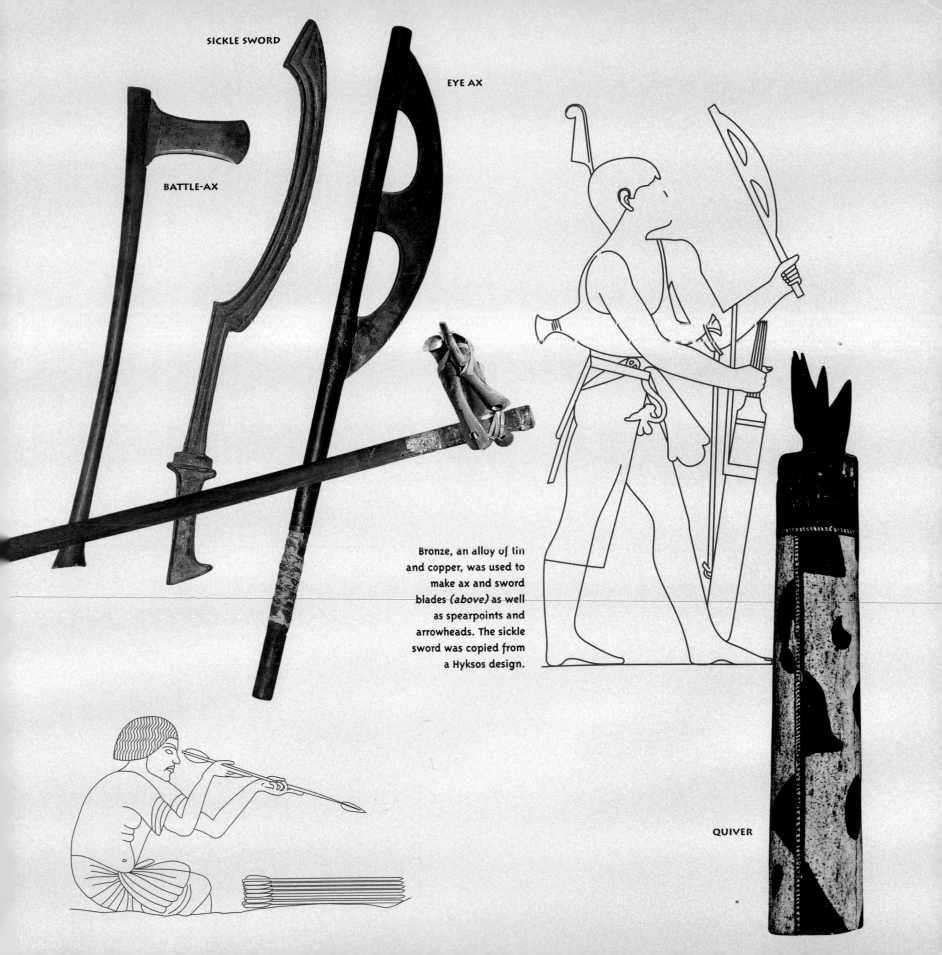

BATTLE-AX

SICKLE SWORD

EYE AX

Bronze, an alloy of tin
and copper, was used to
make ax and sword
blades *(above)* as well
as spearpoints and
arrowheads. The sickle
sword was copied from
a Hyksos design.

QUIVER

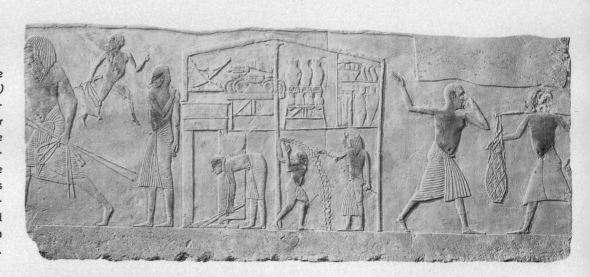

A pavilion at the center of the camp of King Horemhab (*right*) is being prepared for a high-ranking officer. One soldier sweeps the earthen floor while another, supervised by an officer, scatters water to settle the dust. The illustration of Ramses II's camp at Kadesh (*below*) presents a much more detailed depiction of camp life for an Egyptian army on the move.

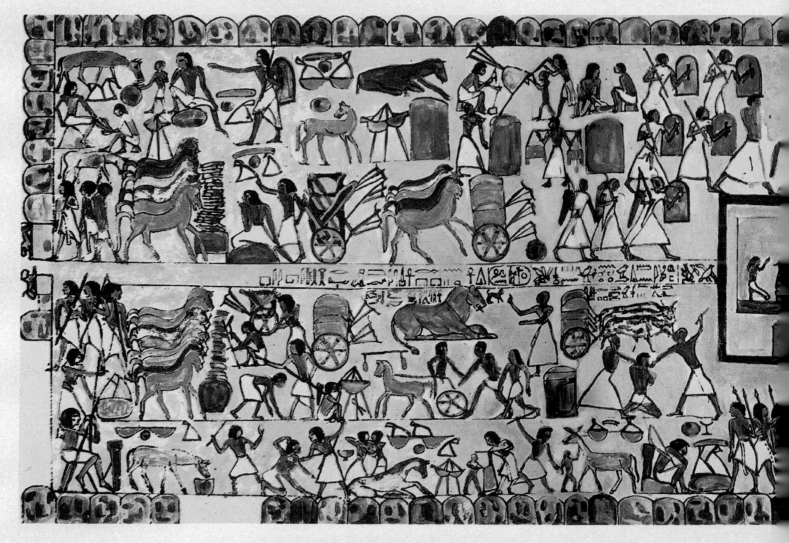

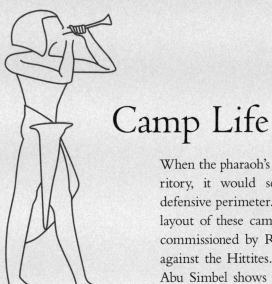

Camp Life

When the pharaoh's army marched through hostile territory, it would set up camp at night behind a defensive perimeter. Much of what is known about the layout of these camps comes from temple wall reliefs commissioned by Ramses II to record his campaigns against the Hittites. The large illustration at left from Abu Simbel shows the Egyptian encampment outside the gates of Kadesh on the eve of battle.

The camp is surrounded by a rectangular barricade of wooden shields. Inside this protective barrier, soldiers guard the entrance road *(far left),* while others attend to the daily routines of camp life: cooking, repairing equipment, and feeding and watering the horses and pack animals. At center right stands the pharaoh's personal enclosure with Ramses represented by a golden cartouche. Just to the left of the enclosure, two Egyptian soldiers are beating a confession out of a Hittite spy picked up along the march. The peaceful nature of the scene is shattered by a surprise Hittite assault on the camp, shown at right. Spear-wielding Egyptian infantrymen rush to the defense as Hittite chariots storm through a breach in the wall of shields.

Soldiers received bread ration tokens made of plastered, painted wood. The tokens came in different shapes, as shown below, depending on the type of bread. The markings may indicate the official reckoning of how many loaves the bearer had coming to him.

CHAPTER FOUR

And None Have Returned

Surrounded by symbols of rebirth, Osiris, king of the dead and god of fertility *(left),* wears his characteristic crown topped by the sun disk, and holds a crook and flail. He is wrapped mummy-tight in white linen, and his face and hands are green, the color of new life. On either side of him is an eye of Horus, an image often painted near the entrance to a tomb that enabled the deceased to look outward. Stakes holding jackal skins filled with milk *(foreground)* await use in resurrection ceremonies.

For some time a woman known as Dedi, the wife of a priest living in the region of Memphis about the 20th century BC, had been worrying over the prolonged illness of her serving maid, Imiu. She could not run her household properly without assistance, and the apparent indifference of her husband, Intef, only sharpened her anxiety. Intef had been of no use at all; he neither tended to the domestic chores nor cared for the ailing servant. It fell to Dedi to manage on her own.

When she could no longer tolerate the situation, Dedi sat down and wrote a letter to her negligent husband, taking him to task for his insensitivity to her suffering. "Why do you want your threshold to be made desolate?" Dedi asked. "If there's no help from you, your house will be destroyed; don't you know that it is this serving maid who maintains your house among men?" Instead of using papyrus, Dedi wrote directly onto the surface of a rough red pottery bowl, starting first on the inside and then, when this could not contain the outpouring of her woes, spilling over to the outside.

Although Dedi had accused him of being insensitive to her concerns, Intef had a fairly good reason for keeping silent: He had died some time earlier. In Dedi's view, a common one, death did not necessarily preclude her husband from helping out around the house. Indeed, in this particular instance, Intef would be of more use to Dedi in the Realm of the Dead. Illnesses such as the one afflicting the housemaid were thought to be the result of the malign influence of hostile spirits. Only by the intervention of her dead husband could Dedi hope to have the serving woman restored to health. "Can you not fight for her day and night?" Dedi asked. "Fight for her! Watch over her! Save her from all those doing her harm! Then your house and your children shall be maintained."

Dedi promised that once the household returned to normal, proper funerary libations would be poured for Intef's spirit, in keeping with the orderly running of a well-maintained household. But she emphasized that this could happen only if Intef heeded her pleas. "Fight for her," she urged. "Now!"

Having finished her letter, Dedi filled the bowl with food and left it in Intef's tomb. In this way, she could be sure that her husband would not overlook it. When his spirit came to partake of the offering, he would naturally read the message and do her bidding, or so Dedi hoped.

Such letters were fairly common in ancient Egypt. The dead and the living maintained a close relationship; those men and women who had passed into the afterlife not only remained part of the community, they were expected to lend their assistance whenever they were called upon to do so. At every stage of their history, the ancient Egyptians clung to the belief, as did Dedi, that their spirits survived death and that, in order for this to happen, their corpses must be preserved at all costs. Over the centuries, the Egyptians would evolve a complex set of attitudes about the journey to the afterworld. The desire for eternal life, which seems to dominate the surviving records of their culture, sprang from a deep passion for life and a wish to see it continue beyond the normal earthly span. To this end the nation funneled a great deal of its wealth, giving employment to a fortunate portion of the population.

The Egyptians began their preparations for the afterlife with their tombs; built to last, these "houses of eternity" were often made of stone, a more durable substance than the mud-brick homes they occupied during the comparatively brief stay on earth. The ambitious men and women who constructed, furnished, and in-

A MASTER ARCHITECT'S GREATEST ACHIEVEMENT

The Step Pyramid at Saqqara, built for the Third Dynasty pharaoh Djoser by his architect Imhotep *(below)*, survives as the oldest stone colossus in the world. Imhotep's innovative design resulted in the first of the Egyptian pyramids and transformed the royal tomb from the single-story, flat mastaba into a multitiered monument that reached toward the sky. Like the pyramids that followed, the Step Pyramid was part of a larger funerary complex *(lower right)*, where royal priests maintained the king's mortuary cult long after his death. Experimentation with pyramid design in the Fourth Dynasty led to the Bent Pyramid at Dahshur, the first smooth-sided true pyramid at Meidum, and, finally, to the three magnificent pyramids at Giza. Structural deficiencies later caused the walls of the Meidum pyramid to collapse.

habited these tombs—and even those who robbed them—were part of the engine that drove Egypt's economy, creating a strong demand for both necessities and luxury goods. The tomb itself could be a simple mud-brick structure, a rock-cut chamber, or a sprawling temple complex. During the Archaic Period and the Old Kingdom, the tombs of the pharaohs took on great importance. These early kings, who would spend eternity traversing the heavens in the company of the gods, were interred in a flat mud-brick, benchlike structure known today as a mastaba. Its simple shape, however, concealed a vertical shaft leading to elaborate offering rooms, a tomb chapel, and a burial chamber belowground. In the reign of King Djoser, during the Third Dynasty, the mastaba gave way to a far grander funeral complex centered on a massive step pyramid. This was the forerunner of the later, so-called true pyramids.

The pyramids symbolized the mound of earth that rose from the primeval waters during the world's creation. They also suggested the sun's rays beaming down to form a staircase to eternity, emphasizing the pharaoh's place in one of Egypt's most important cults, the worship of the sun god Re. In the Fifth and Sixth Dynasties, pyramids became smaller because the kings preferred to channel their resources into supporting the state cult of Re by building temples to this important god. During the Middle Kingdom, the great pharaoh Nebhepetre Mentuhotep II of the 11th Dynasty cut his tomb into a cliff at Deir el-Bahri near Thebes. Against its sheer wall he built his funerary monument, a complex of buildings consisting of three landscaped tiers with a mastaba

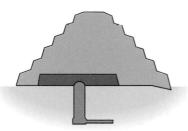

FIRST DYNASTY - MASTABA

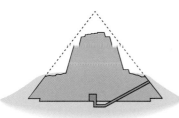

THIRD DYNASTY - STEP PYRAMID

FOURTH DYNASTY - EARLIEST TRUE PYRAMID

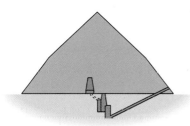

FOURTH DYNASTY - BENT PYRAMID

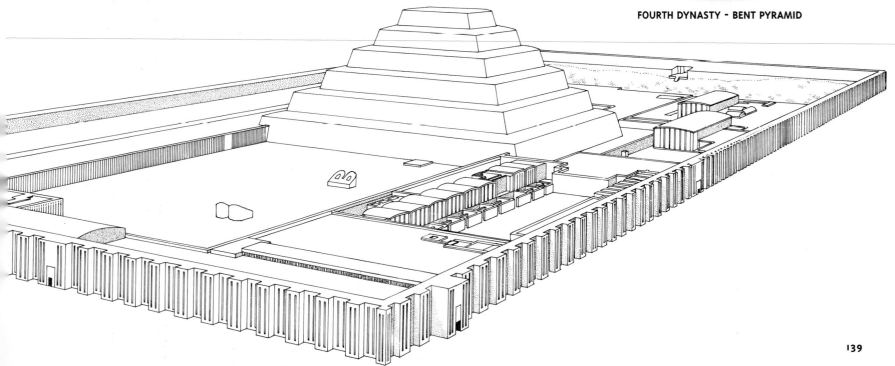

or mound at the top. The new twist was that the mastaba did not contain the tomb, which was carved into the heart of the mountain behind the terraced structure.

In the New Kingdom, royal pyramids were no longer being created. The Theban founders of the 18th Dynasty wanted to be buried on their ancestral grounds and evade the ever present threat of tomb robbers. So they built a royal necropolis on the west bank of the Nile at Thebes. There, starting with Tuthmosis I, Egypt's kings were laid to rest in a series of labyrinthine tombs cut deep into the rocky cliffs, known today as the Valley of the Kings. The rock-cut tombs fit the Theban landscape better than pyramids, but they were no safer, for they too were ultimately despoiled. Some of the more notorious thefts provided moments of high drama, and they reveal how easily potent taboos, and even the awe of the underworld, could break down in the face of greed or need.

Wealthy, high-ranking nobles also wanted lavish trappings for their tombs. As early as the Sixth Dynasty, one such nobleman, a royal courtier named Weni, rose to become governor of Upper Egypt, serving three pharaohs. Following the

To smooth a rough-hewn limestone block, stonemasons stretched a pair of rods like those pictured over the block's surface, with the connecting string pulled taut. A stick was then used as a measure to check if the distance between the taut string and the surface was the same from point to point. High spots were leveled with mallet and chisel, as portrayed below.

Khufu's Great Pyramid (background, right) was slightly taller than that of his son Khafre (center, with intact casing stones at its peak) and more than twice as high as that of Khafre's successor, Menkaure (foreground), who began the small pyramids nearby for his wives.

BUILDING THE GREAT PYRAMID

Shortly after ascending the throne in 2606 BC, the pharaoh Khufu commanded his Overseer of Royal Works to prepare a burial place for the king grander than any of the tombs built by his predecessors. West of the Nile, across from the Old Kingdom capital of Memphis, a choice site on the Giza plateau was surveyed and leveled as a foundation for Khufu's pyramid. Then the limestone bedrock was excavated to make room for a subterranean burial chamber (a plan that was later abandoned).

As the first stones for the pyramid were being cut from nearby quarries, thousands of men began building causeways, erecting storehouses and barracks, and digging a canal to link the foot of the plateau to the Nile. Meanwhile, scribes dispatched orders to outlying provinces for more work crews and arranged for the delivery of tools, timber, rope, food, cooking vessels, and countless other supplies.

Throughout Khufu's 23-year reign, the construction site teemed with laborers struggling to complete the monument before the king's death. Khufu and his architects did not make it easy for them. The royal planners decided to enlarge the structure several times and to relocate the burial chamber from beneath the pyramid to its inner reaches. Day after day, year after year, the quarries rang with the sounds of hammer and chisel on stone, while boats delivered the finest limestone and granite from Tura and Aswan upriver.

From dawn to dusk, sled crews dragged stone monoliths weighing a few tons or more to staging areas at the base of the pyramid. There stonemasons chiseled the blocks to conform to the prescribed dimensions, smoothed the sides, and squared

Egyptian stonemasons used heavy wooden mallets like the one at top to pound their chisels, which were made originally of stone or copper *(above)* and later of bronze.

the corners. Laborers then reloaded the sleds and began hauling them slowly up the clay-and-rubble ramps that flanked the emerging structure.

As the pyramid's working level grew ever higher, teams shifted the blocks from the sleds into their designated positions, fitting them together so snugly that the seams between the outer blocks, or casing stones, were paper thin. Toiling below were legions of toolmakers and storekeepers, cooks and bakers, butchers and brewers, porters and guards, all skillfully directed by ever watchful scribes—the royal project managers. At any one time, as many as 30,000 workers may have been involved in the massive project. Some of them were professional craftsmen, employed at Giza year-round. Most, however, were peasants—not slaves—working as conscripts during the annual Nile flood as an alternative to paying taxes, serving in the military, or performing other mandatory labor for pharaoh and country, such as digging irrigation canals. Proud to be serving the god-king, some carved the names of their work teams—Victorious Gang, Enduring Gang—into the massive stones.

The regimen at Giza was probably no less demanding than that imposed afterward on tomb workers at Deir el-Medina, who toiled nine days straight and rested on the 10th day. In addition, the pyramid builders faced extraordinary hardships. They waded in stagnant canal water that exposed them to parasites. They risked heatstroke, insect bites, and broken bones, and some even met with fatal accidents. Yet the task was not without compensation. Rations of bread, beer, onions, and garlic were doled out three times a day, and the men earned additional payment in wheat or barley seed. With luck, laborers at the end of the long workweek might be rewarded with a feast of grilled fish or fowl, washed down with wine.

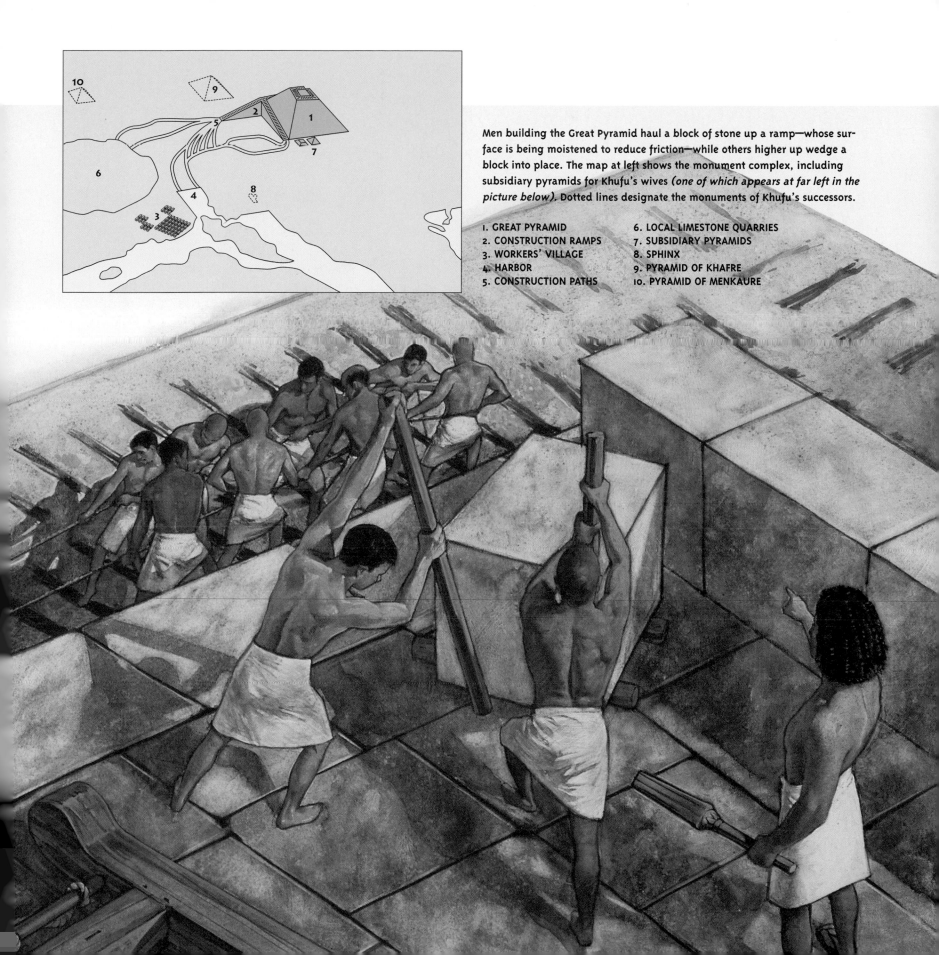

Men building the Great Pyramid haul a block of stone up a ramp—whose surface is being moistened to reduce friction—while others higher up wedge a block into place. The map at left shows the monument complex, including subsidiary pyramids for Khufu's wives (one of which appears at far left in the picture below). Dotted lines designate the monuments of Khufu's successors.

1. GREAT PYRAMID
2. CONSTRUCTION RAMPS
3. WORKERS' VILLAGE
4. HARBOR
5. CONSTRUCTION PATHS
6. LOCAL LIMESTONE QUARRIES
7. SUBSIDIARY PYRAMIDS
8. SPHINX
9. PYRAMID OF KHAFRE
10. PYRAMID OF MENKAURE

The result of all this exertion was a monument of almost superhuman grandeur. Its base was a near-perfect square covering more than 13 acres, with each side measuring 756 feet, give or take a few inches. The finished structure contained more than 2,300,000 stone blocks and rose to a height of 482 feet. Its smooth casing stones—many of which were subsequently pilfered by other monument builders—glittered in the sun, dazzling the peasants in distant fields when they paused in their labors to ad-mire Khufu's marvel.

This Great Pyramid would be justly celebrated by later ages as one of the wonders of the world. But for Khufu and his followers, its true significance was other-worldly. Hidden from view, deep within the structure, lay the tomb cham-ber that would hold the king's remains. And that was only a temporary resting place. Once attendants had deposited the dead pharaoh in his chamber and sealed the entrance, Khufu would embark in spirit on his long-anticipated journey to heaven in the company of the sun god Re.

After Khufu's death, attendants carried his coffin through the courtyard of the mortuary temple at the base of the Great Pyramid *(see diagram, below)* and made their way up the cavernous Grand Gallery *(left and 7 below)* to the King's Chamber, which replaced the earlier subterranean burial vault planned for the king. Once inside the tomb chamber, the attendants placed the coffin in a stone sarcophagus. Then they closed off the burial vault by releasing heavy granite blocks that slid down a groove in the floor of the Grand Gallery and plugged the entrance. Finally, the attendants exited through a narrow escape chute and sealed that behind them to conceal its existence. Despite such elaborate precautions, robbers ultimately found their way in and emptied the tomb chamber.

practice of his peers, he covered the walls of his chapel in Abydos with 50 columns of finely carved hieroglyphs, texts describing his achievements and also the uncommon splendor of his burial furnishings: "When I begged of His Majesty my lord that there be brought for me a sarcophagus of white stone from Tura, His Majesty had a royal seal-bearer cross over with a company of sailors under his command, to bring me this sarcophagus from Tura. It came with him in a great barge of the court, together with its lid, a doorway, lintel, two doorjambs, and a libation table."

Since it was the king who supplied favored courtiers like Weni with burial goods, this description showed that the pharaoh held Weni in the highest regard, and Weni was not reluctant to drive the point home: "Never before had the like been done for any servant," he said, "but I was excellent in His Majesty's heart; I was rooted in His Majesty's heart; His Majesty's heart was filled with me." For Weni and others, such declarations of closeness to the king were more than mere swagger. As a manifestation of the divine, the pharaoh was seen as the core of stability and prosperity in this life as well as in the next. Weni's efforts to link his name with that of

1. EXTERIOR OF GREAT PYRAMID
2. KING'S CHAMBER
3. CHAMBER FOR KING'S KA STATUE
4. SUBTERRANEAN CHAMBER (UNFINISHED)
5. DESCENDING PASSAGEWAY
6. ASCENDING PASSAGEWAY
7. GRAND GALLERY
8. AIR SHAFT (OPENING TO HEAVEN)
9. MORTUARY TEMPLE

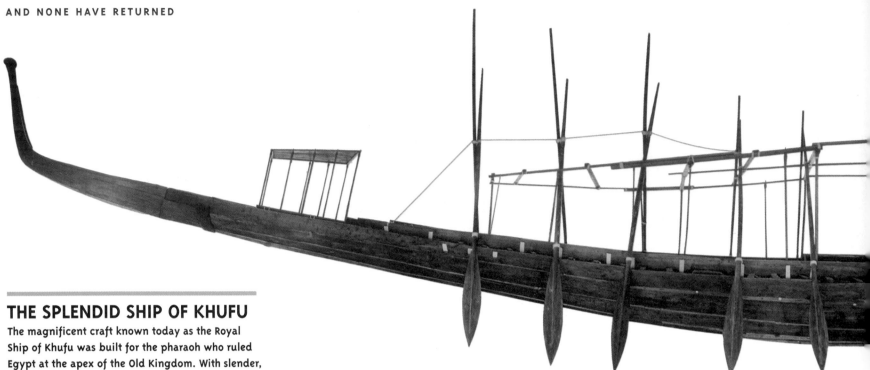

THE SPLENDID SHIP OF KHUFU

The magnificent craft known today as the Royal Ship of Khufu was built for the pharaoh who ruled Egypt at the apex of the Old Kingdom. With slender, curving lines and stem and stern ornaments elegantly carved in the shape of papyrus-reed bundles, Khufu's ship imitates the sacred papyrus raft that, according to myth, ferried the sun god Re across the heavens. This ship may have been built with a similar celestial journey in mind for the departed pharaoh. Rope marks on the hull indicate, however, that the ship was submerged in earthly water at least once. Perhaps it transported Khufu's mummy from the Memphis palace to the Giza necropolis during the royal funeral. If so, the body would have been sheltered in the cabin, protected from the heat by dampened reeds placed across the trellis overhead. A similar canopy was set above the rowers in the ship's aft. Before burial, the boat was disassembled into 1,224 parts, ranging in size from pegs just a few inches long to cedar planks stretching more than 75 feet. For nearly 4,500 years, the boat lay sealed in a stone grave at the foot of the Great Pyramid, where in 1954 its secret chamber beneath the Giza sand was discovered.

the god-king arose from a fervent desire to continue the association in the afterlife.

Not everyone could boast such royal clout as Weni, but even those less favored aspired to build and equip a proper tomb. For many Egyptian nobles, these preparations became a major concern and expenditure. The grave site could also be a focus of family activity, when the Egyptians, on certain festival days, visited their relatives' tombs to feast and present offerings to the dead and to celebrate their continued life after death. It was a way of including their dead kin in the social community of the living.

While the wealthy and powerful sought to prepare themselves for eternity, Egypt's lower classes had to struggle to muster even the most basic requirements for a proper burial. The poorest classes could not afford to build tomb structures. Frequently they couldn't even manage to buy a coffin and would be forced to bury their dead in rudimentary sandpits. Sometimes an older tomb that had been robbed and abandoned proved a convenient and inexpensive place for a family to bury its members. Even some of the great pyramids contain one or two extra bodies tucked away in the corners.

However grand or humble, the tomb served as a meeting place between this world and the next. It was the earthly home of the three spirit forms that survived death: the ba, the ka, and the akh. The ba, depicted as a human-headed bird, was the essence of

the individual's unique characteristics. Separated from the corpse at death, it soared across the sky with the sun god by day, returning to the tomb at night to infuse the mummy with its personal qualities. The ka was envisioned as an individual's life force. Upon death, the ka left the body and traveled to the afterworld. Thereafter it required nourishment, provided by the offerings of the living. It was by virtue of his akh, however, that Dedi's deceased husband could have been of service, for the akh was the spirit capable of interacting with the living and interceding on behalf of live human beings. These three spiritual entities, taken together, formed what we now might call the soul.

The spirits of the departed did not attain a happy immortality automatically, but rather they were transformed through the careful observance of a number of well-defined funeral rituals. Once the spirit of the deceased left its body, it faced extraordinary dangers on its journey toward eternity. Punishing deities lay waiting in the shadows. Gigantic snakes might block the path. Frightening demons could thwart the defenseless traveler.

Protection against the hazards that might crop up on the road to the afterlife could be found in funerary texts. Among these was the Book of the Dead, which included about 192 spells used frequently during the New Kingdom and later. The Book of the Dead reveals the secrets required by spirits in transition from this world to the next, demonstrating in the process the power of words, names, and inscriptions.

The spirit could journey safely through the perils of the underworld only if it knew the correct procedures and appropriate speeches to recite at designated stops along the way. One chapter of the Book of the Dead, for example, provides spells against having one's head cut off. Another is meant to ensure that the deceased will not be forced to eat dung. Some incantations allow the dead person to exist in the fullest possible sense. One, for example, offers tips on taking the form of a falcon whenever the situation calls for it. Such a transformation enhances the person's ability to move about freely and also provides identification with the falcon god Horus, transferring some of that deity's power.

These lavishly decorated, nested coffins belonged to Tamutnefret, a woman of considerable wealth and high social status. Coffins used during the Old and Middle Kingdoms were simpler, rectangular boxes, but by the New Kingdom, these mummy-shaped containers had become very popular.

As part of the process of readying oneself for the afterlife, an Egyptian could either commission a personal version of the Book of the Dead or have his or her name inserted in a ready-made copy of the text. Either way the book would be placed in the tomb for reference on the perilous journey. Such a man was Ani, in whose tomb was found one of the best-preserved papyrus copies of the Book of the Dead. Ani and his wife, Tutu, lived and were buried in Thebes during the 14th century BC. Tutu was a "musician of Amun," a common title for women of good social standing during the New Kingdom. It indicated that she participated in temple rituals, playing instruments or perhaps shaking the rattlelike instrument known as the sistrum during processions. Ani's titles show him to be a well-placed official who was a member of both royal and temple bureaucracies: "True royal scribe, scribe of accounting of the divine offerings of all the gods, overseer of the double granary of the lords of Abydos, scribe of the divine offerings of the lords of Thebes."

Ani's Book of the Dead includes vignettes that accompany the spells, with his name inserted at the appropriate points in the text. These are illustrations describing how Ani would use the spells to safely complete his nether world journey. Among other things, they demonstrate the paramount importance of names. When passing through various great halls and tall gates on the way to eternity, Ani would be expected to know the appropriate underworld name of virtually each piece of wood or stone he encountered. In one vignette, a doorjamb, for example, accosts Ani: "I shall not let you enter through me," says the doorjamb, "unless you tell my name." Properly prepared, Ani answers promptly as required: "Plummet of the place of truth." A pair of left and right door lintels also demand to be identified, and Ani gives the answers, respectively, "Scale pan that carries maat" and "Scale pan of wine." Not to be outdone, the threshold and the door bolt also require that Ani supply their correct names—Ox of Geb and Toe of his mother.

At one stage, Ani is required to furnish the names of his own feet. "You shall not tread upon me," declares a menacing floor. "Why not?" inquires Ani. "I am pure." The floor, however, has its own reasons: "Because we do not know your feet with which you tread on us. Tell them to me." The correct answers are Who enters before Min and Wenpet of Nephthys. "You know us," the floor acknowledges, apparently mollified by this information. "Tread upon us." Ani earns his entrance by revealing his knowledge of the underworld, thus demonstrating his mastery over its forces.

With sufficient money to pay for a proper burial and a copy of the necessary funerary texts in hand, it would seem that virtually anyone could attain eternity. The ultimate challenge, however, was the person's own conduct throughout life. The deceased on the way to paradise had to face judgment in the Hall of Two Truths. This experience could be harrowing indeed, as Ani's vignette illustrates: Having braved all the other terrors of the underworld, Ani now waits to defend himself before an imposing council of gods. Dressed in his finest clothes and white sandals, his eyes properly painted, and his body anointed with fragrant oil of myrrh, he enters the Hall of Two Truths. Head lowered, he stands hesitantly at the center of the grand chamber, scarcely daring to move. An assembly of no fewer than 42 gods, each of whom must be addressed by name, stare down at him from the jury box. Osiris himself, with his wife Isis close behind him, scrutinizes Ani from his throne of judgment. The divine scribe Thoth, hovering to one side, is prepared to record the verdict.

At the center of the chamber lies the greatest danger to be faced, for there, about to be weighed on an imposing set of scales, is Ani's own heart. As the seat of emotion and the repository of intelligence, the heart was thought to carry the dead man's memories. It acted, therefore, as the sole witness in the case for Ani's salvation. While Ani's heart is lowered into one pan of the great scales, a single feather of Maat, the goddess of truth and righteousness, serves to counterbalance it. This is, then, a literal weighing of the heart against truth. Even the faintest trace of deceit or treachery will condemn the defendant. It is a chilling thing to watch, more so because lurking near the scales is a fearsome creature known as Ammit, the Devourer of the Dead. This hybrid monster, with the head of a crocodile, the mane and forequarters of a lion, and the hindquarters of a hippopotamus, stands with its glistening jaws snapping, ready to pounce on the heart and wolf it down if Ani should fail the test.

OSIRIS MADE WHOLE

Through the story of his death and resurrection, Osiris symbolized the triumph of good over evil and the promise of immortality for all Egyptians. According to the ancient myth, Osiris was so powerful and highly esteemed that he inspired jealousy in the heart of his evil brother Seth, who arranged for his murder. At a banquet, Seth presented Osiris with an ornate coffin. When Osiris climbed inside to test the fit, Seth slammed the lid shut and cast the chest into the Nile. Seth ascended the throne, unaware that Osiris's widow Isis had retrieved the coffin and hidden it in the marshes. Upon discovering this, Seth found and dismembered the body and scattered its pieces. But Isis and her sister Nephthys patiently gathered every part except the genitals, which were eaten by fish. With the help of the god Thoth, Isis formed Osiris's broken body into a mummy, created a new penis, and brought her husband back to life. Together they conceived a child, Horus, and Osiris descended into the nether world to rule the dead, while Isis remained on earth to raise their son in secrecy. When he came of age, Horus avenged his father's death by deposing Seth and becoming the new king of Egypt. During their battle, however, Seth tore out one of the eyes of Horus. The god Thoth restored Horus's eye, and it became a popular symbol of protection (above) for both the living and the dead. Reigning pharaohs were associated with Horus and deceased kings with Osiris. In time, all Egyptians would aspire to become one with the body and spirit of Osiris, living as he did in the afterlife.

Ani has prepared for this moment earlier in his journey before reaching the Hall of Two Truths. Almost as soon as he had begun his expedition, he had cried out an appeal to his heart not to betray him: "Oh my heart of my mother! Do not rise up against me as witness! Do not oppose me in the tribunal! Do not rebel against me before the guardian of the scales!" While framed as an appeal, it is also a form of control, for this spell is meant to ensure, magically, cooperation from the deceased's heart.

Now when it is time to address the awe-inspiring jury, one imagines that Ani's voice quivers slightly as he begins to read his statement. Ani declares his innocence to each of the 42 gods in turn. The method of his appeal is the so-called negative confession, a listing of vices that have not been committed: "I have not done crimes against people," he says. "I have not mistreated cattle. I did not begin a day by exacting more than my due. I have not blasphemed a god. I have not robbed the poor. I have not done what the god abhors. I have not maligned a servant to his master." The

The earliest known Pyramid Texts appear below in the tomb of Unas, a Fifth Dynasty pharaoh. Incised and painted in blue on the walls and ceilings of the tomb, the hieroglyphs ensured that Unas would dwell in "lightland for all eternity."

SACRED TEXTS

The ancient Egyptians believed that the right words could help them secure eternal life. People who died without knowing what to say when they stood trial before the gods in the underworld would be lost forever. Those armed with the proper prayers and spells, however, would be protected and transfigured and would join the blessed dead in heaven.

During the Old Kingdom, Pyramid Texts were composed for royalty and inscribed on their tombs *(left)* in order to enable them to ascend to heaven with the sun god Re. In one text,

the king humbly offers himself as a servant to Re. In another, the king boasts that he has earned immortality by seizing "the hearts of the gods" and devouring their knowledge. The deceased faced many challenges on the path to eternity and sometimes had to respond forcefully.

During the First Intermediate Period, the lesser nobility took to inscribing their wooden coffins *(below)* with passages and illustrations adapted from the Pyramid Texts and other sacred sources. People no longer regarded the pharaoh as uniquely qual-

ified for a divine afterlife. They, too, might become one with Re. "I shall sail rightly in my bark," recited the deceased in one such Coffin Text; "I am lord of eternity in the crossing of the sky." The Coffin Texts also identified the deceased with the god Osiris, who ruled the underworld and freed those who uttered the right spells from the terrors of that realm.

By the time of the New Kingdom, many Egyptians were buried with spells inscribed on their linen shrouds or on papyrus scrolls. Nearly 200 such spells were combined in a collection

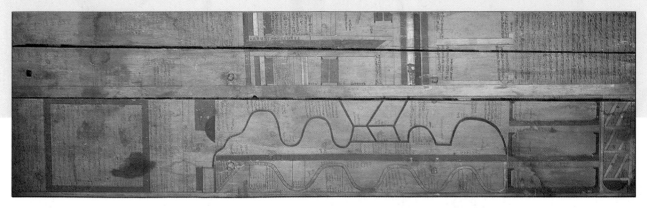

The eyes of the falcon god Horus, painted on the side of a coffin belonging to an official named Gua *(left)*, offer the deceased both protection and the power of sight. A map on the coffin's floor *(below)* shows a safe route through the nether world, complete with advice ranging from table manners in the Realm of the Dead to repelling evil snakes and crocodiles.

that became known as The Chapters of Coming Forth by Day, or the Book of the Dead. For those who could afford a copy of the text, it served as a kind of afterlife insurance policy. So long as the information was entombed with the deceased, he or she would know exactly what to say when standing in judgment before Osiris and the other gods in the Hall of Two Truths and pleading for eternal life.

Royalty of this period had special funerary texts that adorned the walls and ceilings of their tombs in the Valley of the Kings. One such text, called the Am Duat, was an illustrated guide to traversing the perils of the underworld. It provided a detailed record of the 12 hours that the sun god Re spent each night under the earth after setting in the west. Re was shown illuminating the underworld and rising in triumph at dawn—symbolic of the pharaoh's own resurrection.

oration continues in this vein for some time. Perhaps Ani gathers courage as he goes along, for the speech is not meant to be delivered meekly. As he reads off each successive example of his own righteousness, Ani's voice may well grow louder and more forceful: "I have not caused pain. I have not caused tears. I have not killed. I have not ordered to kill. I have not made anyone suffer. I have not damaged the offerings in the temple. I have not copulated nor defiled myself. I have not cheated in the fields. I have not taken milk from the mouths of children."

The declamation eventually touches on such subjects as ownership of cattle and fishing rights. Then as now, few men or women could recite such a list of assertions without fear of contradiction. But this incantation is cast as a magical spell and is therefore supposed to be foolproof in its effect.

The longed-for response, at last, is spoken by the great company of gods: "What you have said is true. The Osiris scribe Ani, justified, is righteous. He has committed no crime nor has he acted against us. Ammit shall not be permitted to prevail over him." And at this point, the crocodile-headed monster, after a final greedy look at the heart lying in the pan of the great scales, would skulk away. The council of gods then proclaims, "Let there be given to him bread and beer which have been issued in the presence of Osiris, and a permanent grant of land in the Field of Offerings."

As can be seen in Ani's vignettes, powerful spells were necessary to guarantee the continued existence of the spirit. But while the magic inherent in the incantations was important, it was critical to preserve the corpse itself. For those who could afford it, this meant mummification, and even the poorest achieved some measure of bodily preservation since the hot, dry sands drew the moisture from the corpses and halted their decay.

The humble as well as the rich aspired to purchase a coffin for the afterlife, and sometimes, for the poor, a single coffin did duty for an entire family. Early coffins of the Old and Middle Kingdoms were rectangular boxes of wood, but during the Middle Kingdom, the anthropoid, or mummy-shaped, coffin came into

fashion and subsequently became the most popular form used during the New Kingdom. Plain coffins for those less well off came already inscribed with funerary texts, but with blank panels left for the owner's name. Curiously, many people left these areas blank, possibly because they were illiterate.

Even the most modest burial included one or two personal possessions, such as a simple bracelet or necklace, or possibly a scarab bezel ring. A toilet kit was also packed for the departing spirit, with perhaps a bottle of perfume, some makeup, and an applicator wand. A few personal utensils and pottery vessels filled with food and drink often rounded out the collection of burial goods. For those who could manage a slightly more upscale funeral, some sticks of furniture might be added to their personal effects, along with whatever tools and instruments they had used in life. A musician would take his or her instrument along to the next world; a seamstress might be buried with her cloth and thread. The food offerings were of a higher quality as well. Al-

though wine was too expensive for the middle classes, stone vessels filled with beer found their way into the funerary meal, along with bread, joints of meat, and the occasional roasted fowl. It might take several years to save up enough money for such a lavish funeral, but it was considered to be well worth the expense.

Customized coffins were usually prepared for the wealthy, who insisted on personalized inscriptions and decorative carvings. Their grave goods were supplemented with a more extensive collection of furniture and jewelry. A rich bureaucrat might bring along his scribe's kit; a military man would carry a small arsenal of weapons into the next world.

It was not necessary to be born into the most elite class to go out in the highest style: In Deir el-Medina, the village of tomb workers near Thebes, a brilliant young man named Kha married a woman called Merit, and through his own labor rose to become the overseer of works, serving three kings of the 18th Dynasty in the 15th century BC. With the same meticulous

attention to detail that had brought about his rise in the here and now, he sought to arrange for the good life in the hereafter.

Kha ordered a splendid set of two nested anthropoid coffins for himself. The innermost box boasted a covering of gold leaf, with delicate inlays of glass meant to suggest lapis, carnelian, and turquoise. A statuette of Kha stood watch over a rich array of papyri, scarabs, and amulets. Some of these might have been given as gifts to the deceased by friends or the officials he served, and for that reason are inscribed with their names, not his.

Kha's burial furniture alone would have equipped an entire household. He stocked his tomb, which he shared with Merit, with two beds, one of them fully made up with a mattress and linens, along with more than 10 chairs and an assortment of lamps and pot stands. Kha did not expect to enjoy the afterlife devoid of bodily functions, for there was a toilet provided, a stool with a wide slit in the middle; the pan below, filled with sand, would be emptied by servants. Kha also intended to continue

Nestled within these desert mountains is the Valley of the Kings *(foreground),* where the tombs of New Kingdom royalty are cut into the cliffs. Egypt's rulers hoped to evade tomb robbery in this remote valley located across the Nile River from the ancient Egyptian capital of Thebes. Overlooking the vast desert necropolis stands the tallest pinnacle in the region, the pyramid-shaped mountain known as the Peak that was revered in ancient times as a goddess-protector of the dead.

removing hair from his body after death, for included among his toilet articles were a bronze razor and tweezers.

He expected his physique in the next world would be a rejuvenated one, since the statuette he had made of himself was that of a young man. To make sure he was well dressed, Kha had more than 100 changes of clothes buried with him, including 50 loincloths, 18 tunics, 26 kilts, and a pair of cloaks. His wife, Merit, entered the afterlife with her dark, braided wig, made of human hair, and a large makeup chest, its glass and alabaster jars filled with oils, creams, and eye paint.

Like those of lesser means, Kha brought the tools of his trade into the afterlife. In keeping with his station in life, Kha equipped himself with several boxes filled with six-color palettes, pens, writing boards, signet rings, a cubit measure, an adz for planing wood, and a scale, consisting of a bronze rod from which weighing pans were suspended. Lest he grow hungry in the

VENERABLE ANIMAL MUMMIES

Egyptians associated animals and their awesome powers with the gods. Since the days of the first pharaohs, the majestic falcon represented Horus, patron of kings. By the Late Period, Egyptians were honoring their patron deities by burying mummies of animals linked with those gods in special cemeteries. People flocked to Bubastis, cult center of the cat goddess Bastet, and left mummified cats there as offerings. Elsewhere, pilgrims offered dogs to the jackal-headed Anubis, crocodiles to Sobek (the crocodile god), fish to Osiris (whose body parts were eaten by fish), and ibises to the ibis-headed Thoth. So many lovers of learning brought offerings to Thoth that his cult cemetery grew to contain more than four million ibis mummies. Many of those birds and other sacred species were raised in captivity and sold to worshipers, who then had the creatures embalmed—often with splendid wrappings and masks—before committing them to their tombs.

DOMESTIC CAT

WILD CAT

DOG

FALCON

CROCODILES

HAWK

FISH

TWO FALCONS

IBIS

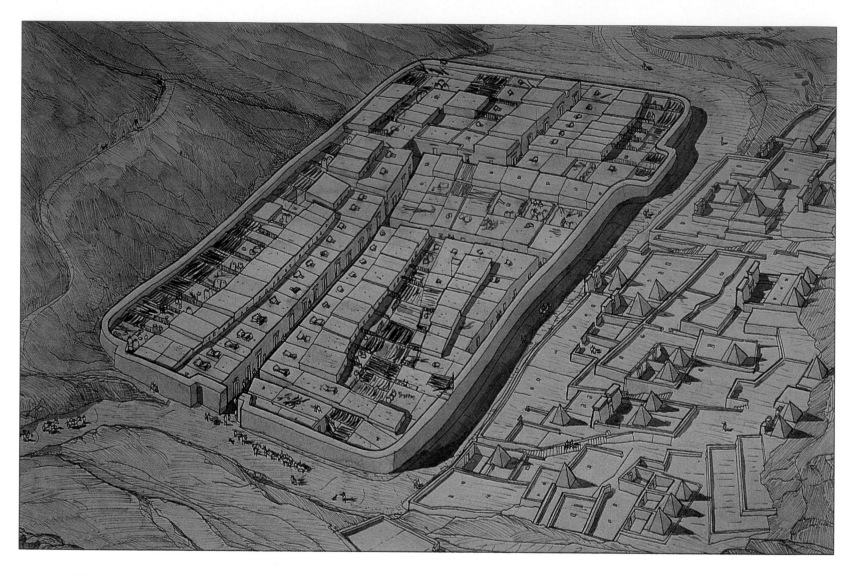

The village of Deir el-Medina, home to generations of New Kingdom workers who built and furnished the tombs in the Valley of the Kings, is shown above in an artist's reconstruction based on the ruins of the ancient buildings. The walled hamlet's one entrance *(foreground)* leads to the main street and the alleys running from it, where some 70 houses are lined up in neat rows. Outside the walls are the chapels and tombs of the villagers.

next world, Kha laid in a virtual storehouse of foods, including preserved meats, wine, bread baked into various animal shapes, vegetable paste, dates and grapes, garlic and onions, juniper and cumin, and even a basket of dung for the kitchen fire.

Along with preparing a final resting place, a tomb owner such as Kha instituted a perpetual mortuary cult, an ongoing memorial designed to keep the name of the deceased alive in the thoughts of the living and to guarantee his or her continued existence in the afterlife. Mortuary priests, known as ka priests, were hired to ensure that libations and food offerings were provided and that the proper rituals were carried out on schedule. Like the tomb itself, the mortuary cult entailed a great deal of expense. Usually the tomb owner set up an endowment, often a parcel of farmland called a mortuary estate, the produce of which would both pay the personnel of the cult and supply the offerings. Such land was not taxed and thus provided a loophole similar to the tax-deductible charitable contributions that are well known today. The mortuary priest, often a relative of the deceased, presided over the smooth running of the cult, and thus he assumed a role of paramount importance to the tomb owner: "He profits you more than your own son," wrote one nobleman.

Unlike the burial chamber, the mortuary chapel was thrown open to the public. An architectural feature known as a false door was built to admit the spirit of the departed, which in theory could pass directly from tomb to chapel even if the two structures were some distance apart. The spirit's presence did not discourage the living. Visitors were urged to come inside, look around, and offer a prayer for the dead man or woman. Some tomb inscriptions, known as Appeals to the Living, exhorted passersby to recite offering prayers for the dead, stressing the cost effectiveness of a piety that required no financial outlay and elicited favor from the gods. In a sense, this was a safety net for the deceased; if the paid priests were negligent in their duties, the prayers and offerings of these walk-in supplicants would do the job.

While monuments might decay and contracts could be broken, magical spells, sculpture, and drawings could survive the neglect of a tomb by a person's descendants. Therefore the simple personal possessions placed in the earliest graves were later bolstered by symbolic objects, including both portraits and statues known as shawabtis, doll-size replicas of servants and craftspersons intended to substitute for the dead person when the gods demanded labor in the afterlife.

Tomb paintings often showed male and female servants preparing offerings of food and carrying them to the deceased. If the actual offerings were to stop for any reason, the painting alone could provide sustenance to the spirit. Offering tables groaning with food were another feature of tomb paintings, even when the actual tables were bare.

It was well to provide symbolically for the spirit, since even the simplest burial was a lure to tomb robbers, who would break into all but the most heavily guarded tombs and strip away the valuable possessions of the deceased. Kha and Merit were among the lucky ones who journeyed through the underworld for several millennia with their possessions intact. Whatever provisions had been made before death proved futile for many tomb owners, the unfortunates whose tombs would be visited by thieves. The robbers would ransack the burial chamber, strip away its

An unshaven carpenter from Deir el-Medina is shown smoothing wood with an adz. Besides carpenters, the royal craftsmen included painters, draftsmen, stonemasons, and sculptors. Fathers taught their skills to their sons to keep the privilege of working for the pharaoh in the family.

treasures, and even cart off the mummy for the jewels and gold that lay under the wrappings, perhaps, in the process, hacking the limbs from the defenseless corpse.

Often the robbers were gangs of highly skilled and well-organized Egyptians, many of them citizens of Thebes and West Thebes and minor temple functionaries. On a few occasions, the thieves who plundered the tombs were the very craftsmen who had constructed them: Some of the royal tomb workers of Deir el-Medina, the town on the ridges above the Valley of the Kings, were, in the late-12th-century-BC reign of Ramses IX, found to be involved in tomb thefts. In this period, gangs of about eight robbers sometimes included stonemasons to breach the tomb walls, water carriers to help in tunneling and hauling away the loot, and metalworkers to melt down the plundered metals in a furnace. A boatman completed the team. In effect, he drove the getaway car, ferrying the gang and their loot away from the Valley of the Kings to the east side of the river.

The job of guarding a tomb required extraordinary vigilance. In many cases, it was difficult even to detect that a robbery had been committed. The gangs usually broke in through a rear wall, leaving the seals on the tomb door undisturbed. In many instances, the robbers didn't have to worry about getting caught at all. A generous bribe to a corrupt priest or high-ranking official would ensure that the authorities looked the other way.

After entering the tombs, the robbers could safely abandon all stealth. Shielded by the thick walls, they could and often did tear the place apart, smashing open the stone sarcophagi and the offering chests, and chopping the gold from the gilded coffins. Even the mummies themselves might be slashed to bits. In some cases, the robbers may have brutalized the corpses for fear of the retribution of the deceased, but more often they were simply in a hurry to get at the jewelry concealed in the folds of linen. For some, even this approach was too subtle. The more brazen robbers just set fire to the densely packed burial chambers. When they returned later, small pools of hardened gold could be plucked from the debris.

"We went to the tomb of Tjanefer, who had been the third priest of Amun," reported one robber during the reign of Ramses IX. "We opened it and brought out his inner coffins, and took his mummy and left it in a corner of the tomb. The inner coffins we took in the boat, along with the rest, to the Island of Amenhotep, and we set fire to them in the night and made off with the gold which we found on them; four *kite* fell to the lot of each man."

Four kite of gold amounted to about one and a quarter ounces. A worker of Deir el-Medina might work four months to earn that much in grain, so it is not difficult to see how the riches of the tombs could offer a temptation, especially in lean times. In Thebes, as government officials turned a blind eye to the plunder, the proceeds of tomb robbery gradually filtered into the city's commerce. Thus, whenever a tomb robber was actually apprehended, the authorities found themselves in a political minefield. No official wished to be seen as negligent in his duties, but a close investigation might well uncover high-level complicity.

A mayor of Thebes named Paser, during the last quarter of the 12th century BC, was determined to restore law and order to the beleaguered city. Paser appears to have had a sense of his own importance, and he bestowed upon himself the imposing title of The Mayor Who Reports to the Ruler. By law, tomb thefts fell under the jurisdiction of Pawero, the mayor of West Thebes, who also served as chief of police for the royal necropolis. So when two accusers, scribes living in Deir el-Medina named Harshire and Pabasa, decided to report a suspected robbery to Paser instead of to Pawero, Paser sensed a golden opportunity to challenge a rival and benefit his region and the nation as well.

Stunning murals found in the tomb of Sennefer, a mayor of Thebes who was buried in the Valley of the Kings, testify to the talents of Deir el-Medina artists. To whitewashed tomb walls they applied hues of black, red, white, yellow, blue, and green, using mineral-based paints that could retain, for millennia, much of their original brilliance.

DECORATING A TOMB

Work began in earnest on a king's tomb as soon as he ascended the throne, but completing a royal tomb often required more time than a pharaoh's reign allowed. The process of decorating the tomb's interior began when plasterers smoothed and whitewashed the newly cut walls and ceilings. Then draftsmen traced red grid lines on the prepared surfaces and made initial outlines of selected images, also in red. Next, a master draftsman superimposed his corrections in black. Relief sculptors with bronze chisels then raised the outlined images by chipping away the background stone. The untimely death of the pharaoh Horemhab forced artists to abandon work on the relief at left, found in his tomb. The sculptors working on raising the images completed only half their task. Had they finished, painters would have come in with their paints and brushes of varying thicknesses (below) to color the images and hieroglyphs. In the pitch-black depths of the mountain, the work of the artisans progressed by the light of a candle cut to burn a particular length of time. When the candle flickered out, the workers knew their shift was over.

By reporting the robbery to Paser, across the river in Thebes, the two scribes hoped to launch an investigation that would draw attention away from Deir el-Medina on the west bank, where a few villagers were implicated in a recent theft. The names offered by the two scribes were those of other gangs of tomb robbers. Still it was an extraordinary act on their part, since the two men faced mutilation and possibly even death if their statements proved false. While technically the responsibility for the safety of the royal ancestors was Pawero's job, the ambitious Paser seized the opportunity to demonstrate his abilities to the king.

Paser initiated an investigation headed by the vizier Khaemweset, the most important governing official after the pharaoh himself. The vizier ordered a group of court officials and military commanders, including Pawero, to inspect the tombs in the Theban necropolis. It was probably not a happy group that trudged out to the Valley of the Kings that day. Many of them felt the exercise to be futile, and the hot August sun beating down on the desert sands made for sweltering discomfort. Nonetheless, the authorities dutifully carried out the vizier's orders. They found that the tomb of King Sobekemsaf II, who had ruled about 1635 BC, some 500 years earlier, had been stripped bare. "The burial chamber was found empty of its lord, likewise the chamber of the great royal wife," reported the official record of the event. "The thieves had laid their hands upon them." The officials rounded up several suspects.

Among the suspected thieves was a coppersmith by the name of Pekharu, who had also been a suspect in a robbery two years earlier. Pekharu's previous interrogation, if it followed the typical pattern, took the form of beating the poor man and twisting his limbs in a torture device. Not surprisingly, a confession had been quickly extracted, and Pekharu had admitted to stealing objects from the tomb of Queen Isis, the wife of Ramses III.

Now Pekharu was trotted out again for the benefit of the vizier, who went to inspect the scene himself the next day, taking the coppersmith with him. With his wrists tied and his eyes blindfolded, Pekharu was led to the center of the royal necropolis by the vizier's guards. There he was released and ordered to identify the tomb of Queen Isis. Having already been subjected to an "examination" at the hands of his captors, Pekharu would have been in no mood to deceive the vizier. The accused man took his bearings and headed straight for a nearby tomb structure. If the vizier had hoped for a confirmation of guilt, he was to be disappointed. Pekharu had identified an open and unfinished tomb where there had never been a burial of any kind.

The vizier ordered his captive to make another attempt, and Pekharu gathered himself and set off once more across the hot sands. This time he made for the abandoned hut of a scribe. Terrified of the vizier's wrath, Pekharu made a desperate plea of innocence: "I know of no place here," he protested, "except this tomb which is open and this house which I pointed out to you."

This seemed to satisfy the vizier. He was disposed to accept the coppersmith's apparent innocence, despite his earlier confession, because the seals on the tomb of Queen Isis did in fact appear to be intact. But the truth of the situation had escaped him. Although the entryway of the queen's tomb showed no signs of tampering, the burial chamber had been entered from the rear and ravaged, and the mummy itself lay in tatters.

For the moment, at least, Mayor Pawero had the upper hand. Mayor Paser's accusations seemed to have been disproved, and Pawero emerged as an attentive official falsely accused of neglecting his duties. While it was clear to everyone that the tomb of King Sobekemsaf II had been robbed, Mayor Pawero was thought to have the situation under control.

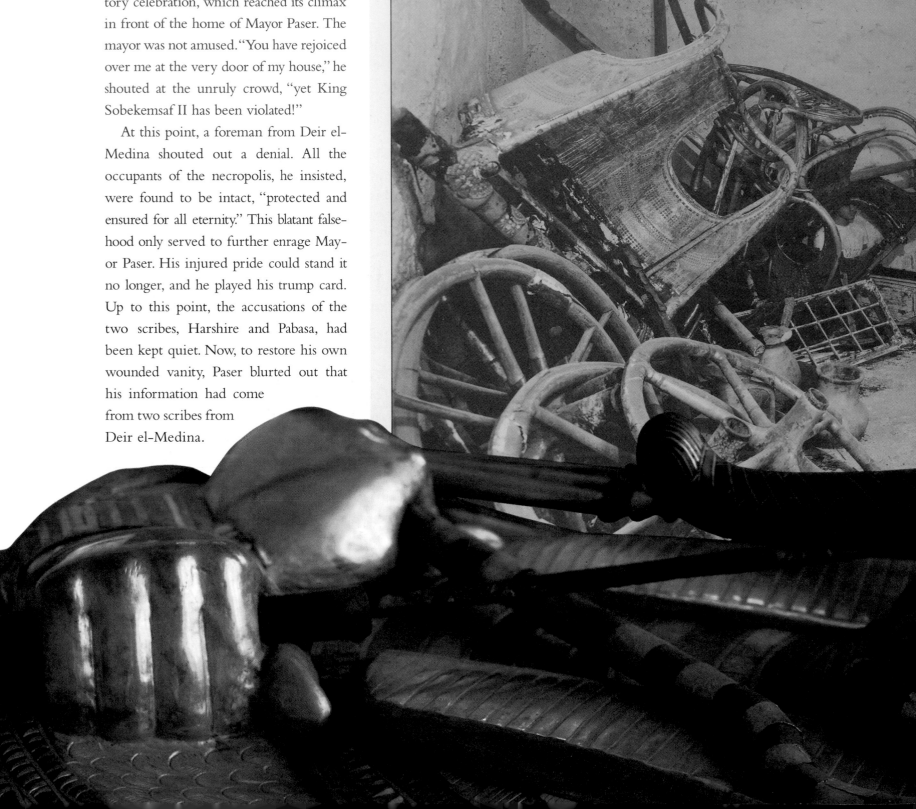

To celebrate this happy outcome, Pa-wero's supporters staged a boisterous victory celebration, which reached its climax in front of the home of Mayor Paser. The mayor was not amused. "You have rejoiced over me at the very door of my house," he shouted at the unruly crowd, "yet King Sobekemsaf II has been violated!"

At this point, a foreman from Deir el-Medina shouted out a denial. All the occupants of the necropolis, he insisted, were found to be intact, "protected and ensured for all eternity." This blatant falsehood only served to further enrage Mayor Paser. His injured pride could stand it no longer, and he played his trump card. Up to this point, the accusations of the two scribes, Harshire and Pabasa, had been kept quiet. Now, to restore his own wounded vanity, Paser blurted out that his information had come from two scribes from Deir el-Medina.

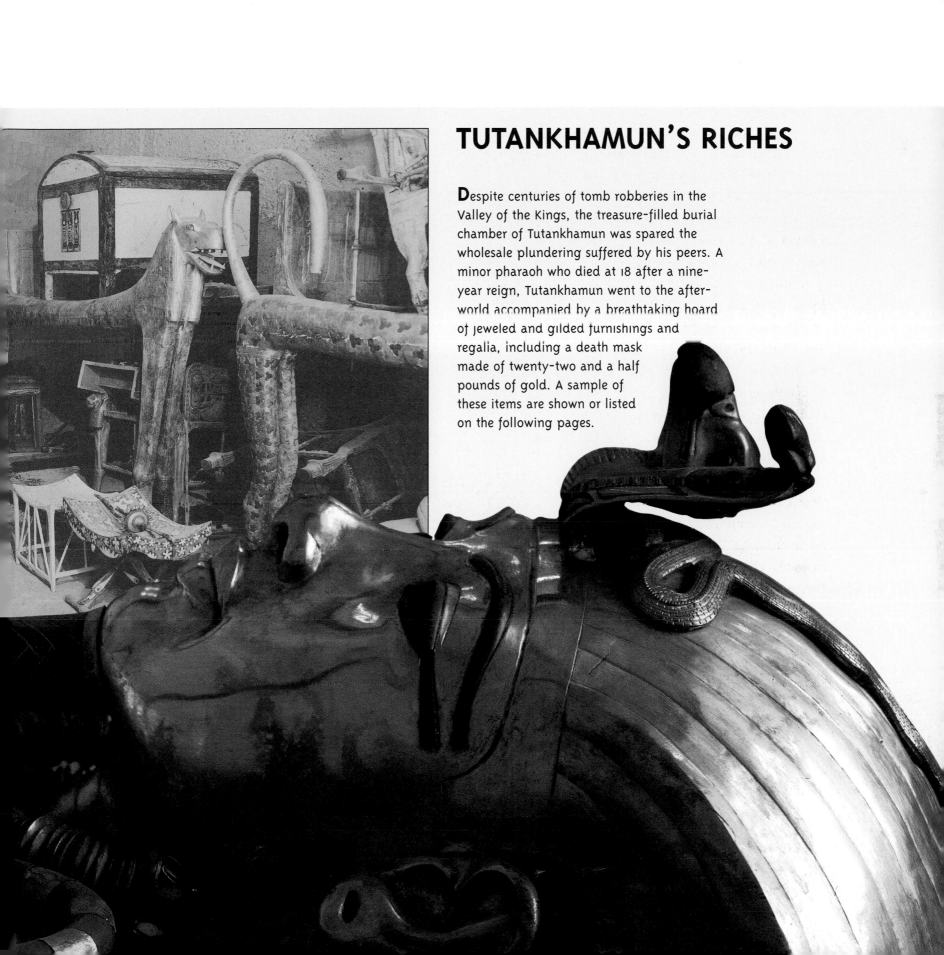

TUTANKHAMUN'S RICHES

Despite centuries of tomb robberies in the Valley of the Kings, the treasure-filled burial chamber of Tutankhamun was spared the wholesale plundering suffered by his peers. A minor pharaoh who died at 18 after a nine-year reign, Tutankhamun went to the after-world accompanied by a breathtaking hoard of jeweled and gilded furnishings and regalia, including a death mask made of twenty-two and a half pounds of gold. A sample of these items are shown or listed on the following pages.

ANUBIS AMULET
ANUBIS FETISH
454 ARROWS AND
  ARROWHEADS
116 BASKETS OF DRIED FRUIT
BEADED LINEN SKULLCAP
17 BLUE FAIENCE PITCHERS
35 MODEL BOATS
46 BOWS
48 BOXES OF OX AND GOOSE
  MEAT
BRACELET WITH CARNELIAN
  SWALLOW
BRONZE RAZORS
2 CALCITE LAMPS

CANOPIC COFFINETTES
6 FELINE-FOOTED BEDS
CEREMONIAL ROBE
6 CHAIRS
6 CHARIOTS
CHILD'S FINE LINEN GLOVE
6 CUBIT MEASURING RODS
EYE OF HORUS BRACELET
FAIENCE PAPYRUS SCEPTER
3 FAIENCE BANGLES
FAIENCE FLORAL PENDANTS
33 FAIENCE BULL FORELEGS
FALCON COLLAR
5 FINGER RINGS
4 GAME BOARDS
GILDED CHEETAH BED
GILDED HATHOR BED
GLASS MANDRAKE FRUIT
3 GLASS VESSELS
GOLD-BLADED DAGGER
2 LIFE-SIZE GUARDIAN STATUES
HAND-SHAPED IVORY CLAPPERS
GILDED SHRINE
HEADREST OF GLASS
HEADREST OF FAIENCE
HEADRESTS OF IVORY
HEADRESTS OF GILDED WOOD
TAWERET BED
HUMAN-HEADED URAEUS
  AMULET
IBEX OIL JAR
IRON-BLADED DAGGER
16 IRON-BLADED CHISELS
IVORY BOOMERANGS
2 JARS OF HONEY
50 BOXES AND CHESTS
LEAF AMULET

LEOPARD-SKIN CLOAK
LINEN HEADDRESS
34 LOINCLOTHS
12 LOAVES OF BREAD
2 MUMMIFIED FETUSES
ORNAMENTAL CASKET
106 GOLD ORNAMENTS WITH
  MUMMY
PAINTED WOODEN BOX
2 QUIVERS
REED-AND-PAPYRUS BOXES
REMAINS OF WOVEN TAPESTRY
  GARMENT
RESIN SCARAB
ROLLS OF FINE LINEN
ROYAL DIADEM
SCARAB CHAIN
SCARAB PECTORAL
SERPENT AMULET
SHIRT COLLAR BAND
8 SHIELDS
SILVER POMEGRANATE VASE
80 STONE VESSELS
12 STOOLS
TASSELED CLOTH BELT
THOTH AMULET
TINY COFFIN WITH LOCK OF
  HAIR FROM TUT'S
  GRANDMOTHER, QUEEN TIY
SHAWABTI BOXES
413 SHAWABTI FIGURES
130 WALKING AND
  FIGHTING STICKS
WATER SKINS
30 WINE JARS
WOODEN OARS
14 WRITING PALETTES

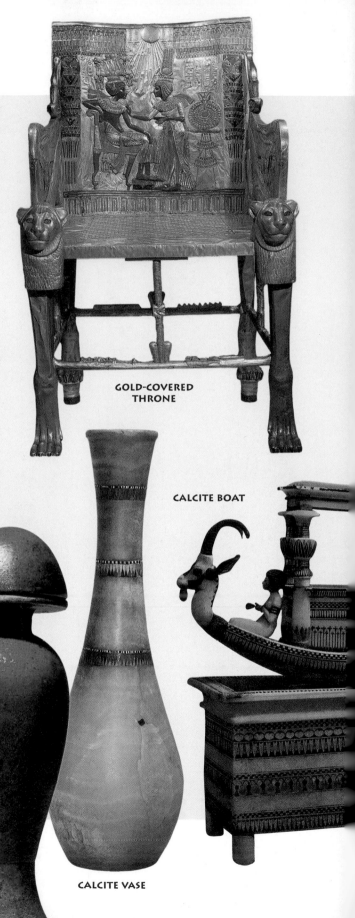

JACKAL GOD
ANUBIS

GOLD-COVERED
THRONE

CALCITE BOAT

CALCITE VASE

CALCITE VASE

FAIENCE WATER
JAR

GOLDEN FAN

VENEERED
WOOD SANDALS

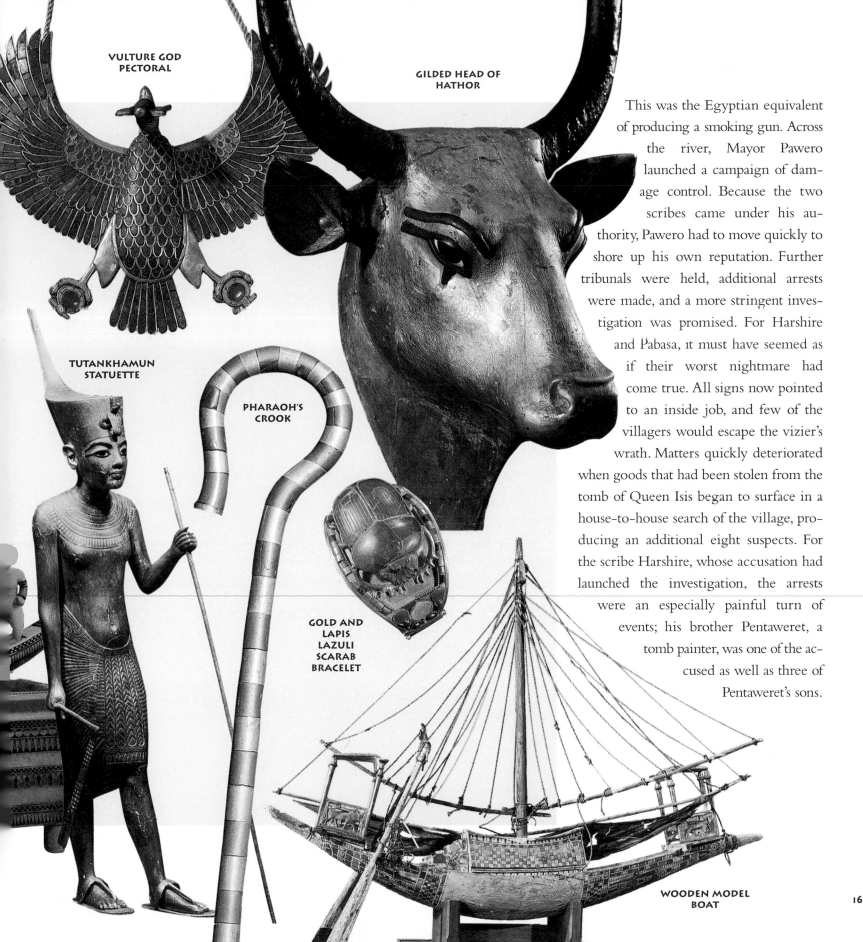

VULTURE GOD PECTORAL

GILDED HEAD OF HATHOR

TUTANKHAMUN STATUETTE

PHARAOH'S CROOK

GOLD AND LAPIS LAZULI SCARAB BRACELET

WOODEN MODEL BOAT

This was the Egyptian equivalent of producing a smoking gun. Across the river, Mayor Pawero launched a campaign of damage control. Because the two scribes came under his authority, Pawero had to move quickly to shore up his own reputation. Further tribunals were held, additional arrests were made, and a more stringent investigation was promised. For Harshire and Pabasa, it must have seemed as if their worst nightmare had come true. All signs now pointed to an inside job, and few of the villagers would escape the vizier's wrath. Matters quickly deteriorated when goods that had been stolen from the tomb of Queen Isis began to surface in a house-to-house search of the village, producing an additional eight suspects. For the scribe Harshire, whose accusation had launched the investigation, the arrests were an especially painful turn of events; his brother Pentaweret, a tomb painter, was one of the accused as well as three of Pentaweret's sons.

Now the vizier's darkest suspicions had been confirmed, and he struck back with the most powerful weapon at his command. He cut off the supply of grain to Deir el-Medina, intending to find out the names of all the guilty workers. Ironically, the vizier had the eight arrested men imprisoned in an empty grain magazine. The rest of the loot soon appeared. The spoils included more than 37 pounds of silver, nearly two pounds of gold, and more than seven pounds of a gold-and-silver alloy called electrum. Quantities of fine linens were also recovered, along with oils, vases of bronze and ebony, and even fragments of the royal coffins. For the average tomb worker, this was truly wealth beyond measure. Even divided eight ways, the profit from one night's robbery would have been the equivalent of anywhere from 25 to 50 years' worth of salary.

The accused men confessed to the robbery, undoubtedly inspired by further beatings and limb twisting. They revealed payoffs made to people at every level of Theban and West Theban society, from temple priests and royal officials to barbers and water carriers. Even the most prominent Theban families were implicated in the scandal. And there could be no denying that the integrity of the Theban government had been tainted.

While the investigation progressed, the supply of grain into the village remained blocked. The villagers tried to make do with fish and stored goods, but the embargo on grain quickly depleted their stocks. "The tomb makers do not work," a scribe recorded; "they are hungry and debilitated."

The stolen treasure had brought the robbers little pleasure. They had splurged on a few luxuries, such as fine clothes, new sandals, meat flavored with oils, and good beer, but apart from these minor extravagances, their greatest expense had been in the payoffs to those higher up on the social ladder. Pawero and his men tracked down every merchant,

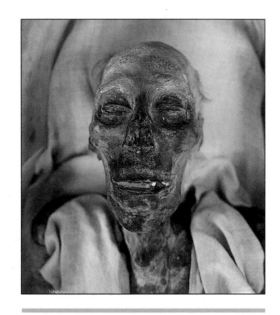

A FAMILY BURIAL

The legendary pharaoh Ramses II, whose unwrapped mummy is shown above, fathered at least 100 children, including an estimated 52 sons. Several of his sons are thought to share a tomb of about 100 rooms in the Valley of the Kings. At the back of the recently excavated tomb (right), a statue of Osiris stands silent watch at the intersection of the T-shaped corridors shown in the floor plan drawing (inset). Near the front of the tomb is a pillared hall; the two rooms leading into it reveal faint wall paintings and reliefs showing Ramses presenting some of his young princes to various deities. One of the descending passages may lead to Ramses' tomb.

weaver, and oil refiner who had received any portion of the stolen goods. Working with a dogged persistence, Pawero eventually recovered every single item of stolen treasure.

At last, the vizier summoned all the villagers to the royal necropolis. There he ordered the seals on the tomb of Queen Isis to be broken, and left the Thebans to contemplate the destruction wrought by their comrades. Several days later, after a committee of workers threw

been roughly handled and a few were cruelly dismembered, but none had yet deteriorated beyond recognition. Prompt action would be needed to prevent further destruction.

A grim task faced the commission. One by one, the mummies of the royal ancestors were brought together in an abandoned tomb. King Amenhotep I, an 18th Dynasty pharaoh, considered by the villagers to be their patron, had been hacked to pieces by axes, the better to strip

> ## "All the kings who rest in the great and noble necropolis are intact; protected and ensured for eternity."

themselves on his mercy, the vizier finally pardoned the village for its crime. "You are right, you workmen of the Necropolis," he declared. The fate of the tomb robbers is unknown. Village records show that they never returned to their homes, and most likely they were executed. Mayor Paser, whose overweening ambition fueled the investigation, appears no further in the official documents. His rival, Pawero, clung to power for many more years. He worked to contain the spread of tomb robbery. Occasionally a gang of thieves was tried and executed, but the problem spiraled out of his control. Not a single piece of stolen merchandise was ever returned to the tomb from which it had been taken. Ramses IX would die before the beleaguered workers could complete his tomb.

About a century and a half after this incident, the entire Theban necropolis had suffered so much plunder that a special commission gathered to assess the problem. By now, all but a handful of the royal tombs had been stripped of their treasures, and there could be no hope of restoring the burial chambers to their former grandeur. Many of the royal mummies themselves, however, had survived the depredations of the tomb robbers. Most had

away jewelry that had set in the hardened embalming resins. The hands and wrists of Queen Nefertari, favorite wife of Ramses II, once dripping with rings and bracelets, had been snapped from her arms. Temple priests labored over the broken bodies, gently straightening the mangled limbs and wrapping the battered corpses in fresh burial shrouds.

When the melancholy work was done, a silent funeral procession made its way under cover of darkness through the black cliffs of western Thebes. There at Deir el-Bahri, in an old burial shaft from the early Middle Kingdom, the ill-used bodies of Egypt's pharaohs were secretly laid to rest. When the coffins were all in place, the weary temple priests sealed the chamber and made their way by the light of torches back toward the city. Behind them, a hush descended over the tombs. Once again the energies and efforts of living Egyptians had been directed toward the preservation of their dead, and of their civilization as well. Egypt would soon lose its preeminent position in the Middle East, but its people maintained their cherished culture, with its hope of immortality, for another millennium before it came under Greek, then Roman, and finally Christian influence.

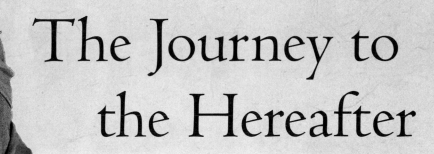

The Journey to the Hereafter

A blissful eternity, to many Egyptians, was one spent soaring through the sky with the sun god by day and returning nightly to a well-supplied tomb. This ideal would be realized after the body had been properly prepared and the appropriate rites administered. At the moment of death, the spirit, or ka, left the body, to be reunited with it after a period of embalming lasting as long as 70 days. The illustrations of this process on the following pages are from a collection of sacred texts known as the Book of the Dead, a copy of which was prepared for a scribe named Ani in the 13th century BC. There were various degrees of extravagance in embalming to fit the purchasing power of the deceased; an affluent person would emerge from the embalmers arrayed like Nesmutaatneru *(detail, left),* a woman wrapped in a finely woven linen shroud, covered with a faience-beaded net and adorned with jeweled amulets.

Terra-cotta masks of the jackal-headed god Anubis *(above)* were worn by the priests who supervised the embalming. The priests watched the process through two eyeholes located under the snout *(left)*.

"Oh flesh of king, do not decay, do not rot, do not smell unpleasant!"

The Embalmers Ply Their Craft

The embalmers were priests required to live and labor outside of town in a workshop called the Wabet, or Clean Place. Trained to perform their tasks with both surgical and ritual precision, they first cut open the body and removed its internal organs. The eviscerated innards were placed in canopic jars *(top right),* carved from alabaster and inscribed with spells that would enable the organs to rejoin the resurrected body. Once inside the jars, each organ was protected by the son of Horus whose head graced the lid: the jackal Duamutef, who guarded the stomach; the baboon Hapi, the lungs; the falcon Qebehsenuf, the intestines; and the human Imsety, the liver. After the organs were removed, the embalmers then covered and stuffed the body with the salt known as natron, and let it dry.

The heart was left in place, while the brain was pulled out through the nose with a hook and discarded. Resin, injected into the head through the nostrils with a funnel *(above),* prevented the skull from collapsing. A special flint knife *(above, left)* was used to make the first incision in the abdomen below the ribs on the left side, as can be seen on this early mummy. All other cutting was done with an ordinary metal blade.

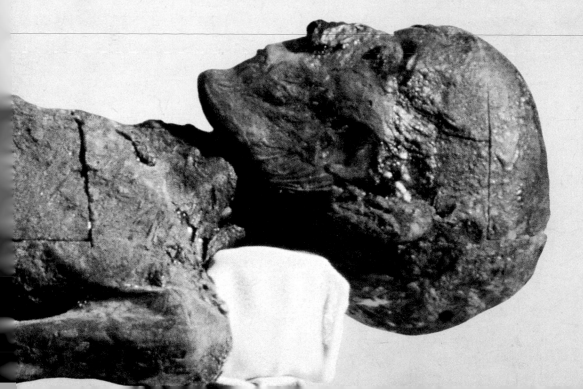

Within the wrappings, the embalmers placed a scarab amulet over the heart. The heart was a key part of gaining entrance to the underworld, and its amulet reflected its worth. The one pictured below is of green jasper set in gold. The gold plaque (*bottom*) covered the embalmer's incision. For protection, it carries an eye of Horus surrounded by the god's four sons.

"Bind with the cloth of Re-Harakhty.
Twenty-two rolls for the right
and the left of the face, to be wound at the level of the ears."

In a scene from Ani's Book of the Dead *(left)*, Anubis balances Ani's heart against a feather from the goddess Maat, who represents truth. Thoth, the ibis-headed god of wisdom, records the result, while behind him Ammit, a crocodile-headed monster, waits to devour the heart if the scales tilt against Ani.

Swaddled in Cloth and Magic

When dry, the body was stuffed with straw or linen to restore its shape, massaged with fragrant unguents, and coated with tar or resin. Using as many as 400 yards of linen, the embalmers then wrapped the mummy according to the strictures of sacred texts. First the head was swathed, followed by the wrapping of each individual finger and toe. Sometimes a tag, such as the one at lower right, was inscribed with a protective spell and tied to the big toe. The legs were bandaged and then the arms, which were crossed over the chest imitating the pose of Osiris, god of the dead. Every layer of wrapping was smeared with resin to hold it in place. Before the final layers went on, a funerary mask was placed over the head and shoulders. Finally, the mummy was laid in the coffin *(far left)*, ready for burial.

Nestled among a mummy's bandages were other amulets, sometimes as many as 100, often jeweled. Frequently included were, above, the eye of Horus for protection, and above that, the ankh, symbolizing the breath of life. The *djed* pillar *(above, left)* represented the backbone of Osiris, a sign of stability and endurance.

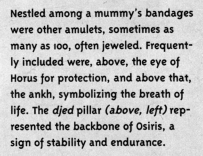

"Westward, westward,
   to the Land of the Just."

176

A Tomb Full of Symbols

The underworld was believed to be located in the west where the sun died every day, and it was on the western bank of the Nile that the dead were often buried. The funeral procession shown at left includes oxen towing a mummy to its tomb, accompanied by priests and relatives. Beside the coffin, a loved one mourns. Awaiting the mummy in the tomb would be a variety of items such as the miniature wooden boat *(below, left),* with its diminutive carved crew standing ready to transport the spirit of the deceased. In these boats, the souls of the nobility made a pilgrimage after death to Abydos to visit the tomb of Osiris.

Relatives of the deceased laid out great feasts in the tombs, such as the dried-out fish and fowl on this stand, found in the Theban tomb of a wealthy man. The food was intended to nourish the ka of the dead man.

Tomb statues like that of King Auibre Hor *(right)* enabled the ka to assume a physical form. The king, striding forward, bears a pair of raised arms on his head to denote the ka within.

Resurrection of the Mummy

When the funeral procession reached the burial chamber, it was time for the all-important Opening of the Mouth ceremony. At the moment of death, the spirit left the body. To achieve rebirth, the ba, the essence of the individual, symbolized by a birdlike being *(right)*, had to return to the corpse to breathe life into the mummy through the mouth. To begin the ceremony, the mummy was set upright in its coffin. The priest, while not actually opening the mouth, touched the mummy's face three times with various tools, rubbed its surface with milk, and embraced the mummy, presenting it with clothing, a haunch of beef, and a bull's heart. Setting a feast before it, he invited the rejuvenated corpse to enjoy it all: "Arise Osiris, take your seat before these myriad offerings." The scene at lower right shows the ba on its way to the tomb after the ceremony.

A forked knife *(right and above)* was one of the tools used in the Opening of the Mouth ceremony. It may have been the same instrument employed to sever a child's umbilical cord, thus reinforcing the theme of rebirth.

"*I am alive. I am strong. I have awakened. My body will not be destroyed in this eternal land.*"

Carved statuettes known as shawabtis *(left)* were set in the tomb to become servants for the deceased. To ensure attentiveness to their afterlife duties, the figurines often were inscribed: "If one calls you at any time you shall say, 'I will do it.' "

A Reward
for the Just

The scribe Ani, whose heart weighed no more than the feather of truth, is pictured twice in this illustration from his Book of the Dead, standing on the far left and kneeling in the center. Having been judged worthy, Ani must go before Osiris for the ultimate reckoning. Horus leads him by the hand into the throne room where Ani, after donning a wig, kneels before the Lord of Eternity. Osiris, gripping his crook and flail, the emblems of authority, sits in final judgment. Behind Osiris stands his wife, Isis, wearing a small throne upon her head. Beside her is her sister Nephthys, dressed in red. The sons of Horus, portrayed here as tiny figures on a lotus blossom, are also present. Horus announces that Ani has been judged in the presence of Thoth and Maat: "I bring Ani to you. His heart is true, having gone forth from the balance, and he has not sinned against any god or any goddess." As a final gesture of humility before he is allowed to join Osiris and achieve immortality, Ani once again proclaims his innocence: "There is no wrongdoing in my body. I have not wittingly told lies."

"Hail to you, you august, great, and potent god, prince forever. May you grant that I be among the living."

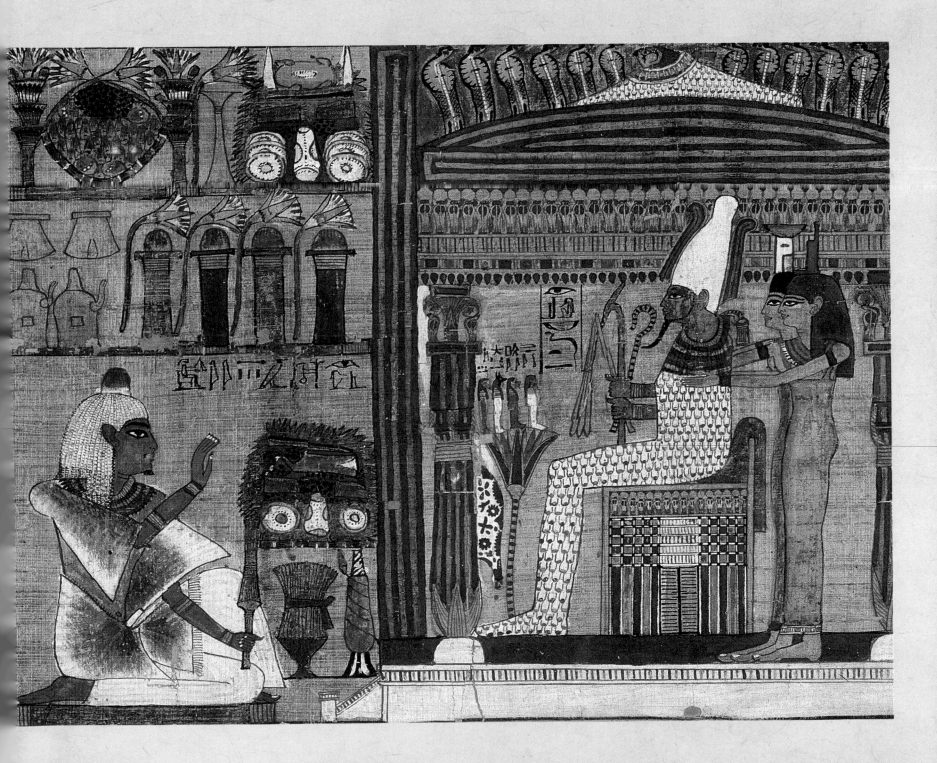

GLOSSARY

Adz: a metal instrument used in funerary rituals, derived from a stonecutting and shaping tool.

Akh: one of the three aspects of the soul; the luminous effective spirit of the deceased, capable of interacting with the living.

Ammit, Devourer of the Dead: a beast that consumed the hearts of unworthy spirits at the judgment of the dead.

Amulet: a charm against bad luck or illness-causing spirits.

Ankh: the hieroglyphic sign for "life."

Apis bull: manifestation of the god Ptah; embodied by a live bull, born with the proper markings, which was worshiped in Memphis and mourned by Egyptians when it died.

Aten: deity in the form of the solar disk, often portrayed with outstretched arms emanating like sunrays; its worship was promoted by King Akhenaten in the 14th century BC.

Ba: one of the three aspects of the soul, depicted as a human-headed bird; the essence of an individual's personality that manifested itself to others.

Bas-relief: low relief; stone-carving technique in which the figure stands out from the background.

Black Land: the fertile country of Egypt; referred to by Egyptians as *kemet,* or "black," for the dark soil that covered the delta and part of the Nile Valley after the annual floods.

Book of the Dead: a collection of spells written on papyrus, tomb walls, and coffins to protect the deceased in the hereafter; in use primarily from the New Kingdom onward.

Canopic jars: four jars that held a mummy's internal organs (liver, lungs, intestines, and stomach).

Cartouche: an oval ring, signifying a magical rope, within which the names of royalty were written and protected.

Cataract: swift, unnavigable rapids; the Nile had six such stretches in ancient Nubia.

Coffin Texts: inscriptions for the protection of the dead written on the inner coffin walls; used primarily during the First Intermediate Period and the Middle Kingdom.

Deben: unit of weight, equivalent to 12 shat (3.2 oz. or 91 g.).

Delta: the area encompassed by the fan-shaped branching of the Nile tributaries, which in ancient times numbered seven; Lower Egypt.

Demotic: latest form of Egyptian writing and language, used from the Late Period through the Roman Period.

Djed pillar: an amulet or symbol in the form of a post capped with three or four horizontal segments representing the backbone of Osiris and the stability and duration of the monarchy.

Dynasty: a line of related kings; 31 roughly successive dynasties were defined by the priest-historian Manetho in the third century BC based on earlier Egyptian traditions.

Electrum: naturally occurring alloy of silver and gold found in Nubia and the southlands, used in jewelry, statuary, and for plating obelisks.

Eye of Horus: the eye lost by the god Horus during his battle with Seth and later restored to him; also known as the wedjat eye, it was a symbol for health and an amulet.

Faience: ceramic material made from crushed quartz and coated with a blue or green glaze, used for jewelry and decorative objects.

Flax: long, slender plant whose fibers were woven into linen or used to make baskets, mats, and ropes.

Frankincense: aromatic tree resin used for incense, imported from lands to the south of Egypt.

Harem: a women's compound associated with the royal palace and some temples, including quarters for queens and other women of distinction.

Heb-Sed: jubilee festival of the king, originally set to mark the 30th year of his reign, but occasionally celebrated more frequently.

Hieratic: simplified form of hieroglyphic writing used by scribes for handwritten documents.

Hieroglyphs: from the Greek for "sacred carvings," the oldest form of Egyptian writing, composed of pictograms (pictures of objects), phonograms (symbols representing sounds), and ideograms (symbols that determine the meaning of words).

High priest: highest ranking official within a temple; known by such titles as the First Prophet of Amun in Thebes, or the Greatest of the Seers of Re in Heliopolis.

Hyksos: from the Egyptian for "rulers of foreign lands," princes from the Near East who conquered Lower Egypt in the 17th century BC and dominated the entire country through the Second Intermediate Period.

Jasper: an opaque variety of quartz, suitable for carving.

Ka: one of the three aspects of the soul; the life force of a person or god; the ka of a dead person had to be fed and sheltered, duties that fell to a ka priest.

Khepresh: the blue leather crown most often seen in depictions of the king in battle; sometimes called the war crown.

Khopesh: a short bronze sword with a sickle-shaped blade.

Kite: unit of weight equivalent to one-tenth of a deben (3.33 oz. or 9.1 g.).

Lotus: common term for various water lilies indigenous to Egypt whose buds and blossoms were the emblem of Upper Egypt and a symbol of rebirth in the afterlife.

Lower Egypt: the region centered on the delta; its symbol was the papyrus.

Mastaba: from the Arabic for "bench," a type of Old Kingdom tomb; rectangular, with sloping sides and a flat roof, it often had many rooms, including an offering chapel and a subterranean burial chamber.

Middle Kingdom: era in Egyptian history covering the years 2061-1668 BC and comprising the 11th through 13th Dynasties.

Mortuary temple: building where the king's funeral was celebrated; thereafter, rituals were regularly performed in the temple to guarantee his continued existence in the afterlife; originally the temple was built adjoining the tomb, but during the New Kingdom, the two sites were separated to guard against tomb robbery.

Mummy: the preserved remains of a corpse, treated with dehydrating salts and wrapped in linen bandages.

Myrrh: fragrant tree resin used as incense and to perfume oils.

Natron: a naturally occurring compound of sodium carbonate, sodium bicarbonate, and other agents used by the Egyptians for rinsing out the mouth and bathing, for manufacturing faience, and for dehydrating the body during mummification.

Necropolis: from the Greek for "city of the dead," cemetery or cluster of cemeteries associated with a town or city, containing graves or tombs or both.

New Kingdom: period in Egyptian history from 1560-1070 BC, comprising the 18th through 21st Dynasties.

Obelisk: tall, tapered, four-sided monolith with a pyramid-shaped peak, associated with the power of the sun god; most were carved from pink granite quarried in Aswan and were either capped or clad entirely in electrum to reflect the rays of the sun.

Obsidian: dark green or black glass formed by volcanic activity; often used for jewelry, amulets, or for the eyes of statues.

Old Kingdom: period of Egyptian history from 2705-2213 BC, comprising the Third through Eighth Dynasties.

Opet: New Kingdom festival celebrated at Thebes to sanctify the king and reaffirm his relationship to the god Amun; it was marked by a great procession from the Great Temple of Amun at Karnak to the Temple of Luxor.

Ostracon: from the Greek for "potsherd" (plural, ostraca), limestone fragment or piece of broken pottery used for writing on; a cheap alternative to papyrus.

Papyrus: a tall aquatic reed, and the paperlike sheets made from it; the papyrus flower was the symbol of Lower Egypt and was often used as a decorative motif.

Pharaoh: from the Egyptian for "great house," a term originally referring to the royal palace and applied by extension to the king.

Ptolemaic Period: the last period of pharaonic rule, from 332 BC–30 BC, during which Macedonian kings governed Egypt; also known as the Greek Period.

Pylon: a massive structure at the entrance to a temple, serving as a gateway and often carved with images of the king.

Pyramid: structure with a square base and four sloping, triangular sides meeting at a peak; used as a tomb for royalty during the Old and Middle Kingdoms and for nonroyalty during the New Kingdom.

Pyramid Texts: texts written on the walls of chambers inside the royal pyramids, relating funeral rites and magical spells to guarantee the immortality of kings in the afterlife.

Pyramidion: pyramid-shaped capstone placed atop a pyramid or obelisk; often decorated with hieroglyphic texts.

Quern: hand-operated mill for grinding grain.

Red Land: the rocky, reddish desert beyond the narrow strip of irrigated land adjacent to the Nile.

Sarcophagus: container for a corpse; the term originally referred to a large stone receptacle that held one or more smaller, wooden coffins but was later applied to any coffin, whether made of wood, stone, gold, silver, or some other material.

Scarab: an amulet or stamp-seal carved to resemble the dung beetle of the same name, associated with regeneration; a so-called heart scarab amulet, with a hieroglyphic inscription on its underside, was placed within a mummy's bandages to ensure resurrection in the afterlife.

Sea Peoples: seafaring people of the Aegean and Eastern Mediterranean who conquered Anatolia, Syria, Phoenicia, and Canaan before they attempted unsuccessfully to invade Egypt in 1175 BC.

Shat: unit of weight, equivalent to one-twelfth of a deben (.26 oz. or 7.58 g.).

Shawabti: literally "answerer," a carved or molded figurine of a person, included with other funerary equipment from the Middle Kingdom onward to answer for the deceased in the afterlife and perform tasks as required.

Shen: in hieroglyphic inscriptions, a circle of rope with overlapping ends, symbolizing eternity and protection; in elongated form, it became a cartouche, protectively encircling kings' names.

Sistrum: a musical instrument producing a jangling sound, used by queens and priestesses in religious ceremonies to please the goddess Hathor and other deities.

Sopdet: Egyptian name for the star Sirius, whose rising into the dawn sky after a 70-day period of invisibility roughly coincided with the commencement of the annual Nile floods and so marked the beginning of the new year.

Sphinx: a symbol of royal power that took the form of a seated lion, often with the head of a pharaoh; the most famous example is the Great Sphinx, carved from a stone outcropping at Giza.

Stele: a commemorative stone slab or wooden marker bearing inscriptions or illustrations.

Upper Egypt: the southern part of the country, extending along the Nile from Memphis to the First Cataract; its symbol was the lotus, or water lily, and its protective goddess was Nekhbet, who took the form of a vulture.

Uraeus: the rearing-cobra insignia featured on the brow of the king's crown, symbolizing protection for the king and doom for his enemies.

Valley of the Kings: a valley west of Thebes used as a burial site for pharaohs of the New Kingdom; although carved deep into the rock to discourage grave robbers, nearly all the tombs were ransacked in antiquity.

Valley of the Queens: Burial site for royal wives and children, situated 1.1 miles (1.8 km) southwest of the Valley of the Kings.

Vizier: the highest-ranking state official serving the pharaoh; he was responsible for administration, including the economy and legal matters; originally, there was a single vizier, but later there were two, one for Lower Egypt and one for Upper Egypt.

Wedjat eye: see Eye of Horus.

GODS OF ANCIENT EGYPT

Amun: originally the patron god of Thebes; associated with the ram but often portrayed as a man, wearing a headdress with two feathered plumes; when Theban princes gained control of Egypt, Amun rose to prominence and merged with Re, becoming Amun-Re.

Anubis: god of the dead and mummification, with the head of a jackal; as Lord of the Necropolis, Anubis was a protector of tombs.

Bastet: cat-headed goddess who personified joy and motherly protection.

Bes: dwarflike god of domestic security, joviality, and fertility.

Geb: god of the earth and vegetation; brother and husband of the sky goddess Nut.

Hathor: a goddess of many facets, usually depicted in the form of a cow; she inspired music, dancing, and love and played a nurturing role as the divine mother of the reigning pharaoh; she could also be vengeful, taking the form of a savage lioness.

Horus: falcon god whose cult was originally centered at Hierakonopolis; also known as Harakhty, or Horus of the Horizon; the son of Isis and Osiris, Horus ruled Egypt through his physical incarnation, the king.

Isis: goddess who personified the virtues of the wife and mother; she offered protection to the deceased, having been instrumental in restoring the body of her brother and husband, Osiris, after he was dismembered by his murderous brother, Seth.

Khons: moon god, son of Amun and Mut; depicted as a young man.

Maat: goddess of truth and justice, whose name was synonymous with the concept of universal order; she regulated the seasons, the movements of the stars, and the relationships between individuals and gods and was invoked when judgments were made, both in the civil courts and in the afterlife.

Mut: goddess who served as Amun's divine consort.

Nephthys: sister of Isis, Osiris, and Seth and protector of the dead.

Nut: sky goddess whose body made up the heavens; she swallowed the sun god Re every night, and he was reborn from her womb every morning.

Osiris: god of fertility and of eternal life after death; murdered and dismembered by his brother, Seth, but restored by his wife, Isis, he reigned supreme in the next world, offering eternal life to all deserving humans.

Ptah: creator god, patron of artisans.

Re: sun god; he became identified with Horus under the title Re-Harakhty, depicted as a hawk-headed human wearing a solar disk; also became identified with Amun under the title Amun-Re.

Seth: god of chaos and storms who murdered his brother, Osiris, and battled with his nephew, Horus; depicted with a doglike head and associated with many dangerous animals, including the hippopotamus.

Shu: primeval god of air and sunlight, who fathered the sky (Nut) and the Earth (Geb) and set them apart.

Sobek: crocodile god, associated with water and fertility.

Thoth: god of writing and wisdom, master of magical spells, and patron of scribes; associated with the moon, he was often portrayed with the head of an ibis.

PRONUNCIATION GUIDE

Aapehty (ah-ah-PET-tee)
Ahhotep (ah-HO-tep)
Ahmose (ah-MO-zeh)
Akhenaten (AH-ken-AH-ten)
Amenhotep (AH-men-HO-tep)
Amenmesse (AH-men-MESS-eh)
Amennakht (AH-men-nockt)
Aneksi (AH-nek-see)
Ani (AN-ee)
Ankhesenamun (AHNK-es-en-AH-mun)
Apophis (ah-PO-fis)
Auibre Hor (ow-EEB-ray HOR)
Ay (EYE)
Dedi (DED-ee)
Djoser (JO-zer)
Gua (GWA)
Harshire (har-SHE-ray)
Hatshepsut Khenemetamen
(HOT-shep-soot KENEM-et-AH-men)
Hattusilis (HOT-too-SILL-iss)
Hau (HOW)
Hay (HA-ee)
Hekanakht (HEK-ah-NOCKT)
Herodotus (hair-OD-uh-tus)
Hesire (HES-ee-ray)

Hesysunebef (HES-ee-su-NEB-ef)
Hetepet (HET-eh-pet)
Horemhab (HOR-em-hahb)
Inherka (in-HAIR-kah)
Imhotep (im-HO-tep)
Imiu (IM-ee-yoo)
Ipuy (IP-oo-ee)
Iutenheb (IW-ten-heb)
Iyneferet (ee-NEF-er-et)
Kenherkhepeshef (KEN-hair-KEP-esh-ef)
Khaemweset (KAH-em-WES-et)
Khafre (KAHF-ray)
Khufu (KOO-foo)
Menkaure (men-COW-ray)
Mentuhotep (MEN-too-HO-tep)
Merisu (MEH-ree-soo)
Muwatallis (MOO-wah-TAH-lis)
Naunakht (now-oo-NOCKT)
Neferenpet (NEF-er-EN-pet)
Neferhotep (NEF-er-HO-tep)
Nefertari (NEF-er-TAR-ee)
Nefertiabet (NEF-ert-YAH-bet)
Nefertiti (NEF-er-TEE-tee)
Nesmutaatneru (NES-moot-ah-AHT-neh-roo)
Pabasa (pa-BAH-sa)
Paneb (PAH-neb)
Paser (PAH-ser)

Pawero (pah-WAIR-oh)
Pekharu (peh-KAR-oo)
Pendua (pen-DOO-ah)
Penmaat (pen-MAH-AHT)
Pentaweret (PEN-ta-WAIR-et)
Ramses (RAM-sees)
Sennedjem (sen-NEH-jem)
Sennefer (sen-NEH-fer)
Senusret (sen-OOS-ret)
Seqenenre Tao II
(SEK-eh-NEN-ray TAH-ow)
Seti (SET-ee)
Sihathor (SEE-HATH-or)
Sinuhe (SIN-oo-ay)
Sitamun (sit-AH-mun)
Smenkhare (SMENK-kah-ray)
Snefru (SNEF-roo)
Sobekemsaf II (SO-bek-EM-saff)
Tamutnefret (TAH-moot-NEF-ret)
Tiy (TEE)
Tjanefer (cha-NEF-er)
Tutankhamun (TUT-ankh-AH-mun)
Tuthmosis (tut-MO-sis)
Unas (OO-nahs)
Wabet (WAH-bet)
Wabkhet (WAHB-ket)
Weni (WEH-nee)

PICTURE CREDITS

ACKNOWLEDGMENTS

The editors wish to thank the following individuals and institutions for their valuable assistance in the preparation of this volume:

Elvira d'Amicone, Museo Egizio, Turin; Carol Andrews, Department of Egyptian Antiquities, British Museum, London; Ramsey Atitullah, Photographic Service, British Museum, London; Achille Bianchi, Rome; Jean-Luc Bovot, Département des Antiquités Égyptiennes, Musée du Louvre, Paris; Maurice Bucaille, Paris; Rosemarie Drenkhahn, Kestner Museum, Hannover, Germany; Dina Faltings, German Institute of Archaeology, Cairo; Joanna Galas, Muzeum Narodowe, Warsaw, Poland; Jean-Claude Golvin, Paris; François Gourdon, Antony; Cristiana Morigi Govi, Museo Civico Archeologico, Bologna; Zahi A. Hawass, Director General of the Giza Pyramids and Saqqara, Cairo; A. A. M. van der Heyden, The Netherlands; Heidrun Klein, Bildarchiv Preussischer Kulturbesitz, Berlin; Wojciech Kolataj, Polish Archaeological Mission, Alexandria, Egypt; Jean-Paul Lacombe, Editions Gallimard, Paris; Olof Landstrom, Stockholm, Sweden; Jacques Livet, Paris; Gioia Meconcelli, Museo Civico Archeologico, Bologna; Roland Mourer, Muséum d'Histoire Naturelle, Lyons, France; Ingeborg Müller, Staatliche Museen zu Berlin-Preussischer Kulturbesitz; F. Pawlicki, Center of Polish Mediterranean Archaeology, Cairo; Lino Pellegrini, Milan; Luisa Ricciarini, Milan; John G. Ross, Cortona, Italy; Anna Maria Donadoni Roveri, Museo Egizio, Turin; Brigitte Schmitz, Roemer und Pelizaeus Museum, Hildesheim; N. J. D. Smith, London; John Taylor, Department of Egyptian Antiquities, British Museum, London; Elisabetta Valtz, Museo Egizio, Turin; Tania Watkins, Department of Egyptian Antiquities, British Museum, London; Kent Weeks, ARCE, Cairo.

BIBLIOGRAPHY

BOOKS

Adams, William Y. *Nubia: Corridor to Africa.* London: Penguin Books, 1977.

The Age of God-Kings: Time Frame 3000-1500 BC, by the Editors of Time-Life Books (Time Frame series). Alexandria, Va.: Time-Life Books, 1987.

Aldred, Cyril. *Tutankhamun's Egypt.* New York: Charles Scribner's Sons, 1972.

Ancient Egypt: Discovering Its Splendors. Washington, D.C.: National Geographic Society, 1978.

Andrews, Carol, ed. *The Ancient Egyptian Book of the Dead.* Transl. by Raymond O. Faulkner. London: British Museum Publications, 1985.

Angeloglou, Maggie. *A History of Make-Up.* New York: Macmillan, 1970.

An Introduction to Ancient Egypt. London: British Museum Publications, 1979.

Arnold, Dieter. *Building in Egypt.* New York: Oxford University Press, 1991.

Aufrere, Sydney, Jean-Claude Golvin, and Jean-Claude Goyon. *L'Égypte Restituée.* Paris: Editions Errance, 1991.

Badawy, Alexander. *A History of Egyptian Architecture.* Berkeley: University of California Press, 1968.

Baikie, James. *Egyptian Papyri and Papyrus-Hunting.* London: Religious Tract Society, 1925.

Baines, John, and Jaromír Málek. *Atlas of Ancient Egypt.* New York: Facts On File Publications, 1980.

Barbarian Tides: Time Frame 1500-600 BC, by the Editors of Time-Life Books (Time Frame series). Alexandria, Va.: Time-Life Books, 1987.

Benson, Douglas S. *Ancient Egypt's Warfare.* Chicago, 1994.

Bierbrier, Morris. *The Tomb-Builders of the Pharaohs.* London: British Museum Publications, 1982.

Breasted, James Henry:
Ancient Records of Egypt. Vols. 2 and 3. Chicago: University of Chicago Press, 1906.
The Edwin Smith Surgical Papyrus. Chicago: University of Chicago Press, 1930.
A History of Egypt: From the Earliest Times to the Persian Conquest. New York: Charles Scribner's Sons, 1909.

Brothwell, Don R., and A. T. Sandison. *Diseases in Antiquity.* Springfield, Ill.: Charles C. Thomas, 1967.

Bryan, Cyril P., transl. *Ancient Egyptian Medicine: The Papyrus Ebers.* Chicago: Ares Publishers, 1974 (reprint of 1930 edition).

Bucaille, Maurice. *Mummies of the Pharaohs: Modern Medical Investigations.* Transl. by Alastair D. Pannell and Maurice Bucaille. New York: St. Martin's Press, 1990.

Budge, E. A. Wallis. *Egyptian Magic.* New York: Bell Publishing, 1991.

Casson, Lionel, and the Editors of Time-Life Books. *Ancient Egypt* (Great Ages of Man series.) Alexandria, Va.: Time-Life Books, 1978.

Cerny, Jaroslav:
A Community of Workmen at Thebes in the Ramesside Period. Cairo: Institut Français d'Archéologie Orientale, 1973.
The Valley of the Kings. Cairo: Institut Français d'Archéologie Orientale, 1973.

Clarke, Somers, and R. Engelbach. *Ancient Egyptian Masonry: The Building Craft.* London: Oxford University Press, 1930.

Clayton, Peter A. *Chronicle of the Pharaohs.* London: Thames and Hudson, 1994.

D'Auria, Sue, Peter Lacovara, and Catharine H. Roehrig, eds. *Mummies and Magic: The Funerary Arts of Ancient Egypt.* Boston: Museum of Fine Arts, 1988.

David, A. Rosalie:
The Ancient Egyptians: Religious Beliefs and Practices. London: Routledge & Kegan Paul, 1982.
Discovering Ancient Egypt. New York: Facts On File Publications, 1993.
The Egyptian Kingdoms. New York: Peter Bedrick Books, 1988.

Davies, N. de Garis. *The Tomb of the Vizier Ramose.* London: Egypt Exploration Society, 1941.

Dayagi-Mendels, Michal. *Perfumes and Cosmetics in the Ancient World.* Jerusalem: Israel Museum, 1989.

de Cenival, Jean-Louis. *Le Livre Pour Sortir le Jour.* Paris: Musée d'Aquitaine et Réunion des Musées Nationaux, 1992.

Desroches-Noblecourt, Christiane. *Tutankhamen: Life and Death of a Pharaoh.* London: Penguin Books, 1989.

Dodson, Aidan. *Monarchs of the Nile.* London: Rubicon Press, 1995.

Dothan, Trude, and Moshe Dothan. *People of the Sea: The Search for the Philistines.* New York: Macmillan, 1992.

Dunand, Françoise, and Roger Lichtenberg. *Mummies: A Voyage through Eternity.* New York: Harry N. Abrams, 1994.

Edwards, I. E. S. *The Pyramids of Egypt.* Harmondsworth, U.K.: Penguin Books, 1985.

Edwards, I. E. S., C. J. Gadd, and N. G. L. Hammond, eds. *The Cambridge Ancient History.* Vol. 1. Cambridge: Cambridge University Press, 1971.

El Mahdy, Christine. *Mummies, Myth and Magic in Ancient Egypt.* New York: Thames and Hudson, 1989.

Egypt and the Ancient Near East. New York: Metropolitan Museum of Art, 1987.

Egypt: Land of the Pharaohs, by the Editors of Time-Life Books (Lost Civilizations series). Alexandria,

Va.: Time-Life Books, 1992.

Egyptian Museum Berlin. Mainz: Verlag Philipp von Zabern, 1992.

Erman, Adolf. *Life in Ancient Egypt.* Transl. by H. M. Tirard. New York: Benjamin Blom, 1969.

Estes, J. Worth. *The Medical Skills of Ancient Egypt.* Canton, Mass.: Watson Publishing, 1993.

Fagan, Brian M. *The Rape of the Nile.* New York: Charles Scribner's Sons, 1975.

Fakhry, Ahmed. *The Pyramids.* Chicago: University of Chicago Press, 1961.

Faulkner, R. O., transl. *The Ancient Egyptian Pyramid Texts.* Oak Park, Ill.: Bolchazy-Carducci Publishers, 1969.

Foster, John L., transl. *Love Songs of the New Kingdom.* Austin: University of Texas Press, 1974.

Frankfort, Henri. *The Birth of Civilization in the Near East.* New York: Barnes & Noble, 1951.

Gardiner, Alan. *Egypt of the Pharaohs.* London: Oxford University Press, 1961.

Ghalioungui, Paul:
Magic and Medical Science in Ancient Egypt. Amsterdam: B. M. Israël, 1973.
"Medicine in Ancient Egypt." In *An X-Ray Atlas of the Royal Mummies.* Ed. by James E. Harris and Edward F. Wente. Chicago: University of Chicago Press, 1980.
The Physicians of Pharaonic Egypt. Cairo: Al-Ahram Center for Scientific Translations, 1983.

Golvin, Jean-Claude, and Jean-Claude Goyon. *Karnak: Ägypten.* Tübingen: Ernst Wasmuth Verlag, 1990.

Grimal, Nicolas. *A History of Ancient Egypt.* Transl. by Ian Shaw. Oxford: Blackwell, 1992.

Grunfeld, Frederic V., ed. *Games of the World.* New York: Holt, Rinehart and Winston, 1978.

Gunn, Fenja. *The Artificial Face: A History of Cosmetics.* New York: Hippocrene Books, 1973.

Harer, W. Benson. "Health in Pharaonic Egypt." In *Biological Anthropology and the Study of Ancient Egypt.* Ed. by W. Vivian Davies and Roxie Walker. London: British Museum Publications, 1993.

Harris, James E., and Kent R. Weeks. *X-Raying the Pharaohs.* New York: Charles Scribner's Sons, 1973.

Harris, J. R., ed. *The Legacy of Egypt.* Oxford: Clarendon Press, 1971.

Hart, George:
Ancient Egypt. New York: Alfred A. Knopf, 1990.
Pharaohs and Pyramids: A Guide through Old Kingdom Egypt. London: Herbert Press, 1991.

Hawass, Zahi A. *The Pyramids of Ancient Egypt.* Pittsburgh: Carnegie Museum of Natural History, 1990.

Hayes, William C. *The Scepter of Egypt.* Part 1. New York: Harry N. Abrams, 1953.

Haynes, Joyce L. *Nubia: Ancient Kingdoms of Africa.* Boston: Museum of Fine Arts, 1992.

Hicks, Jim, and the Editors of Time-Life Books. *The Empire Builders* (The Emergence of Man series). New York: Time-Life Books, 1974.

Hobson, Christine. *The World of the Pharaohs.* New York: Thames and Hudson, 1987.

Hornung, Erik:
Idea Into Image: Essays on Ancient Egyptian Thought. Transl. by Elizabeth Bredeck. New York: Timken Publishers, 1992.
The Valley of the Kings: Horizon of Eternity. Transl. by David Warburton. New York: Timken Publishers, 1990.

James, T. G. H.:
An Introduction to Ancient Egypt. London: British Museum Publications, 1979.
Pharaoh's People: Scenes from Life in Imperial Egypt. Chicago: University of Chicago Press, 1984.

Janssen, Jac. J. "The Role of the Temple in the Egyptian Economy during the New Kingdom." In *State and Temple Economy in the Ancient Near East.* Vol. 2. Ed. by Edward Lipinski. Leuven: Departement Oriëntalistiek, 1979.

Janssen, Jack, and Rosalind Janssen. *Egyptian Household Animals.* Buckinghamshire, U.K.: Shire Publications, 1989.

Jenkins, Nancy. *The Boat beneath the Pyramid.* New York: Holt, Rinehart and Winston, 1980.

Jones, Dilwyn. *Boats.* London: British Museum Publications, 1995.

Kaster, Joseph, ed. and transl. *Wings of the Falcon: Life and Thought of Ancient Egypt.* New York: Holt, Rinehart and Winston, 1968.

Kees, Hermann. *Ancient Egypt: A Cultural Topography.* Ed. by T. G. H. James. Chicago: University of Chicago Press, 1961.

Kemp, Barry J. *Ancient Egypt: Anatomy of a Civilization.* London: Routledge, 1989.

Killen, Geoffrey. *Egyptian Woodworking and Furniture.* Buckinghamshire, U.K.: Shire Publications, 1994.

Kitchen, K. A. *Pharaoh Triumphant.* Warminster. U.K.: Aris & Phillips, 1982.

Landström, Björn. *Ships of the Pharaohs.* London: Allen & Unwin, 1970.

Lepre, J. P. *The Egyptian Pyramids.* Jefferson: N.C.: McFarland, 1990.

Lesko, Barbara S. *The Remarkable Women of Ancient Egypt.* Berkeley, Calif.: B. C. Scribe Publications, 1978.

Lesko, Barbara S., ed. *Women's Earliest Records from Ancient Egypt and Western Asia.* Atlanta: Scholars Press, 1989.

Lesko, Leonard H., ed. *Pharaoh's Workers: The Villagers of Deir el Medina.* Ithaca, N.Y.: Cornell University Press, 1994.

Lichtheim, Miriam. *Ancient Egyptian Literature: A Book of Readings.* 3 vols. Berkeley: University of California Press, 1973-1980.

Lurker, Manfred. *The Gods and Symbols of Ancient Egypt.* London: Thames and Hudson, 1980.

Macaulay, David. *Pyramid.* Boston: Houghton Mifflin, 1975.

Majno, Guido. *The Healing Hand: Man and Wound in the Ancient World.* Cambridge, Mass.: Harvard University Press, 1975.

Málek, Jaromír. *In the Shadow of the Pyramids.* Norman: University of Oklahoma Press, 1986.

Manniche, Lise:
An Ancient Egyptian Herbal. Austin: University of Texas Press, 1989.
Music and Musicians in Ancient Egypt. London: British Museum Publications, 1991.

Martin, Geoffrey T. *The Hidden Tombs of Memphis.* London: Thames and Hudson, 1991.

McDowell, A. G. *Jurisdiction in the Workmen's Community of Deir El-Medîna.* Leiden: Nederlands Instituut Voor Het Nabije Oosten, 1990.

Meltzer, Edmund S., ed. *Letters from Ancient Egypt.* Transl. by Edward F. Wente. Atlanta: Scholars Press, 1990.

Mertz, Barbara:
Red Land, Black Land: Daily Life in Ancient Egypt. New York: Peter Bedrick Books, 1990.
Temples, Tombs and Hieroglyphs. New York: Peter Bedrick Books, 1990.

Milton, Joyce. *Sunrise of Power: Ancient Egypt, Alexander and the World of Hellenism.* New York: HBJ Press, 1980.

Montet, Pierre. *Everyday Life in Egypt: In the Days of Ramesses the Great.* Transl. by A. R. Maxwell-Hyslop and Margaret S. Drower. Philadelphia: University of Pennsylvania Press, 1981.

Moran, William L., ed. and transl. *The Amarna Letters.* Baltimore: Johns Hopkins University Press, 1992.

Murnane, William J. *The Road to Kadesh.* Chicago: Oriental Institute of the University of Chicago, 1990.

Newby, P. H. *Warrior Pharaohs.* London: Faber and Faber, 1980.

O'Connor, David:
Ancient Nubia: Egypt's Rival in Africa. Philadelphia: University of Pennsylvania Museum, 1993.
A Short History of Ancient Egypt. Pittsburgh: Carnegie Museum of Natural History, 1990.

Parker, Richard A. *The Calendars of Ancient Egypt.* Chicago: University of Chicago Press, 1950.

Parkinson, R. B. *Voices from Ancient Egypt.* Norman:

University of Oklahoma Press, 1991.

Peet, Thomas Eric. *The Great Tomb-Robberies of the Twentieth Egyptian Dynasty.* Hildesheim: Georg Olms Verlag, 1977.

Pinch, Geraldine. *Magic in Ancient Egypt.* London: British Museum Publications, 1994.

Pritchard, James B., ed. *Ancient Near Eastern Texts Relating to the Old Testament.* Princeton, N.J.: Princeton University Press, 1969.

Quirke, Stephen, and Jeffrey Spencer, eds. *The British Museum Book of Ancient Egypt.* New York: Thames and Hudson, 1992.

Ramses II: Magnificence on the Nile, by the Editors of Time-Life Books (Lost Civilizations series). Alexandria, Va.: Time-Life Books, 1993.

Redford, Donald B. *Akhenaten: The Heretic King.* Princeton, N.J.: Princeton University Press, 1984.

Reeves, Carole. *Egyptian Medicine.* Buckinghamshire, U.K.: Shire Publications, 1992.

Reeves, C. N. *Valley of the Kings.* London: Kegan Paul International, 1990.

Reeves, Nicholas. *The Complete Tutankhamun.* New York: Thames and Hudson, 1990.

Robins, Gay. *Egyptian Painting and Relief.* Buckinghamshire, U.K.: Shire Publications, 1986.

Rodenbeck, Max. *Egypt: Gift of the Nile.* New York: Harry N. Abrams, 1991.

Roehrig, Catharine H. *Mummies and Magic.* Boston: Museum of Fine Arts, 1988.

Romano, James F. *Death, Burial, and Afterlife in Ancient Egypt.* Pittsburgh: Carnegie Museum of Natural History, 1990.

Romant, Bernard. *Life in Egypt in Ancient Times.* Transl. by J. Smith. Geneva: Editions Minerva, 1978.

Romer, John:
   Ancient Lives. New York: Henry Holt, 1984.
   People of the Nile. New York: Crown Publishers, 1982.

Sadek, Ashraf Iskander. *Popular Religion in Egypt during the New Kingdom.* Hildesheim: Gerstenberg Verlag, 1987.

Säve-Söderbergh, Torgny. *The Navy of the Eighteenth Egyptian Dynasty.* Uppsala: Almquist and Wiksells, 1946.

Schmidt, Heike C., and Joachim Willeitner. *Nefertari.* Mainz: Verlag Philipp von Zabern, 1994.

Schott, Sigfried. *Das schöne Fest vom Wüstentale.* Wiesbaden: Akademie der Wissenschaften und der Literatur, 1952.

Shaw, Ian. *Egyptian Warfare and Weapons.* Buckinghamshire, U.K.: Shire Publications, 1991.

Shaw, Ian, and Paul Nicholson. *The Dictionary of Ancient Egypt.* New York: Harry N. Abrams, 1995.

Smith, G. Elliot. *Catalogue Général des Antiquités Égyptiennes.* Cairo: Institut Français d'Archéologie Orientale, 1912.

Smith, William Stevenson. *Ancient Egypt.* Boston: Museum of Fine Arts, 1960.

Spencer, A. J. *Death in Ancient Egypt.* London: Penguin Books, 1982.

Stadelmann, Rainer. *Die Ägyptischen Pyramiden.* Mainz: Verlag Philipp von Zabern, 1985.

Stead, Miriam. *Egyptian Life.* London: British Museum Publications, 1986.

Strouhal, Eugen. *Life of the Ancient Egyptians.* Norman: University of Oklahoma Press, 1992.

Trigger, B. G., et al. *Ancient Egypt: A Social History.* Cambridge: Cambridge University Press, 1983.

Vercoutter, Jean. *The Search for Ancient Egypt.* New York: Harry N. Abrams, 1992.

Vernus, Pascal. *Affaires et Scandales sous les Ramsès.* Paris: Pygmalion, 1994.

Vinson, Steve. *Egyptian Boats and Ships.* Buckinghamshire, U.K.: Shire Publications, 1994.

Watson, Philip J. *Egyptian Pyramids and Mastaba Tombs of the Old and Middle Kingdoms.* Buckinghamshire, U.K.: Shire Publications, 1987.

Wente, Edward. *Letters from Ancient Egypt.* Atlanta: Scholars Press, 1990.

White, Jon Manchip. *Everyday Life in Ancient Egypt.* London: B. T. Batsford, 1963.

Wildung, Dietrich. *Egyptian Saints.* New York: New York University Press, 1977.

Wilkinson, Charles K. *Egyptian Wall Paintings.* New York: Metropolitan Museum of Art, 1983.

Wilson, Hilary. *Egyptian Food and Drink.* Buckinghamshire, U.K.: Shire Publications, 1988.

Yadin, Yigael. *The Art of Warfare in Biblical Lands.* Vols. 1 and 2. New York: McGraw-Hill, 1963.

PERIODICALS

Blackman, Aylward M. "Oracles in Ancient Egypt." *Journal of Egyptian Archaeology,* 12, 1926.

Capart, J., A. H. Gardiner, and B. Van De Walle. "New Light on the Ramesside Tomb-Robberies." *Journal of Egyptian Archaeology,* 22, 1936.

Cerny, Jaroslav. "Papyrus Salt 124 (Brit. Mus. 10055)." *Journal of Egyptian Archaeology,* 15, 1929.

Dodson, Aidan. "Rise and Fall of the House of Shoshenq." *KMT,* 1995.

Edgerton, William F. "The Strikes in Ramses III's Twenty-Ninth Year." *Journal of Near Eastern Studies,* July 1951.

Faulkner, R. O. "The Battle of Megiddo." *Journal of Egyptian Archaeology,* 28, 1942.

Gordon, Andrew H. "Origins of Ancient Egyptian Medicine." *KMT,* Summer 1990.

Gore, Rick. "Ramses the Great." *National Geographic,* April 1991.

Hamblin, Dora Jane. "A Unique Approach to Unraveling the Secrets of the Great Pyramids." *Smithsonian,* April 1986.

Leek, F. Filce. "Teeth and Bread in Ancient Egypt." *Journal of Egyptian Archaeology,* 58, 1972.

Lemonick, Michael. "Secrets of the Prince's Tomb." *Time,* May 29, 1995.

Lesko, Barbara S. "Women's Monumental Mark on Ancient Egypt." *Biblical Archaeologist,* March 1991.

McIntyre, Glen V. "Rameses III & the End of Empire." *KMT,* Fall 1990.

Preston, Douglas. "Annals of Archeology: All the King's Sons." *The New Yorker,* January 22, 1996.

Reeder, Greg. "Up at the Giza Plateau." *KMT,* Winter 1991-1992.

Ringle, Ken. "Tomb with a View." *The Washington Post,* June 15, 1995.

Roberts, David. "Age of Pyramids." *National Geographic,* January 1995.

Schwabe, Calvin W. "Origins of Ancient Egyptian Medicine." *KMT,* Fall 1990.

Stevens, John M. "Gynaecology from Ancient Egypt: The Papyrus Kahun." *The Medical Journal of Australia,* December 20-27, 1975.

Smith, Stuart Tyson. "They *Did* Take It with Them." *KMT,* Fall 1991.

Urschel, Joe. "More Rooms Found in Huge Egyptian Tomb." *USA Today,* November 30, 1995.

Wente, Edward F. "A Letter of Complaint to the Vizier To." *Journal of Near Eastern Studies,* 20, 1961.

Wilford, John Noble. "Vast Tomb of Ramses II's Many Sons Is Discovered." *The New York Times,* May 16, 1995.

OTHER SOURCES

Allen, James P., et al. "Religion and Philosophy in Ancient Egypt." Yale Egyptological Studies 3, 1989.

Bonnet, Charles, ed. "Kerma, Royaume de Nubie." Exhibition catalog. Geneva: Musée d'Art et d'Histoire, 1990.

"The British Museum Book of Ancient Egypt." Catalog. New York: Thames and Hudson, 1992.

"Documents of the Egyptian Empire (1580-1380 B.C.). Collection. Victoria, Australia: Australian Institute of Archaeology, 1981.

"Égypte." Guides Gallimard. Éditions Nouveaux-Loisirs, October 1994.

Kemp, Barry J. "Temple and Town in Ancient Egypt." In "Man, Settlement and Urbanism." Seminar proceedings. London University, 1972.

Leca, A. P. "La Medecine Egyptienne au Temps des Pharaons." Discussion. Paris, 1971.

INDEX

Numerals in italics indicate an illustration of the subject mentioned.

Hapi (son of Horus): *173, 174*
Harems: 63, 94; Amenhotep III's, 80-81
Harpist: blind, *39*
Harshire (scribe): 161, 163, 164, 167
Hathor (goddess): *28, 53,* 73, *167*
Hatshepsut (pharaoh): *10, 62,* 63-66, *65,* 69, *75,* 80; Punt expedition, *118-121;* quoted, 70
Hattusilis III (Hittite king): 127
Hawk mummy: *157*
Hay (foreman): 36
Headache remedy: *41*
Health problems and remedies: *38-41*
Heart: amulet over, *174;* weighing of, 29, 149-150, *174-175*
Heb-Sed ritual, pharaoh's: 85-87
Hekanakht (landowner): 18-22, 24, 26
Herodotus (Greek historian): quoted, 45
Hesire (physician): *40*
Hesysunebef (Paneb's stepbrother): 42-43
Hetepet (Hekanakht's relative): 24
Hieratic script: *84*
Hieroglyphs: *84;* cartouches, *8-12,* 84, *85;* for *female, 45;* for *scribe, 81*
Hippopotamuses: faience, *24;* game board shaped like, *97;* tusk, wand from, *57*
Hittites (people): Ramses II and, 92, 123-127, *126-127, 134-135*
Horemhab (pharaoh): 90; camp, *134;* tomb decoration, *162*
Horus (god): *8,* 28, *29, 85,* 147, 149, *180;* eye of, *9, 41, 136,* 149, *151, 174, 175;* sons of, *173, 174, 181*
Hounds and jackals (game): *97*
Housing: *20,* 31, *76;* in Punt, *120*
Hunro (weaver): 42-43
Hunting: 77; family outings, *50, 95*
Hyksos (people): 10, 70, 106-110; crown, *9;* weaponry, copying of, 109, *132-133*
Hymn to the Aten (Akhenaten): 88, 91

I

Ibis mummy: *157*
Imhotep (Djoser's architect): *138*
Imiu (servant): illness of, 137, 138
Imsety (son of Horus): *173, 174*
Incense: priest holding, *68*
Incense trees: Hatshepsut's, *120-121*
Infant: suckling of, *52*
Inherka (grandfather): tomb scene, *56-57*
Intef (priest): widow's letter, 137-138
Ipi (royal official): estates, 19
Ipuy (sculptor) and family: *32-33,* 33-34

Irrigation canals: *16-17*
Isis (goddess): *29,* 149, *181;* temple, *12*
Isis (Ramses III's wife), tomb of: thefts from, 163, 167-168, 170
Isis-knot amulet: *53*
Israelites (people): Ramses II and, 92
Iutenheb (Hekanakht's second wife): 24
Ivory: chair, *31;* clappers, *100;* game board, *97*
Iyneferet (Sennedjem's wife): *54*

J

Jars: canopic, *173;* cosmetic, *34;* water, *166*
Jasper: scarab amulet, *174*

K

Ka (spirit): 147, *176, 177*
Kadesh, Syria: battle, 123-127, *134-135;* ruler of, campaign against, 114, 116, 118, 121, 123
Kamose (pharaoh): 108; quoted, 108, 109
Ka priests (mortuary priests): 158, 159
Karnak temple complex, Thebes: *66-69;* festivals, 72, 73, 75; wall art, *62-63, 122*
Kawit, Queen: *35*
Kenherkhepeshef (Naunakht's husband): 44
Kha (overseer of works) and wife: 155; burial goods, *34,* 155-156, 158
Khaemweset (vizier): 163, 167-168, 170
Khafre (pharaoh): monuments, *8, 140-141*
Khufu (pharaoh): Great Pyramid of, 9, *141-145;* Royal Ship of, *146-147*
Knives: embalmer's, *173;* for Opening of the Mouth ceremony, *178*
Kohl: *34*
Kumma fortress, Nubia: *112-113*
Kushites (Nubians): 107, 110-111, 115

L

Leopard skins: priests wearing, *33, 46, 176*
Libyans (people): captives, *11*
Love poems and songs: 36, 50, 51, 88, 96
Luxor temple complex, Thebes: *10,* 75

M

Maat (goddess): *29,* 175
Mail, coat of: *125*
Mallet: stonemason's, *141*
Maps: on coffin, *151;* Great Pyramid complex, 143; Nile, *13;* Nubia, 114; Punt, route to, 118; Thebes, 13

Marketplace: 30, *43*
Marriage: 36, 46, 50; ending, 41-43
Masks: of Anubis, *172;* plaster, *86-87;* Tutankhamun's, *11,* 165
Mastabas: *139*-140
Medical problems and remedies: *38-41*
Medjay (Nubian archers): 109, 113-114
Megiddo, battle of: 114, 116, 118, 121, 123
Mehen (game): *96*
Menkaure (pharaoh): pyramids, *140-141*
Mentuhotep II (pharaoh): *9;* funerary monument, 139-140
Merisu (Hekanakht's eldest son): letters to, 19-21, 22, 24, 26
Merit (Kha's wife): 155; belongings, *34,* 156
Meryt (Sennefer's wife): *51*
Middle Kingdom (2061-1668 BC): timeline *9,* 10, 18-19, 104; army, 104-106, *105;* funeral complex, 139-140; Hekanakht, 18-22, 24, 26; home, *20;* Nubian forts, *9,* 111, *112-113,* 113-114, *115;* texts, 82, 107
Military: 103-127, *128-135;* Ahmose, *106,* 108-111; armor, *105, 124, 125;* camp life, *134-135;* Hyksos, conflict with, 106-110; infantrymen, *105, 128,* 129, 131; marines, 108-109, 110, *128-129;* Middle Kingdom army, 104-106, *105;* Nubian forts, *9,* 111, *112-113,* 113-114, *115;* Old Kingdom, 104; under Ramses II, 123-127, *126-127, 134-135;* under Ramses III, 11, 103-104; reward to, *110-111;* training, *130-131;* under Tuthmosis III, 103, 114, 116, 118, 121, *122,* 123; weapons, 103, *105,* 106-107, *131, 132-133*
Mortuary cults and priests: 158-159
Mortuary temples: Amenhotep III's, 77, 79, 81; Great Pyramid's, *145;* Hatshepsut's, *64-65, 120-121;* Ramses III's, scenes from, 103-104, *128*
Mud brick: 79; homes built from, *20,* 31
Mummies: *171, 174,* 175; amulets, *171, 174, 175;* animal, *156-157;* in funeral procession, *176-177;* Opening of the Mouth, *178;* Ramses II, *168;* restoration of, 170; Seqenenre Tao II, *108;* spinal problems, *38*
Musicians: at banquet, *100-101;* blind, *39;* sistrum players, *73*
Mutnodjmet, Queen: 52

Muwatallis (Hittite king): 124, 125
Myths: creation, 8, *27*

N

Narmer (king): palette, *8*
Naunakht (woman): 44; will, 44, *47*
Nearuna (military task force): 126-127
Nebamun (physician): with family, *95;* tomb, paintings from, *95, 98-101*
Neferhotep (foreman): 31-32, 36, 37-38, 41
Neferenpet (scribe): *69*
Nefertari (Ramses II's wife): 92, *97;* mummy's restoration, 170
Nefertiabet, Princess: *46*
Nefertiti (queen; Akhenaten's wife): *11,* 88, *89,* 91
Nephthys (goddess; Isis's sister): 149, *181*
Nesmutaatneru (woman): mummy, *171*
New Kingdom (1560-1070 BC): *10-11,* 70, 111. *See also individual people, places, and things*
Nile River: *6-7, map* 13, 18; flooding of, 15, 26, 72; flood plain, *16-17*
Nubia and Nubians: 111, *map* 114, 115, *116-117;* Abu Simbel temple, *92-93;* forts, *9,* 111, *112-113,* 113-114, *115;* Kushites, 107, 110-111, 115; pharaoh, *12*
Numerals, hieroglyphic and hieratic: *84*
Nut (sky goddess): *27*

O

Oasis, Fayum: *16-17*
Oils and ointments: 33; box for, *34*
Old Kingdom (2705-2213 BC): *8-9,* 70, army, 104; healing arts, *40;* musician, *101;* pyramids, *8, 9, 138-145;* Pyramid Texts, *150,* 151
Opening of the Mouth ceremony: *178*
Opet Festival: Thebes, 72, 73, 75
Osiris (god): *136,* 149, 151, *181;* backbone, representation of, *175;* offering to, *157;* pharaohs portrayed as, *29,* 65
Osorkon II (pharaoh): as Osiris, *29*
Oxen: mummy towed by, *176-177*

P

Pabasa (scribe): 161, 163, 164, 167
Paintbrushes: *162-163*
Palace, Amenhotep III's: 79; floor painting, *79*
Palettes, scribes': *81, 83;* use of, *82*
Paneb (stonemason): 26, 31-32, 35-38, 41-42, 43-44

TIME® LIFE BOOKS

Time-Life Books is a division of Time Life Inc.

TIME LIFE INC.
PRESIDENT and CEO: George Artandi

TIME-LIFE BOOKS
PRESIDENT: John D. Hall
PUBLISHER/MANAGING EDITOR: Neil Kagan

WHAT LIFE WAS LIKE
On the Banks of the Nile

EDITOR: Denise Dersin
DIRECTOR, NEW PRODUCT DEVELOPMENT:
Curtis Kopf
MARKETING DIRECTORS: Pamela R. Farrell;
Joseph A. Kuna

Deputy Editors: Paula York-Soderlund, Loretta Y. Britten
Design Director: Cynthia T. Richardson
Text Editors: Charlotte Anker, Stephen G. Hyslop,
James Michael Lynch, Glen Ruh
Art Directors: Mary Gasperetti (principal), Alan Pitts
Associate Editors/Research and Writing:
Kristin Dittman, Sharon Kurtz, Trudy W. Pearson
Senior Copyeditor: Ann Lee Bruen
Technical Art Specialist: John Drummond
Picture Coordinator: Catherine Parrott
Editorial Assistant: Patricia D. Whiteford

Special Contributors: Karin Kinney (editing); Patricia
Cassidy, Maggie Debelius, Sarah Labouisse, Rita Thievon
Mullin, Mark Rogers, Myrna Traylor-Herndon, Barry
N. Wolverton (research-writing); Bill McKenney, Ellen
L. Pattisall (design); Anthony Allan, Ronald H. Bailey,
Daniel Stashower (chapter text); Jocelyn Lindsey,
Maureen McHugh, Laura Werner (research); Barbara
L. Klein (index).

Correspondents: Maria Vincenza Aloisi (Paris), Christine
Hinze (London), Christina Lieberman (New York).
Valuable assistance was also provided by: Dick Berry
(Tokyo), Angie Lemmer (Bonn), Ann Natanson (Rome),
Nihal Tamraz (Cairo), Saskia Van De Linde (Amsterdam),
Caroline Wood (London).

Vice President, Director of Finance: Christopher Hearing
Vice President, Book Production: Marjann Caldwell
Director of Publishing Technology: Betsi McGrath
Director of Photography and Research: John Conrad Weiser
Director of Editorial Administration: Barbara Levitt
Production Manager: Marlene Zack
Quality Assurance Manager: Miriam P. Newton
Chief Librarian: Louise D. Forstall

Consultants:
Peter Piccione is an Egyptologist and Near Eastern historian and is widely recognized as an authority in the
specialized field of the religious significance of ancient
Egyptian games and athletics. A member of the faculty
of Northwestern University, Dr. Piccione also teaches at
the University of Chicago's Oriental Institute. His current fieldwork includes the excavating and documenting
of the tombs of Ray and Ahmose in Western Thebes,
where he has served as director of the American
Research Center in Egypt Theban Tombs Project since
1990. A popular lecturer on the society and culture of
ancient Egypt, he is perhaps best known as the decipher-
er of the Egyptian board game, senet, and has created a
version of it called "King Tut's Game" for modern use.

Thomas Mark Dousa is presently a doctoral candidate in
Near Eastern languages and civilizations at the University of Chicago; his dissertation topic deals with healing practices in Late Period Egypt. His interests as an
Egyptologist include Egyptian language, especially mon-
umentary texts of the first millennium BC and demotic
script; Egyptian religious practices; and interconnections
between Egypt and the classical world.

Library of Congress Cataloging-in-Publication Data
What Life Was Like On the Banks of the Nile, Egypt
(3050-30 BC)/by the editors of Time-Life Books.
    p. cm.
    Includes bibliographical references and index.
    ISBN 0-8094-9378-0
    1. Egypt—Civilization—To 332 B.C. 2. Egypt—
Civilization—332 B.C.-638 A.D. I. Time-Life Books.
DT61.W467 1996   96-12894
932—dc20   CIP

Other Publications:
HISTORY
The American Story
Voices of the Civil War
The American Indians
Lost Civilizations
Mysteries of the Unknown
Time Frame
The Civil War
Cultural Atlas

SCIENCE/NATURE
Voyage Through the Universe

COOKING
Weight Watchers® Smart Choice Recipe Collection
Great Taste~Low Fat
Williams-Sonoma Kitchen Library

DO IT YOURSELF
The Time-Life Complete Gardener
Home Repair and Improvement
The Art of Woodworking
Fix It Yourself

TIME-LIFE KIDS
Family Time Bible Stories
Library of First Questions and Answers
A Child's First Library of Learning
I Love Math
Nature Company Discoveries
Understanding Science & Nature

For information on and a full description of any of the
Time-Life Books series listed above,
please call 1-800-621-7026 or write:

Reader Information
Time-Life Customer Service
P.O. Box C-32068
Richmond, Virginia 23261-2068

This volume is one in a series on world history that uses
contemporary art, artifacts, and personal accounts to
create an intimate portrait of daily life in the past.

Other volumes included in
the *What Life Was Like* series:

In the Age of Chivalry, Medieval Europe,
  800 - 1500 AD
When Rome Ruled the World, The Roman Empire,
  100 BC - 200 AD
At the Dawn of Democracy, Classical Athens,
  508 - 322 BC
When Longships Sailed, Vikings,
  800 - 1100 AD